ENDORSERS Worldview Dynamics

Richard's book is a must-read for anyone engaged in enabling human evolution toward life-affirming futures for all life on Earth. His book is well-written, concise, easy to read, insightful and unique; a truly vital contribution to the necessary [r]evolution in human consciousness now demanded by the systemic challenges we face.
Giles Hutchins, Author of *Future Fit* and co-author of *Regenerative Leadership*, Chair of The Future Fit Leadership Academy

This is a work of inspiration and impeccable timing, as we transit from one worldview to another. *Worldview Dynamics and the Well-Being of Nations* should be compulsory reading for anyone who would like to take a good look at the future we are about to embark upon. Richard's book is an invaluable guide.
Lawrence Bloom, Secretary General, Be Earth Foundation

Richard Barrett gives us a tantalizing glimpse of a splendid future that awaits us – when we are at last ready to dedicate our individual flourishing to a world that works for all.
Rev. Deborah Moldow, Founder, Garden of Light and Director of the Evolutionary Leaders Circle of the Source of Synergy Foundation

This book builds on some of Barrett's best thinking. His clear writing and concise analysis help us understand more about how we're placed in the world and how we might advance to a deeper awareness and consciousness. He challenges us to not only reconsider our own worldview, but to place that worldview next to that of others so we can understand the greater whole of which we are all a part.
Jed Emerson, Blended Value

This book is a game-changer which should be required reading for every political leader. An understanding of the concept of worldviews is essential for anyone wanting to initiate personal or cultural transformation. It

provides us with a way forward – how we can move beyond our personal and cultural limitations to celebrate our essential unity.
Wendy Ellyatt, Chief Executive, Flourish Project – Co-Chair, Global Council, Wellbeing Economy Alliance

In *Worldview Dynamics and the Well-Being of Nations*, Richard Barrett has taken his wealth of knowledge on personal and organizational transformation into the arena of societal transformation. His Global Consciousness Indicator for nations allows us to make the evolution of human consciousness conscious. Richard Barrett's vision for our challenging times is a bright light shining on what others have yet to recognize.
Björn Larsson, CEO, The ForeSight Group

This book is a must-read for every national leader who wants to understand and lead their people to a more sustainable life on Earth.
Tor Eneroth, Director of Cultural Transformation, Barrett Values Centre

This powerful text is exactly what the world needs to transition to a new way of being. Its timing is critical and its message essential for leaders everywhere, especially those in government at all levels.
Clive Wilson, author of *Designing the Purposeful World: The Sustainable Development Goals as blueprint for humanity* and *Designing the Purposeful Organization: How to inspire business performance beyond boundaries*

In order to solve the complex challenges of the current world, we need a more mature awareness of values, a profound understanding of the evolutionary stages of human consciousness, and a large map of the collective stages of development. I bow to the work of Richard Barrett, for he has succeeded in uniting all three elements in his work. A must-read for every leader.
Veit Lindau, CEO, homodea.com

You hold in your hand an important book. It provides a synthesis and navigational tool for those who seek to understand the deeper underlying operational structures and dynamics that guide us and our world.
Robert Dellner, Managing Partner, I³Partners Ltd, Originator of Integral Impact Investments

I can only hope that leaders from all walks of life, from global to local, will listen to the wisdom, and absorb the data, contained in *Worldview Dynamics and the Well-Being of Nations*. Most importantly, I hope they take action as a result. Our times demand it.

Brad Rendle, Principal, The Rendle Company, *Designing Commerce Naturally*

In this outstanding book, Richard Barrett addresses the question, how can humankind flourish in the 21st century? His deep insights into psychological and cultural literacy create the foundation on which individuals and nations can thrive. This book is a must-read for all who are engaged in raising the level of human consciousness awareness, which our world so desperately needs.

Dr Neil Hawkes, Founder of The International Values-based Education Trust (IVET) and Values-based Education International (VbE)

Richard Barrett takes his insights from decades of values-based work on the evolution of human consciousness, to help nations undertake the journey to well-being in a way that will sustain the planet as well as move toward a unified humanity. He not only has a research-based framework for diagnosing the level of consciousness, but also clear action steps that will move each nation forward. A must-read for global and national leaders at this critical time.

Nilima Bhat, co-author *Shakti Leadership* and *My Cancer Is Me*; founder-director, The Shakti Fellowship

For more than two decades, Richard Barrett has been a world leader in the assessment and practical application of values. His innovative ideas and tools have produced significant, measurable benefits for organizations all over the world. His latest book takes this work to a new level. *Worldview Dynamics and the Well-Being of Nations* can greatly benefit political, business and academic leaders, as well as anyone interested in better understanding the consciousness of nations and its impacts on society.

Frank Dixon, Global System Change

Richard Barrett's latest book, *Worldview Dynamics and the Well-Being of Nations*, is a must-read for anyone trying to make sense of the state of our world today. It is at the same time a history book and a guide for creating a future where people and planet can flourish – charting the ebb and flow of evolution. Highly recommended in these troubled times.
Ruth Steinholtz, AretéWork

At a time where humanity is at a crossroad facing many important challenges, Richard Barrett's book provides a map which can help us find innovative and more conscious solutions so we can create a promising future for the next generations.
Stephane Leblanc, Founder and CEO, International Centre for Conscious Leadership

With *Worldview Dynamics and the Well-Being of Nations* Richard Barrett continues sharing his important insights about the link between the development of national consciousness and the development of the consciousness of the leaders and the people. He shows how different worldviews arise. He suggests that the increasing recognition of the climate crisis could be the trigger for the development of a new worldview which he calls Humanity Awareness.
Richard Kokholm-Erichsen, author of *Optimisme som Strategi* (Optimism as Strategy), Poet, Coach and Human Awareness activist

In line with his previous books, Richard Barrett gives us another passionate invitation to participate in the process of transforming our society into humanity. Aware that the world we create and care for is a fractal of our inner world, Richard invites us to align the needs of our ego with the yearnings of our soul.
Héctor Infer, Founder and Managing Partner, TransformAction
Global Partner Faculty, Barrett Values Centre

The important information in this book is presented within an awareness that there are stages of maturity of human consciousness. We are overly ready for this new consciousness.
Terry Mollner, Pioneer of Socially Responsible Investing

The depth of interconnectedness of Richard's Seven Levels of Consciousness Model for individuals, teams, leaders, organizations, communities and nations becomes even more apparent in this book. While the potential pathways for a sustained evolution of consciousness need to occur in all these areas, advances in one or two will eventually impact the whole.
Tom Brady, Founder and Co-Creator, The XLR8 Team, Inc. and The *EVOL*ution of Business, Founder, Conscious Capitalism Rochester

This book is a seminal contribution to the emergence of a planetary culture and the emergence of a worldview which Richard characterizes as Humanity Awareness. Our very survival depends on understanding and embodying the central ideas of this book.
David Lorimer, Programme Director, Scientific and Medical Network

Richard Barrett's book is an original attempt to address the inadequacy of current measures of human progress. His recognition that people and nations exist at different levels of consciousness rejects the stereotypes of simplistic typologies and impels us to reflect more carefully on subtle differences between countries and cultures advancing on different paths toward a common ultimate evolutionary destination. It is an important attempt to develop a unifying measure of the subtle and intangible aspects of consciousness.
Garry Jacobs, Chief Executive Officer, World Academy of Art & Science

When Richard launched his methodology for culture organizations based on the Seven Levels of Consciousness Model more than twenty years ago, he started a worldwide movement that has changed the way we see values, beliefs and culture in organizations. Now, Richard has done it again. This book provides a revolutionary way to see the complexities of the world. It should be mandatory reading for researchers as well as political and corporate leaders.
Nany Bilate, www.behavior.com.br

We are currently at a turning point, where traditional economic and political theory are proven to no longer work. *Worldview Dynamics and the Well-Being of Nations* provides a new framework for measuring

the well-being of nations which anticipates an evolutionary shift in consciousness that will reorient and redefine business strategies and global politics. This is a must-read for leaders who can see the challenges we face today, but do not yet see a solution. Richard Barrett is truly a thought leader.
Peta Milan, Director, Transcendent Media Capital and Jade Eli Technologies

Richard Barrett has once more proved to be a global thought leader. In his new book, he reveals the revolutionary metric that helps nations to discover the overall level of well-being experienced by their citizens. A must-read for everyone who is looking for answers to where the world is now and where it is heading.
Miša Lukić, New Strategy, Founder and Chief Business Designer

Worldview Dynamics and the Well-Being of Nations provides a compelling, compassionate and inspiring vision for humanity.
Justin Blake, Supporting Transformational Learning and Leadership and The Global Goals

Both intensely personal and globally prescient, *Worldview Dynamics and the Well-Being of Nations* is a must-read for everyone who cares about the fate of humanity and the Earth.
Lawrence Ford, Shaman of Wall Street, CEO of Conscious Capital, and Founder and Chairman of Future Capital

As a strong believer in the importance of the development of consciousness, I am very inspired by the new work of Richard Barrett on the well-being of nations. This book has given me a deep insight into how the stages of psychological development have an impact on the worldviews of nations.
Wendy van Tol, consulting leader, PWC Netherlands and responsible for culture transformation in the Europe Advisory Leadership team

If we – politicians, governmental leaders, business leaders, activists, entrepreneurs, environmentalists, scientists (read everyone) – would read this book, apply the insights and make use of the map and compass of

societal evolution that Richard so elegantly provides we would be able to solve our biggest challenges.
Åsa Norell, educational revolutionary at the world-renowned school Hyper Island

For skeptically hopeful change makers, this is a book for our time. Richard Barrett provides a pragmatic scaffolding for shaping productive conversations about addressing the needs of our interconnected global community. While we are all a part of one global system, our worldviews about this truth are different. Barrett gives us a timely reminder that when we care for the well-being and needs of others, we care for ourselves.
Andrei Hedstrom, CEO, SweetRush Inc.

Richard offers with simplicity and brilliance a guide to unlocking the real dilemma of global well-being and a pathway to becoming more whole. This book is a must for every human being and leader who cares to make a difference.
Ina Gjikondi, MPS, MA, PCC, Director, Executive Education & Coaching, Center for Excellence in Public Leadership, The George Washington University

Richard Barrett explores new and innovative ways of applying his Seven Levels of Consciousness Model to create his new Global Consciousness Indicator. This indicator offers a consistent way of comparing nations. It enables us to follow the progress and development within nations as well as the world as a whole. *Worldview Dynamics and the Well-Being of Nations* is a valuable source for everyone who wishes to make sense of the state of affairs and development of well-being within the nations of the world.
Dr Bjarni S. Jonsson, Management Consultant and Social Entrepreneur

This book is a masterpiece of impressive and creative research work. Finally, we can measure the well-being of the citizens of a nation. A must read for every teacher and parent, and business and political leader.
Else Nollet, Global Partner and Trainer, Barrett Values Centre

WORLDVIEW DYNAMICS

DYNAMICS

AND

THE WELL-BEING OF NATIONS

RICHARD BARRETT

ISBN: 978-1-6847-1599-2 (sc)
ISBN: 978-1-6847-1600-5 (e)

Interior Image Credit: Pete Beebe

Lulu Publishing Services rev. date: 01/09/2020

Dedication

To all those involved in supporting the
evolution of human consciousness

TABLE OF CONTENTS

LIST OF ILLUSTRATIONS

LIST OF TABLES

ACKNOWLEDGEMENTS

Like all my other books, my soul had a big hand in writing this book. Not only did it give me daily 'downloads' about what to write, it also orchestrated an unbelievable number of synchronistic events that served to orient my thinking at significant moments in the preparation of the book. Each event provided new ideas, new insights and new inspirations. Most importantly, my soul brought exactly the right people into my life who could support and help me with the development of the concepts presented in this book.

One of these people was Zoe Andrews. I bumped into Zoe 'by chance' one night in the refectory of University College London. We were both there to attend a seminar on mindfulness. Zoe is an engaging, dynamic 21-year-old with an inquiring mind. Despite the 50-year difference in our ages, we hit it off. I found out she was taking a year off university and, more importantly, she was a wizard at spreadsheets. Six months later I hired her to work on building the spreadsheets of the Global Consciousness Indicators (GCI)® for 145 nations for the years 2014, 2016 and 2018. You can see the results of this work in Part 2 of this book and at www. barrettacademy.com. I had already laid the foundations for the GCI two years earlier with the help of another friend and extremely bright young entrepreneur, Darshita Gillies.

Another person who has been helping me for more than two decades is my friend Pete Beebe. Pete is a gifted designer and spiritual leader, dedicated to the Lakota Red Road. His creative and spiritual work are best represented by his passion for helping people find out who they are and how to fully bring themselves into the world. He has designed the covers for most of my books and is responsible for the design and update of the

Barrett Academy of Advancement of Human Values website. Pete is always there for me and, no matter how tight the deadline, he never lets me down.

It is important when you are a writer to also have trusted people around you to read your manuscripts – to make sure the ideas you are trying to get across make sense. To this end, I have a great team – Christa Schreiber, Patrik Somers Stephenson and Tor Eneroth. They have read almost everything I have written. All three of them are a never-ending source of support with their valuable feedback. I also want to thank David Green for his detailed comments on the final draft of this book.

Christa Schreiber is a clinical psychologist, a Director of the Barrett Academy for the Advancement of Human Values, and a co-facilitator of the Living Your Soul's Destiny workshop. She is also my wife – a loving, constant support who puts up with my strangeness, makes my life work and keeps me grounded.

In addition, I want to pay tribute to the inspiration of Dr Clare Graves (1914–1986), a professor of psychology and the originator of a theory of adult human development that was later developed and popularized by Dr Don Beck and Dr Christopher Cowan under the name of Spiral Dynamics. Unfortunately, I never met Dr Graves. I am sure we would have had much to talk about. What I find interesting is that although our theories had different origins they arrived at a similar destination.

FOREWORD

Richard Barrett has been a pioneering researcher and practitioner in human psychological development for many decades. As founder of the Barrett Values Centre he spearheaded cutting-edge approaches to building values-driven organizations. As Director of the Academy for the Advancement of Human Values he is developing new techniques for measuring global consciousness. This, his latest book, draws upon his research into the well-being of nations.

This important and timely work asks the vital question: How can political, institutional and organizational leaders understand and hold the space for the diverse developmental needs and worldviews of their supporters, workers and employees by developing governance practices and policies that enable people to live fulfilling lives?

His research helps us to explore how leaders can create conditions conducive to individual and collective worldview development by creating a new narrative for our global society, which he calls humanity awareness.

His model of collective human development explains the history of the evolution of human consciousness and why our nations are currently mired in and torn apart by partisan politics. Rather than pulling the collective towards the advancement of individual and communal psychological development – new levels of well-being – we find our dominant political and organizational leadership mind-set conflicted, confused and corrosive; it's in desperate need of an upgrade.

I believe the rise of the extreme Right and extreme Left marks the death-throes of a worldview that is unable to deal with the global challenges of the day. What lies ahead of us, in this hour of humanity's reckoning, is uncertain; yet Richard's insights give nourishment to what can grow through us if we so choose.

One of Richard's greatest gifts is his ability to convey complex, multi-faceted concepts at the heart of human psychological development with clarity, tractability and precision, avoiding academic evasions while drawing upon the wisdom of the ages. His research on ego–soul dynamics, the stages of psychological development, cultural entropy, evolutionary intelligence and humanity awareness for instance, is not just insightful and original; it gives us a map of human development that everyone can relate to and benefit from.

As Richard notes, to deal with the socio-economic and ecological crises now facing humanity on a global scale, a higher-order level of human awareness is required. Humanity is on the cusp of a momentous change.

Richard's book is a must-read for anyone engaged in enabling human evolution towards life-affirming futures for all life on Earth. His book is well written, concise, easy to read, insightful and unique; a truly vital contribution to the necessary [r]evolution in human consciousness now demanded by the systemic challenges we face.

Thank you, Richard, for your vital contribution to humanity's evolution and the ultimate survival of not just *Homo sapiens* but the diverse fabric of life on Earth, which is at peril due to human egotism.

Giles Hutchins
Author of *Future Fit* and co-author of *Regenerative Leadership*,
Chair of The Future Fit Leadership Academy.

PREFACE

One of the things I have discovered over the past 20 years is that a person's sense of well-being is dependent on their ability to satisfy the needs of the stage of psychological development they are at.[1] A baby at the surviving stage of development has different needs to a young child at the conforming stage of development, which are different again to the needs of a teenager at the differentiating stage of development, and so on.

The ability to satisfy the needs associated with a particular stage of psychological development is in turn dependent on the social environment in which a person lives – the values[2] and beliefs[3] of their parents, the community in which they are raised, the school they attend, the workplace where they earn their living, the religion they adopt and the worldview of the nation where they live. The values and beliefs in each of these environments either support or hinder a person in getting their psychological needs met and thereby have a strong influence on their sense of well-being.[4]

Among all these environments the one that is the most pervasive and dominant is the worldview[5] of the community or nation in which a person lives. If the worldview of a community or nation supports people in getting their needs met, they will feel a sense of well-being; if it doesn't, they won't.

Let me give you an example. Several years ago, I mapped the values

---

[1] Throughout the book, I will frequently shorten the term 'seven stages of psychological development' to either 'seven stages of development', or more simply, 'stages of development'.

[2] See Glossary for a definition of values.

[3] See Glossary for a definition of beliefs.

[4] Richard Barrett, *Everything I Have Learned About Values* (London: Fulfilling Books), 2018.

[5] See Glossary for a definition of worldview.

of the people of Iceland and the people of the United Arab Emirates (UAE). When I compared the results, I was a little incredulous. I could not understand why the people of Iceland, who live in the number one democratic nation in the world, had a significantly higher level of cultural entropy* – a lack of well-being – than the people of the UAE, who live in an authoritarian regime.[6]

I struggled for several years to make sense of these results. Then, one day, I had a flash of insight. I realized that the people of the UAE were at a lower stage of psychological development than the people of Iceland. The people of the UAE were living inside a worldview that enabled them to get their needs met at the stage of psychological development they were at, whereas the people of Iceland, who were at a higher stage of development, were living inside a worldview that did not allow them to get their needs met. Hence the level of well-being of the citizens of the UAE was higher than the level of well-being of the citizens of Iceland.

The measure of cultural entropy in Iceland was taken just before Iceland went bankrupt in 2008. What had happened was that the worldview of the leaders of the nation and the Icelandic bankers had dropped to the point (Wealth Awareness) where it was no longer in alignment with the worldview of the people (People Awareness).[7],[8] This lack of alignment showed up as a high level of cultural entropy.

Wherever there is a high level of cultural entropy in a community, organization or nation it is a sign that people's needs are not being met. The cause is always a lack of alignment between the worldview of the people and the worldview of the leaders.

What I have concluded from over 20 years of mapping the values of leaders, organizations and nations is the following:

- When the worldview of the leaders aligns with the dominant worldview of the people, the people feel a sense of well-being and the organization, community or nation operates with a low level of cultural entropy.

---

[6] See Glossary for a definition of cultural entropy.

[7] Richard Barrett, *Everything I Have Learned About Values* (London: Fulfilling Books), 2018, p. 88.

[8] See Chapter 4 for a detailed explanation of Wealth Awareness and People Awareness.

- When the worldview of the leaders does not align with the dominant worldview of the people – when it is lower – the people do not feel a sense of well-being and the organization, community or nation operates with a high level of cultural entropy. In such situations, the high level of cultural entropy – lack of well-being – will eventually cause the organization, community or nation to fail or will force the organization, community or nation to adopt a higher-order worldview.

What is well-being?

Based on my research, I have come to the conclusion that well-being is *the feeling we get when we can satisfy the needs of the stage of psychological development we are at and also satisfy the needs of the stages of psychological development we have passed through.*

Therefore, as long as we continue to grow and develop, finding a sense of well-being will be a moving target; once we have learned to satisfy the needs of one stage of development and feel a sense of well-being, we will move to the next stage of development, where we may lose our sense of well-being until we have learned how to satisfy the needs associated with that stage of development.

This potential roller-coaster of well-being is quite normal as long as we are growing and developing. But what happens if we get stuck: if, for whatever reason, we fail to master the needs of a stage of development or are blocked by circumstances in reaching a stage of development? This is what happened to my father; because of the situation he found himself in, he was never able to reach the individuating stage of development. Consequently, he never self-actualized and never fulfilled his potential.

When my father was a teenager his father died. Although he was a bright scholar, my father had to leave school at 16 to earn a living to support his mother and himself. He became a mechanic. He spent his life repairing trucks. He died quite young in his late fifties. He never had the chance to individuate and never felt a strong sense of well-being. Because of his low income, he was always anxious about satisfying our family's basic needs. He desperately wanted a better life for me, his only child, than the life he had. His one wish was that I should go to university. That is what he had wanted for himself, but his mother's survival needs had taken precedence.

Strange how history repeats itself. When my father died my stay-at-home mother and I had no income. I was 17; I had good grades, and I was beginning to explore the idea of going to university. I will never forget what happened next.

My mother said to me my father's wish was that I should go to university, and if I could find a way of paying for my studies, she would find a way of surviving. She took a job as a caretaker at the local chapel and I applied to the local education authority for a grant to cover my university fees and living expenses. I got the grant. Within three years of graduating, I had paid off the mortgage on my mother's house and we both regained a sense of well-being. In addition, spending four years at university gave me the freedom to begin to explore my gifts and talents: I individuated and eventually self-actualized.

Now to get back to my point about well-being being a moving target. Imagine that there are seven stages of psychological development.[9] It is highly likely that at some point in our lives we will struggle to meet the needs of one of these stages of development. Or alternatively, because of a change in circumstances, we will no longer be able to meet the needs of a stage of development we have passed through.

Let's say there is an economic downturn, like there was in 2008; you lose your job and you are no longer able to meet your survival needs – you find it difficult to pay your bills. If this happened, you would undoubtedly become anxious and stressed; you may even become depressed. If you continue to struggle for a long time to meet your survival needs, you may at some point consider committing suicide.

It is not surprising, therefore, since each stage of development has its own needs that the number of needs we must satisfy increases as we get older. Satisfying these needs can become increasingly onerous, particularly for men or women who are the main breadwinners of a family. Consequently, the incidence of suicide increases with age. In most Western countries it reaches a peak around the end of the fifth stage of development (the self-actualizing stage) in our early fifties.

[9] The seven stages of psychological development are explained in detail in Chapter 3.

Not surprisingly, we find an inverse pattern in measures of happiness and well-being. Research studies[10] show that we are at our happiest in our early twenties and late sixties, and we are at our unhappiest as we approach our mid-fifties – towards the end of the self-actualizing stage of development.

Therefore, if we wish to increase the level of well-being in a community or nation, we must not only create an environment that nurtures people's self-actualization needs, we must also create an environment that nurtures all the other stages of development as well, particularly people's survival, safety and security needs.

In order to understand the implications of this statement it will be useful to describe the needs we must meet in order to feel a sense of well-being at each stage of psychological development.

Well-being at each stage of development

If you are a baby at the first stage of development, and all your physiological needs are being met, you will experience a feeling of well-being. If your physiological (survival) needs are not met, you will experience distress. This is also true later in life. You must be able to meet your survival needs to feel a sense of well-being.

Let's now assume that you are a child at the conforming stage of development, and all your safety needs are being met – you feel loved, protected and a sense of belonging. Let's say your survival needs are also met. In this case you will experience a feeling of well-being. If your safety needs are met but your survival needs are not met, or your survival needs are met but your safety needs are not met, you will not experience a feeling of well-being. Imagine how distressed you would feel if you could not meet either your survival or your safety needs. No matter what age you are, you must be able to meet both your survival *and* safety needs to feel a sense of well-being.

Let's assume you are now a teenager at the differentiating stage of development and all your security needs are being met – you feel respected, recognized and acknowledged by your peer group and your parents. Let's

---

[10] https://www.brilliantlivinghq.com/happiness-and-age/

also say your survival and safety needs are also met, in which case you will experience a feeling of well-being. If, on the other hand, one of your three sets of needs are not met – survival, safety or security – you will not experience a feeling of well-being. Imagine how distressed you would feel if you could not meet any of these needs. You would be so preoccupied about meeting these fundamental needs that you would not be able to focus on the needs of the fourth (individuating) stage of development.

This is the experience of most people on the planet. They find it difficult to meet their survival, safety and security needs. Consequently, like my father, they never get the opportunity to explore the fourth stage of their psychological development; they never get to individuate.

Let's assume that you are a young adult, in your mid-twenties or early thirties, and you are fortunate enough to live in a nation where you can get your survival, safety and security needs met. You will now want to find freedom and autonomy to become independent and accountable for your life; to adopt the values and beliefs that are meaningful to you, rather than the values and beliefs of your parents or the community in which you were raised. You will want to individuate.

If you are successful, and you can also meet your survival, safety and security needs, then you will feel a sense of well-being. If you are successful at individuating, but for whatever reason you are no longer able to meet your survival, safety or security needs, then you will not feel a sense of well-being. The contrary is also true; if you can meet your survival, safety and security needs but cannot meet your individuating needs, you will not feel a sense of well-being. This was the situation that precipitated the Arab Spring.

Young adults from the Arab nations of North Africa and the Middle East had studied abroad and come home to relatively high-paying private sector jobs that allowed them to meet their survival, safety and security needs. They now wanted the freedom to explore their own values and beliefs; they wanted to individuate. Unfortunately, they came up against authoritarian regimes that were operating from a lower stage of development. Although they demonstrated over several weeks, their needs were not recognized. Many of these people left their respective countries because they were being prevented from growing and developing. They could only find well-being by settling in a country that was operating from a higher stage of development that allowed them to individuate.

This was also the case in the former USSR (and in all communist countries). If people showed any signs of embracing the fourth stage of development – individuating – finding the freedom and autonomy they needed to adopt the values and beliefs that were meaningful to them, rather than the values and beliefs of their parents or the community in which they were raised, they were sent to the Gulag Archipelago.

Now let's assume you have reached your forties and you have the good fortune to live in a nation where you can meet your survival, safety and security needs as well as having the freedom to explore your individuation needs. You will want to self-actualize – find a sense of meaning and purpose to your life. If you successfully self-actualize, you will find a sense of joy and purpose to your life. If, on the other hand, you self-actualize but struggle to meet your survival, safety and security needs, then your sense of well-being will disappear.

Self-actualizing is the most difficult and most anxiety-producing stage of development: this is when the incidence of suicide begins to peak. This stage of development is particularly difficult for women because they often put their partner's needs, their children's needs and an aging parent's needs before their own needs. Consequently, they find it difficult to focus on their own needs.

Once you have successfully mastered your self-actualizing needs, things tend to get a little easier if you can go on satisfying your survival, safety and security needs. At the sixth stage of development – the integrating stage of development – you will find a sense of well-being by connecting empathetically with others to make a difference in the world. At the seventh stage of development – the serving stage – you will find a sense of well-being by contributing to the common good – being of service through acts of kindness and compassion to all those you meet.

There are currently no nations that have created the conditions required to support citizens in meeting their self-actualization needs – finding meaning and purpose in their lives. There are, however, nine nations that have created the conditions required to support citizens in meeting their individuation needs. In all other nations, almost everyone, except the rich, struggle to meet their survival, safety and security needs. What can be done about this?

Finding an answer to this question is what this book is about: how to create the conditions that support people in satisfying not just their survival, safety and security needs but also their individuation and self-actualization needs. The last chapter describes what such a nation would look like.

Politics and well-being

The idea that people grow in stages, and each stage has specific needs, throws a new light on the central question of political thought: How can human beings best govern themselves?

This question assumes we can determine whether one way of governing is better than another – in other words, there is some form of objective morality that enables people to judge a good governance system from a bad governance system.

Viewed through the lens of history, it is obvious that this has never been the case. Morality has always been subjective; it has always reflected the cultural norms and the cosmology[11] of the worldview of the ruling classes in authoritarian regimes, or the dominant worldview of the people in democratic regimes. In an authoritarian regime, the dominant worldview reflects the stage of psychological development of the leader; in a democratic regime, the dominant worldview reflects the stage of psychological development of the people.[12]

When the stage of psychological development of the leader in an authoritarian regime or the stage of psychological development of the people in a democratic regime shifts to a higher level, a new way of governing is required that aligns with the values and beliefs of the new stage of psychological development. For example, in the UK, when women were given the vote, we shifted to a new stage of psychological development, and a new more inclusive governance system was created.

This insight leads me to pose a more nuanced question: *How can*

---

[11] See Glossary for a definition of cosmology.
[12] Chapter 3 provides a description of the Stages of Psychological Development.

human beings best govern themselves so they can get their most important needs met? (With the understanding that their most important needs are the needs of the stage of psychological development they have reached.)

This puts politics in a new light. If everyone in a human group structure is at the same stage of psychological development, and therefore has a similar worldview, then they will have the same needs, and politics becomes simply about what is the best way to satisfy these needs.

This was perhaps true when we lived in clans or tribes, but it is not true in our modern world. It is more normal for people to be at different stages of psychological development and have different worldviews, particularly in democratic regimes. In this case, *politics becomes about managing competing worldviews* – determining which groups win (get their needs met) and which groups lose (don't get their needs met).

In a two-party system, such as in the US and to a large extent the UK, this way of governing is divisive: it sets one group against the other and prevents social cohesion. A multi-party governance system with a coalition government and proportional representation is less divisive because everyone gets some of their needs met – in a coalition government there is always an element of give and take.

If politicians are to be effective, they must know and understand the worldviews of the constituents they represent. Only then can they fully engage in promoting policies that meet the needs of the people.

There is a problem, however; every politician also has a worldview. This creates a conundrum: To what extent can politicians represent the worldviews of their constituents if they and the different constituent groups they represent hold different worldviews? The answer is they can't. So, what is to be done? When we understand that the stages of psychological development are not only age related but also worldview related, then the answer becomes obvious.

However, I think the answer may be too radical to expose at the beginning of this book, because for many readers it will require a fundamental shift in worldview. I have therefore saved my thoughts on the solution to this conundrum until the last chapter when you, the reader, will hopefully have managed to stop looking through your worldview and have started looking at your worldview alongside other worldviews.

For the moment, let me leave you with this challenging thought. If you don't understand the concept of worldviews, and you are a politician, then you really need to read this book. Your effectiveness as a politician depends on it.

PART 1

A THEORY OF WORLDVIEWS

The first part of this book looks at theories that explain the evolution of human consciousness. In Chapter 1, I make the link between the evolution of our collective sense of identity and the evolution of worldviews. In Chapter 2, I describe the situations and circumstances that triggered new collective identities and worldviews, and discuss why, until recent times, worldviews have been slow to evolve. In Chapter 3, I describe the three belief systems – personal, cultural and cosmological – that make up a worldview and which of these belief systems are dominant in each worldview. In Chapter 4, I describe the six existing worldviews – Clan Awareness, Tribe Awareness, State Awareness, Nation Awareness, Wealth Awareness and People Awareness, and the three emergent worldviews that will manifest in future decades and centuries – Humanity Awareness, Earth Awareness and Unity Awareness. In Chapter 5, I conclude the first part of the book with a description of the factors that cause worldviews to evolve and regress.

1

IDENTITY AS THE FOUNDATION
OF WELL-BEING

Throughout history, most of the suffering humans have experienced has been caused by our limited sense of identity. Whenever we've had anxieties about our survival, safety or security, we've clung more tightly to the group we identify with – we have become more clannish, tribalistic, racist or nationalistic. Why do we do that? Because our best chance of surviving has always been to belong to a group. Our sense of identity becomes more important to us when we feel our survival, safety or security is under threat.

Amartya Sen, Nobel Laureate for Economics, agrees. In *Identity & Violence: The Illusion of Destiny*,[13] Sen points out that the identity we assume can have a significant influence over our thoughts and actions; in particular, an overly strong association with any form of ethnic identity can lead us to perform acts of violence against others who do not share the same ethnic identity. Sen's main thesis is that we have a choice about the identity we assume.

Sen provides the following example. 'A Hutu labourer from Kigali may be pressured to see himself only as a Hutu and incited to kill Tutsis, and yet viewed from a larger perspective, he is not only a Hutu, but also a Kigalian, a Rwandan, an African, and a human being.'[14] The points Sen is making are: a) we can choose our identity; and b) the choice we make can significantly affect our life experiences.

---

[13] Amartya Sen, *Identity & Violence: The Illusion of Destiny* (London: Penguin Books), 2006.
[14] Ibid., p. 4.

While theoretically Sen's Hutu labourer does have a choice about his identity, in practice, if he wants to increase his chances of survival and feel safe – and who doesn't want to survive and feel safe – he doesn't have a choice. Allegiance to his tribe and staying close to other Hutus is the only 'choice' he has. Choosing to see himself as a citizen of the planet or an African would not increase his chances of survival or safety while he is living in Kigali and Rwanda.

Throughout history, minority groups all over the world have invariably, at some time or another, become the target of oppression. The Protestants in England in the 16th century, the Jews in Germany in the 1930s, the Catholics in Northern Ireland in the 1960s and the Moslem Bosniaks living in Serbia in the 1990s can all attest to the suffering they experienced as ethnic/religious minorities.

There are two ways of eliminating oppression: either members of the dominant group expand their sense of identity to integrate the minority groups, or if such an accommodation is not possible, members of the minority group separate themselves from the dominant group by establishing their own independent, self-governing territory.

A third more radical way of dealing with the identity problem is for one group, usually the dominant group, to systematically remove other ethnic, racial and/or religious groups from their territory. This is called ethnic cleansing.

This leads me to ask the question, why do humans place such a high level of importance on identity? The answer is simple: because *identity is the foundation of well-being.* Our basic well-being arises from our ability to meet what Abraham Maslow called our deficiency needs – our survival, safety and security needs.

Being part of a group generates reciprocal altruism – everyone in the group cares about the needs of the other members of the group. Everyone knows their survival, safety and security is enhanced when they can call on other members of their group for support. Whoever we identify with, we care for; whoever we don't identify with, we separate ourselves from.

So, what would need to happen for everyone in the world, no matter which ethnic group they belong to, which country they live in and which religion they espouse, to feel free to choose a more expansive sense of identity? The answer is that firstly they would need to be able to satisfy their deficiency needs, and secondly they would need to satisfy their self-actualization needs.

Deficiency needs and growth needs

In the middle of the 20th century Maslow developed a theory that linked well-being to the satisfaction of needs. He postulated that well-being comprises five components. Each component acts as a foundation for the subsequent component. His five components of well-being, in order of importance, are – physiological needs, safety needs, love/belonging needs, self-esteem needs and self-actualization needs (see Figure 1.1).

Self-actualization
The desire to become the best one can be

Self-esteem
Respect, status, recognition, power

Love and belonging
Family, friendship, sense of connection

Safety needs
Employment, protection, resources

Physiological needs
Air, water, food, shelter, reproduction

Figure 1.1: Maslow's Hierarchy of Needs

Maslow divided his hierarchy of needs into two parts – deficiency needs at the base of his pyramid and growth needs at the top. The first two levels of his hierarchy represent our physiological needs – survival and safety. The next two levels represent our emotional needs, and the top level represents our self-actualization needs.

Maslow stated that every level is a foundation for the subsequent level. Therefore, we must learn to satisfy the needs at one level before we can successfully gratify our needs at the next level. Furthermore, we must learn to master our deficiency needs before we can focus on our growth needs: our deficiency needs always take precedence over our growth needs. Thus, only when we master our deficiency needs can we focus on our growth needs.

The order in which we learn to satisfy our deficiency needs is biologically dependent. We spend the first two years of our lives learning how to satisfy and manage our physiological survival needs; we spend the next five to six years learning how to satisfy and manage our emotional safety needs; and we spend our teenage years learning how to satisfy and manage our security needs.

If we reach our early twenties and have been successful in learning to master our deficiency needs, we spend the rest of our lives learning how to master our growth needs. If we are not successful at mastering our deficiency needs our minds remain fixed at the levels of consciousness where we experienced the greatest deficit of needs.

The reason why learning to master our deficiency needs is biologically dependent is because of the physiological development of our brain and the associated psychological development of our mind.

The first brain to develop is the reptilian brain (the body mind). The body mind is dominant during the first two years of our life.[15] The focus of the body mind is on learning to keep the body alive. The second brain to develop is the limbic brain (the emotional mind). The emotional mind is dominant during the next five to six years of our life. The focus of the emotional mind is on learning how to keep us safe in the parental and family framework of our existence. The third brain to develop is the neocortex (the rational mind). The rational mind is dominant during the next 14–16 years or our life. The focus of the rational mind is on learning how to keep us feeling secure in the cultural framework of our existence.

Biologically speaking, we have a fully functioning mind only when

---

[15] It becomes dominant towards the end of the first trimester of pregnancy.

we reach our early twenties. By this point, our mind has been fully programmed to meet our deficiency needs. The programming we receive is totally dependent on our parental and cultural conditioning. Only if we have been successful in learning how to master our deficiency needs do we go on to learn how to master our growth needs. If we struggled to meet our deficiency needs, we will stay focused on trying to satisfy those needs for the rest of our lives and we may never learn how to master our growth needs.

The Seven Levels of Consciousness Model[16]

From 1995 to 1996, I worked on simplifying and expanding Maslow's Hierarchy of Needs to use it as a tool for measuring the consciousness of individuals, organizations and nations. I made three changes:

- A shift in focus from needs to consciousness.
- An expansion of the concept of self-actualization.
- Relabelling the basic needs.

Changing from needs to consciousness

It was evident to me that when people have underlying fear-based beliefs about being able to meet their deficiency needs, their subconscious mind will stay focused on finding ways to satisfy these needs.

Survival consciousness

For example, when a person has a subconscious fear-based belief at the survival level of consciousness, no matter how much money they earn, they will always want more. For them enough is never enough. Because of their early experiences they feel they cannot trust the universe to provide for them. Therefore, they must stay vigilant, earn as much as they can and watch every penny they spend. Such people can remain focused at the survival level of consciousness all their lives, even though compared with others they are financially well-off.

---

[16] https://www.valuescentre.com/barrett-model/

Relationship consciousness

When a person has a subconscious fear-based belief at the love and belonging level of consciousness, no matter how much love and affection they get, they will always want more. They cannot get enough. They want to experience the love and affection that was not accorded to them in their childhood. Such people can remain focused at the love and belonging level of consciousness all their lives, even though they may be in a long-term loving relationship.

Self-esteem consciousness

When a person has a subconscious fear-based belief at the self-esteem level of consciousness, no matter how much praise or accolades they get, they will always want more. They cannot get enough. They want to experience the respect and recognition that was not accorded to them in their teenage years. Such people can remain focused at the self-esteem level of consciousness all their lives, even though their accomplishments are frequently acknowledged by the people around them.

These three considerations led me to recognize that the fear-based beliefs that we learn during the first 24 years of our life, which we use to interpret our reality, strongly influence the levels of consciousness we operate from during our adult years; they keep us focused on our deficiency needs, not allowing us to explore our growth needs.

Expanding the concept of self-actualization

The second change I made was to give more definition to Maslow's concept of self-actualization. I achieved this by integrating the concepts of Vedic philosophy into Maslow's model and expanding self-actualization from one level to three.

According to Vedic philosophy we can experience seven states of consciousness. The first three – waking, dreaming and deep sleep – are part of everyone's daily experience. The next four are dependent on the level of self-actualization we reach.

In the fourth state of consciousness, we recognize we are more than an ego[17] in a physical body. By contemplating the question Who am I? we begin to recognize that we are also a soul.[18]

In the fifth state of consciousness, we learn to fully identify with the motivations of our soul. We give more focus to exploring our natural gifts and talents and we begin to experience a fear-free state of psychological functioning.

In the sixth state of consciousness, we become aware of the deep level of connection we have to other people. We realize that there are no 'others' because at a deeper level of being we are all energetically connected.

In the seventh state of consciousness, we become one with all there is. The self fuses with every other aspect of creation in a state of oneness. There is no separation between the knower and the object of knowing.

The frequency of our experiences of these higher states of consciousness depends on the degree to which we have released the fear-based beliefs we learned during our childhood and teenage years. As we make progress in releasing our fears and mastering our deficiency needs, we gain more access to the higher states of consciousness. We begin at the transformation level and from there we go through three stages of self-actualization.

Transformation

The fourth state of Vedic consciousness corresponds to Carl Jung's concept of *individuation*. I call this level of consciousness *transformation*. Transformation occurs when we find the freedom and autonomy to be who we are: when we begin to inquire into our true nature. We learn to make our own choices; to develop our own voice, independent of the values and beliefs of our parental and cultural conditioning, and thereby become the author of our own life. This is an important preliminary step before we enter the first level of self-actualization.

The first level of self-actualization

The fifth state of consciousness in Vedic philosophy corresponds to the first level of self-actualization. I refer to this level of consciousness as

---

[17] See Glossary for a definition of Ego.
[18] See Glossary for a definition of soul.

internal cohesion. At this level of consciousness, our ego motivations merge with our soul motivations. We want to identify our unique gifts and talents and find our personal transcendent purpose – our calling or vocation in life. We become a soul-infused personality wanting to lead a values-driven and purpose-driven life.

The second level of self-actualization

The sixth state of consciousness in Vedic philosophy corresponds to the second level of self-actualization. I refer to this level of consciousness as *making a difference.* At this level of consciousness, we begin to feel a sense of empathy towards the disadvantaged; we want to use our unique gifts and talents to support and help them; we want to improve the world. We learn that we can make a bigger difference if we connect and collaborate with others who share the same values and the same sense of purpose.

The third level of self-actualization

The seventh state of consciousness in Vedic philosophy corresponds to the third level of self-actualization. I refer to this level of consciousness as *service.* We arrive at this level of consciousness when our pursuit of making a difference becomes a way of life. We begin to feel a sense of compassion for the world. Wherever we are, we want to be of service to others – we just want to help in any way we can. At this level of consciousness, we learn to show love and kindness in all situations; we learn to be at ease with uncertainty and tap into the deepest source of our wisdom.

While I fully realize the correlations I have made between Vedic philosophy and Maslow's concept of self-actualization are not exact, they are sufficiently close to provide insights into the motivations and underlying spiritual significance of the process of self-actualization.

Relabelling the lower levels of consciousness

The last change I made to Maslow's Hierarchy of Needs was to combine Maslow's physiological and safety levels into a single *survival* level, and rename the love/belonging level *relationship consciousness.* Since the fundamental biological purpose of developing strong relationship bonds is to feel protected and safe, I often refer to the relationship level of consciousness as the safety level.

Although I left the self-esteem level unchanged, I frequently refer to this level of consciousness as the security level because our self-esteem and the level of confidence we feel are usually related to the respect and recognition we get from others: we feel more secure when we are held in high regard by our peers.

The Seven Levels Model

This is how I created the Seven Levels Model. The first three levels focus on our deficiency needs – survival, relationship (safety) and self-esteem (security); the last three levels focus on our growth needs – internal cohesion, making a difference and service.

Bridging the gap between our deficiency needs and our growth needs is the transformation level of consciousness. This is where we begin to release the limiting fear-based beliefs we learned during our formative years and start to align our ego motivations with our soul motivations. Figure 1.2 shows the Seven Levels of Consciousness Model.

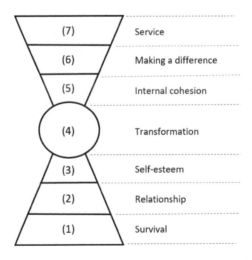

Figure 1.2: The Seven Levels of Consciousness Model

It is important to understand that when people or groups operate from the first three levels of consciousness, their sense of well-being will always be linked to the gratification of their deficiency needs. Only when they have learned how to satisfy and master these needs are their minds free to focus on the gratification of their transformation and growth needs.

We achieve well-being at the transformation level when we find freedom and autonomy to be who we really are. We achieve well-being in the upper levels of consciousness when we find a meaning and purpose to our lives; when we connect with others and make a difference in their lives; and when we can be of service to our family, community, country or the well-being of the Earth. The joy we experience from gratifying our growth needs makes us want to do more.

In order to achieve full spectrum well-being – what I often refer to as flourishing – we must learn to satisfy our deficiency needs, our transformation needs and our growth needs.

The point I want to make is this: *we can only fully satisfy our growth needs by expanding our sense of identity beyond our limited ethnic, racial or religious identity and embracing our full human identity.*

The evolution of identity

Since the time of our earliest ancestors, our species has experienced five significant expansions of identity. During the period of hunter/gatherers, we identified with a small family grouping of 20–30 people. I will be referring to this level of identity as Clan Awareness. At this level of identity/awareness everyone worked together to get their survival and safety needs met.

During the time of the agricultural revolution, we identified with our tribe. In order to survive, keep safe and feel secure we subsumed our clan identity within our tribal identity – different clans learned to live together in the same tribe. I will be referring to this level of identity as Tribe Awareness. Everyone in the tribe supported each other in getting their survival and safety needs met.

During the early period of empire building, we identified with our city state. We subsumed our tribal identity within our state identity – different ethnic groups learned to live together within the same state. I will be referring to this level of identity as State Awareness. At this level of identity/ awareness only the most powerful and wealthy got their survival, safety and security needs met. Everyone else struggled to survive.

During the late period of empire building, we identified with our nation and each nation adopted a unique religion. There were Christian nations, Islamic nations, etc. We subsumed our ethnic and religious identities inside our national identity. I will be referring to this level of identity as Nation Awareness. At this level of identity/awareness only the wealthy and those in positions of authority got their deficiency needs met. Everyone else struggled to survive.

After the Reformation, European nations began to break the link between national identity and religious identity. Religions began to fragment, and science began to replace religion as the overriding cosmology.[19] Nations became secular; more materialistic and less spiritual.

At the same time, the world began to get 'smaller' – more connected physically and financially. Global commerce became increasingly important. Wealth became the new global identifier. Just as formerly religious affiliation had been a key differentiator of identity, now levels of wealth became the primary differentiator of identity, both within nations and between nations. Ever since State Awareness, wealth had always been an important identifier, but in Wealth Awareness it became more pervasive; more than just a division between rich and poor, it was also a division between income levels – low income, moderate income and high income. I will be referring to this level of identity as Wealth Awareness. At this level of identity/awareness only the rich, famous and most educated and industrious were able to master their survival needs. Inequalities between the rich and poor increased significantly in the worldview of Wealth Awareness.

Some nations decided to reduce income inequality by providing social safety nets and welfare for all citizens, rich and poor alike. They redistributed incomes through progressive taxation schemes where the rich paid more than the poor. They also began sharing their national income with poor countries through development aid. I will be referring to this level of identity as People Awareness. This is the first level of

---

[19] See Glossary for a definition of cosmology.

identity/awareness where the State gave everyone an opportunity to get their deficiency needs met. For the first time in human history the masses had the opportunity to focus on their growth needs.

These five shifts in identity, from Clan Awareness to Tribe Awareness, from Tribe Awareness to State Awareness, from State Awareness to Nation Awareness, from Nation Awareness to Wealth Awareness and Wealth Awareness to People Awareness, resulted in a progressive expansion of social integration.

In Clan Awareness around 30–40 people shared the same identity. In Tribe Awareness around several hundred to several thousand shared the same identity. In State Awareness several million shared the same identity. In Nation Awareness, Wealth Awareness and People Awareness tens of millions shared the same identity.

There are three new levels of identity/awareness on the horizon: Humanity Awareness, Earth Awareness and Unity Awareness. In Humanity Awareness we will learn to live together and support our collective well-being as members of humanity. In Earth Awareness we will learn to identify with, and support, the well-being of all non-human life forms on planet Earth. In Unity Awareness we will learn to identify with all there is.

The glue of identity

Every level of identity/awareness has its own special 'glue', the factor that enables an individual to distinguish 'us' – the group they belong to – from 'them' – the group they do not belong to – to distinguish those they can trust from those they cannot trust. We call those we can trust our 'in-group' and those we cannot trust our 'out-group'. In times of scarcity or conflict, we consolidate our links to our in-group and cut our links to our out-group.

There are five main factors that constitute the glue of our primary identity:

- Ethnicity
- Shared territory
- Shared language

- Shared religion
- Place of birth.

Inside each level of identity/awareness we also find sublevels of identity. Just as we learn to trust those who share our primary identity more than those with a different primary identity, we also learn to trust those who share our sublevel identity more than those at other sublevels.

There are six main factors that differentiate sublevels of identity:

- Close blood relatives
- Distant blood relatives
- Individuals who have demonstrated their allegiance to the leader
- Individuals with special talents (advisors and wisdom keepers)
- Social class (landowners, commercial traders, artisans, labourers)
- Wealth (upper, middle and lower class).

In more recent times other sublevels of identity have become important. These include:

- Age
- Gender
- Sexual orientation.

In this book, I introduce two further sublevels of identity:

- Stage of psychological development
- Worldview.

As I will show later, in many respects these two sublevels of identity – stages of psychological development and worldviews – are synonymous.

Worldviews/stages of psychological development are important because they are the most important differentiators of people within a nation and the most important differentiators of people between nations. Therefore, as I stated in the Preface, modern-day politics is about managing the competing worldviews of groups in a nation, and international politics is about managing the competing worldviews of nations. Groups or nations with similar worldviews will find it easier to collaborate than groups or nations with dissimilar worldviews.

The identity of Clan Awareness

The glue of identity in Clan Awareness is **kinship** – close blood relatives. Members of the family (clan) are regarded as 'us' and members of every other family (clan) are regarded as 'them'. There are two main sublevels of identity in Clan Awareness – those with special knowledge, wisdom and experience and the rest of the clan members.

The identity of Tribe Awareness

The glue of identity in Tribe Awareness is **ethnicity** – those who share the same blood line, speak a shared language, share a common cultural heritage (meaningful traditions and rituals) and live in a common territory are regarded as 'us'. Everyone with a different ethnicity is regarded as 'them'. There are three main sublevels of identity in Tribe Awareness – those with close blood ties to the chief, those with special knowledge and talents (the wise and experienced who are held in high regard; members of the tribal council of elders) and the other members of the tribe.

The identity of State Awareness

The glue of identity in State Awareness is **statehood** – the state in which we were born and raised. This is ethnicity without a shared bloodline. Those who belong to the same state are regarded as 'us'; everyone else is regarded as 'them'. There are five main sublevels of identity in State Awareness – those with close blood ties to the leader, those who have demonstrated their allegiance to the leader, those who have special knowledge and talents that are held in high regard by the leader, the social class a person belongs to (the type of work they do) and gender.

The identity of Nation Awareness

The glue of identity in Nation Awareness is **citizenship.** If we share the same citizenship, we are regarded as one of 'us'; if we don't share the same citizenship, we are regarded as one of 'them'. Thus, it is possible to have people of different ethnicities sharing the same identity, although those who belong to the core ethnicity of the nation tend to look upon other ethnicities as foreigners. They tolerate their presence in their shared national identity but may not want them as neighbours or wish to befriend them.

There are five main sublevels of identity in Nation Awareness – those with close blood ties to the leader, those who own large tracts of land, those who have demonstrated their allegiance to the leader (head of State, king, queen or religious leader), those who follow the State religion, and gender. If you are a woman *or* you don't follow the State religion, you may be the object of discrimination. If you are a woman *and* you don't follow the State religion, beware! In olden times you might have been labelled a witch and finished up being burned at the stake.

The identity of Wealth Awareness

The glue of identity in Wealth Awareness is **status**. Wealth, achievement, competence and qualifications are more important than ethnicity.

There are three main sublevels of identity in Wealth Awareness – the upper class, the middle class and the lower class; a hierarchy based on wealth, income and privilege. The upper class consists of the richest and most influential people – royalty, the famous and the well-educated (those who went to prestigious fee-paying schools) as well as those appointed to positions of public office at the national level. The middle class consists of merchants, businesspeople and anyone with a higher education who has been successful in life. The lower class consists of people who are working class, poor or physically/mentally disadvantaged who never had a higher education and had to make their way in life without support or help.

The identity of People Awareness

The glue of identity in People Awareness is **country of residence**. Unlike the other levels of identity/awareness, there are no significant sublevels of identity. Everyone who makes their home in the country and becomes a citizen is treated equally and fairly. There are no hierarchies of privilege and very little discrimination based on gender, religion or sexual orientation.

The identity of Humanity Awareness

The glue of identity in Humanity Awareness goes beyond ethnicity, citizenship, status and residence: it is our **shared humanity**. This is the first true transnational identity. Everyone is considered equal; everyone is treated with respect; everyone is treated fairly. The main sublevel of identity in Humanity Awareness is stage of psychological development.

Worldviews

Each transition to a higher level of identity/awareness required a new 'operating system' – a more inclusive way of governing and administering human affairs. The values and beliefs that lie at the core of each operating system are what I will be referring to in the remainder of this book as worldviews.

A worldview is a set of values and beliefs that enable people to give meaning to their experiences and help them make decisions which allow them to get their needs met within the collective belief structures of their existence.

A worldview is 'larger' than a culture.[20] Groups of people all over the world can share the same worldview but belong to different cultures. For example, even though the worldview of Tribe Awareness can be found in ethnically homogenous groups all over the world, each tribe has its own culture – its own language, dress code, rituals and traditions. Despite these cultural differences they all share the same worldview.

In groups operating from the worldviews of Clan, Tribe and State Awareness, different worldviews are not tolerated. In countries operating from the worldview of Nation Awareness, which are mostly flawed democracies, people with different worldviews may be tolerated but not readily accepted. In countries operating from the worldviews of Wealth Awareness and People Awareness, which are full democracies, people with

---

[20] See Glossary for the definition of culture.

different worldviews are readily accepted if they live by the rules of the society.

Summary

Here are the main points of this chapter.

1. Whoever we identify with, we care for. Whoever we don't identify with, we separate ourselves from.
2. We all have two sets of needs – deficiency needs and growth needs.
3. Our species has experienced five significant expansions of identity/awareness. A new expansion of identity is rapidly approaching – from People Awareness to Humanity Awareness.
4. Every level of identity/awareness has its own 'glue'.
5. The glue of identity in Clan Awareness is kinship.
6. The glue of identity in Tribe Awareness is ethnicity.
7. The glue of identity in State Awareness is statehood.
8. The glue of identity in Nation Awareness is citizenship.
9. The glue of identity in Wealth Awareness is status.
10. The glue of identity in People Awareness is country of residence.
11. The glue of identity in Humanity Awareness is our shared humanity.
12. Each transition to a higher level of identity/awareness required a new 'operating system' – a more inclusive way of governing and administering human affairs.
13. Each level of identity/awareness has its own worldview.

2

THE EMERGENCE OF
NEW WORLDVIEWS

Until recent times worldviews had been slow to evolve. The worldview of Clan Awareness began with the arrival of *Homo sapiens* around 200,000–300,000 years ago and was the dominant worldview until Tribe Awareness emerged around 12,000 years ago. Tribe Awareness was the dominant worldview for around 6,500 years until State Awareness emerged about 5,500 years ago. State Awareness was the dominant worldview for around 3,700 years until Nation Awareness emerged about 1,800 years ago. Nation Awareness was the dominant worldview for around 1,300 years until Wealth Awareness emerged about 500 years ago. The worldview of People Awareness began to emerge about 200 years ago. The worldview of Humanity Awareness began to emerge about 60 years ago. The focus of the seven worldviews and the timeline of their emergence are shown in Table 2.1.

Table 2.1: Focus and timeline of the emergence of new worldviews

Worldview		Focus of worldview	First Emergence
7	Humanity Awareness	Finding meaning through self-expression and creativity.	20th century
6	People Awareness	Collective freedom through equality and accountability.	19th century

5	Wealth Awareness	Personal security through status and influence.	16th century
4	Nation Awareness	Personal security through authority and education.	6th century
3	State Awareness	Personal security through power and strength.	4,000 BCE
2	Tribe Awareness	Collective safety through loyalty and belonging.	10,000 BCE
1	Clan Awareness	Collective survival through sharing and reciprocity.	Earlier than 10,000 BCE

The increasing progression in the frequency of the emergence of new levels of identity/awareness (worldviews) raises three important questions:

- Why have worldviews historically been resistant to change?
- Why are worldviews beginning to emerge more rapidly?
- What triggered the emergence of each new worldview?

Why have worldviews historically been resistant to change?

The reason why worldviews have historically been resistant to change is because they have a self-reinforcing feedback loop. From birth to adulthood, children are programmed by their parents to live inside the worldview of the community in which they are raised. When these children become adults, they in turn programme their children to live inside the same worldview. Generation after generation adopts the same worldview because that is the only way they know how to survive and keep safe. This feedback loop is shown in Figure 2.1.

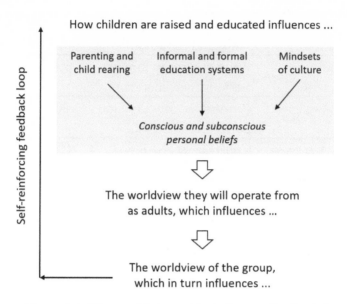

Figure 2.1: The worldview self-reinforcing feedback loop

To my mind, the most significant aspect of the self-reinforcing feedback loop is the way in which children are raised and educated. During the first 20 years of our lives we go through a process of emergent learning – a form of psychological conditioning in which we learn how to survive, keep safe and feel secure in the parental and community frameworks of our existence. This process goes on for around 20 years because that is the time it takes for our three brains to grow and develop.

The reptilian mind/brain (body mind) begins to operate towards the end of the first trimester of gestation and is our dominant decision-making interface with the external world until we reach the age of about 18 months. During this period, our body mind learns how to react to whatever is happening in our physical environment to keep us alive.

The limbic mind/brain (the emotional mind), which has been growing and developing in the background, then becomes the dominant decision-making interface with the world and stays dominant until around the age of seven. During this period, we learn how to react to what is happening in our close family environment to keep us safe. Parenting skills, child-rearing practices and education programmes have a significant impact on the beliefs we learn during this period of our life.

The neocortex (rational mind), which has been growing and developing in the background, then becomes the dominant decision-making interface with the world and goes on growing and developing until around 24 years of age. During this period the rational mind learns how to reflect on and respond to what is happening in our close community environment to generate a feeling of security. The relationships we have with our peers significantly impact the beliefs we learn during this period of our life.

By the time we reach our early twenties, we are fully indoctrinated into the worldview of our parents, the culture of our community and the beliefs of the peer group with which we associate. We have learned the values, beliefs and rules of behaviour that are necessary for us to survive, keep safe and feel secure in our parental, community and peer group frameworks of existence.

The way we learn during this period of our lives is through our experience of love and fear. When our needs are taken care of, we feel loved. When our needs are not taken care of, we become anxious and fearful. Every repeated experience of getting our needs met, or not getting our needs met, builds synaptic connections in our brains.

If we have repeated experiences of not getting our needs met – if we frequently feel abandoned, unloved or insecure, we will develop subconscious and/or conscious fear-based beliefs. If, on the other hand, we have repeated experiences of getting our needs met – if we always feel protected, safe and secure – we will develop subconscious and/or conscious love-based beliefs.

The love- and fear-based beliefs we learn during the first 24 years of our life become deeply embedded in our mind because this is when our mind is growing and developing. Consequently, what we learn when we are growing up about how to get our survival, safety and security needs met tends to stay with us for the rest of our life.

Until around 150 years ago, embracing a worldview that was different to that of our parents, the community in which we lived or our nation was not an option unless we were willing to risk our life, our safety or our livelihood.

Why are worldviews beginning to emerge more rapidly?

What changed this situation was the gradual advent of democracy, allowing both men *and* women to vote for their local representative in parliament and also stand for election.

Democracy not only gave people a voice in how they were governed, it gave them the freedom to explore a different worldview to that of their parents, the community in which they were raised and the worldview embraced by their nation.

For the first time in human history people had the freedom to choose a worldview that was more in alignment with their own values and beliefs. This freedom of thought is the main reason why worldviews are emerging more rapidly.

However, not everyone has this freedom. According to the Economic Intelligence Unit, only 4.5% of the world's population currently live in a 'full democracy'. These are the nations where civil liberties and basic freedoms are respected and reinforced by a political culture conducive to the thriving of democratic principles. In full democracies people are free to embrace the worldview that aligns with their values and beliefs on one condition: that they stay within the law.

Another 43.2% of the world's population live in 'flawed democracies', where basic civil liberties are honoured, but public media may be influenced by politicians. These nations also have other faults, such as an underdeveloped political culture and low levels of political participation. In flawed democracies politicians frequently use fear to manipulate people's choices and promote their personal agendas.

Another 16.7% of the world's population live in 'hybrid regimes', where elections are neither free nor fair. These nations commonly have governments that apply pressure on political opponents; they have non-independent judiciaries, widespread corruption, harassment and pressure placed on the media. Alternative worldviews to those embraced by the leaders are suppressed and freedom of expression is actively discouraged.

The remaining 35.6% of the world's population live in 'authoritarian regimes' where there is no political pluralism. These are nations that are governed as absolute monarchies or dictatorships. The media is controlled by groups associated with the ruling regime, the judiciary is not independent and there is censorship and suppression of any criticism of the government. In authoritarian regimes the worldview of the nation is the worldview of the leader. No other worldview is permitted.

What triggered the emergence of each new worldview?

The emergence of new worldviews can be frequently traced back to a triggering event – a tipping point – that occurred decades or centuries earlier. The triggering event throws into relief the limitations of the dominant worldview, thereby precipitating a shift in conscious awareness that challenges the status quo and leads to the emergence of a new worldview.

The leaders or the masses become disaffected because they are not able to satisfy their emergent needs. As the level of disquiet grows, the momentum for change increases. Once the limitations of the old worldview are laid bare by the triggering event, there is no going back. It is inevitable that a new worldview will emerge – it is just a matter of time.

Whenever a new worldview emerges there is always resistance. In one camp are those who are wedded to the status quo – the adherents to the old worldview. These are the people who are unwilling to let go of the benefits and privileges the old worldview gives them. In the other camp are those who seize the opportunity to satisfy their emergent needs.

This raises an important question in my mind. What were the significant events that sparked the emergence of each worldview? What caused nomadic and semi-nomadic clans to shift into the worldview of Tribe Awareness? What caused tribes to shift into the worldview of State Awareness? What caused the leaders of states to shift to the worldview of Nation Awareness? What caused the leaders of nations to shift to the worldview of Wealth Awareness? What caused the leaders of nations to shift to the worldview of People Awareness, and what will cause the people of nations all over the world to shift to the worldview of Humanity Awareness?

It is sometimes difficult to identify a single triggering event. Very often it is a series of events. However, there is usually one event that stands out – an event that precipitates action. Table 2.2 shows the triggering events that are generally believed to have spurred the emergence of new worldviews.

Table 2.2: Events that triggered the emergence of new worldviews

Worldview		Triggering event
7	Humanity Awareness	Recognition of the climate crisis in the 21st century.
6	People Awareness	The French Revolution, the abolition of slavery and the adoption of women's voting rights in the late 19th and early 20th centuries.
5	Wealth Awareness	The adoption of secularism in the 16th century.
4	Nation Awareness	The adoption of a State religion in the 4th and 7th centuries.
3	State Awareness	Climate change in Africa and East Asia 5,500 years ago.
2	Tribe Awareness	Agriculture in the fertile crescent of the Levant 10,000 years ago.
1	Clan Awareness	The emergence of *Homo sapiens* 200,000–300,000 years ago.

The emergence of *Homo sapiens*

Clan Awareness is the first worldview to be associated with anatomically modern humans. Our early ancestors lived in small, mobile kinship groups. The depth of the kinship bonds – helping each other to survive and keep safe – was the key reason for the emergence of Clan Awareness.

Some clans never shifted to the worldview of Tribe Awareness because they lived in isolated communities. Their territories were never disputed, and they were always able to sustain their lifestyle inside their physical framework of existence.

Agriculture

When clans began to settle in areas suitable for growing food crops and keeping herds of animals – enduring food security – populations began to expand. Kinship groups in the same area intermarried and formed tribes with a shared ethnic identity. This was the beginning of Tribe Awareness.

Some tribes have not moved to the worldview of State Awareness because their territory was either too remote or lacking in resources to be taken over by a larger, more powerful tribe.

Climate change I

Around 10,000 years ago, when the glaciers of the last Ice Age began to retreat, monsoon rains started to sweep across the arid deserts of North Africa (the Sahara region) and East Asia. The rains turned the deserts into fertile lands. Tribes expanded into these areas and established human settlements. Around 5,000 years later, as the glaciers retreated, the rains stopped, and the deserts returned.

The shift in climate caused mass migrations from the desert regions to adjacent fertile areas, triggering competition for territory. Armies were formed, and wars ensued. This was the start of empire building for the purpose of obtaining power. It was also the time when women became subservient to the needs of men. We entered the era of State Awareness.

Some states have not moved to the worldview of Nation Awareness because they are governed by self-serving, corrupt leaders who are unwilling to give up control of their country.

The adoption of a State religion

Around 300 AD the King of Armenia adopted Christianity as the State religion and shortly thereafter in 380 AD Christianity was adopted as the State religion of the Roman Empire. Around 630 AD Muhammad the prophet of Islam succeeded in uniting the tribes of Arabia into a single religious polity.

The marrying of Church and State into a political unity in Europe and the Middle East was the beginning of the worldview of Nation Awareness. It brought order to the political chaos of State Awareness and made religious principles the cornerstone of the administration of justice. This was the start of empire building for the purpose of religious domination.

Some nations have not moved to the worldview of Wealth Awareness because the leaders, the aristocracy and the 'establishment' are unwilling to give up their privileges and/or their religious authority.

The adoption of secularism

Secularism emerged in Europe in the 16th century when human reason triumphed over religious dogma. This opened the door to scientific investigation, took religion out of the administration of justice and made wealth the measure of a person's worth. Respect and recognition were given to those who had the most riches, made the most important scientific discoveries and achieved popular notoriety in some way or another. This was the start of the worldview of Wealth Awareness and empire building for the purpose of commercial interests.

Some nations have not moved to the worldview of People Awareness because the governing elites, their financial backers and corporate interests are unwilling to give up the influence they have over government policymaking.

The adoption of women's voting rights

There were multiple factors that led to the gradual emergence of the worldview of People Awareness. These included the French Revolution, the abolition of slavery and the adoption of women's voting rights. This last factor can be regarded as the tipping point that triggered full democracy.

Up to the late 19th century democracy was the exclusive purview of men. Women were not allowed to vote, nor stand for election as representatives of the people. Increasingly vociferous and violent demonstrations by women's movements changed this situation. Gradually nations began to recognize women's right to participate in the governance of the community and the nation.

The first nation to grant such rights to women was New Zealand (1893). This was quickly followed by Australia (1902), Finland (1906), Norway (1913), Denmark and Iceland (1915), Canada (1917), Germany and Austria (1918), the Netherlands and Luxembourg (1919), and Sweden (1921). For the most part these are the nations that are now operating from the worldview of People Awareness and the upper levels of Wealth Awareness – the nations that are getting ready to graduate to People Awareness. Full voting rights were not accorded to women in the UK and the US until 1928.

Climate crisis II

The only thing that will trigger the shift from People Awareness to Humanity Awareness is a crisis of global proportions. That crisis is now upon us: it is called the climate crisis. The climate crisis will trigger the worldview of Humanity Awareness because it affects every human being on the planet. To combat this threat, we must embrace a higher-order level of identity/awareness – one that supports the future well-being of the human race.

The first nations to shift to Humanity Awareness are likely to be those nations operating from People Awareness. The glue of identity in People Awareness is country of residence. The glue of identity in Humanity Awareness is our shared humanity. It is the first transnational identity because it includes all human souls.

So, what is preventing nations currently operating from the worldview of People Awareness shifting to Humanity Awareness? The answer to this question is simple – it is because they cannot do it alone. The worldview of Humanity Awareness demands that we rise above our identity differences and work together for the good of the whole. We will only be able to do this if we let go of our ego-driven, power-seeking partisan politics and shift to a higher level of identity/awareness that embraces everyone.

Have we experienced such a movement before? Yes, but not of the same magnitude. My example is regional, not global. At the end of World War II, the nations of Europe began to cooperate with each other to form the European Economic Community, which later became the European Union (EU). The primary purpose of this collaboration was to prevent a third World War. In this regard, it has been successful. However, as I will explain in Chapter 8, the EU is still a work in progress and because of worldview differences it is in danger of falling apart.

Summary

Here are the main points of this chapter.

1. Historically, worldviews have been resistant to change.
2. New worldviews are now emerging more rapidly because of the advent of democracy.
3. The emergence of new worldviews can be traced back to a triggering event.
4. The triggering event for the emergence of Tribe Awareness was agriculture.
5. The triggering event for the emergence of State Awareness was climate change.
6. The triggering event for the emergence of Nation Awareness was the creation of monarchies and/or the adoption of a State religion.
7. The triggering event for the emergence of Wealth Awareness was secularism.
8. The triggering event for the emergence of People Awareness was the emancipation of women.
9. The triggering event for the emergence of Humanity Awareness will be the climate crisis.

3

HOW DO WE CREATE
OUR WORLDVIEW?

Every individual has a personal worldview, and every human group structure (community, organization and nation) has a collective worldview. In democratic group structures, the collective worldview represents the worldview of the majority. Other worldviews are tolerated to the extent that they do not incite people to break the law or disrupt the workings of the society. In authoritarian regimes, the collective worldview represents the worldview of the leader: other worldviews are not tolerated.

The question I now want to explore is this: How can two people raised in the same town, going to the same school, finish up adopting different worldviews? To answer this question, we need to dissect worldviews into their component parts.

The three components of worldviews

Worldviews are comprised of three types of belief system: a personal belief system, a cultural belief system and a cosmological belief system. Every worldview is a blend of these three belief systems (see Figure 3.1) and each belief system operates in a specific context and in a particular time frame (see Table 3.1).

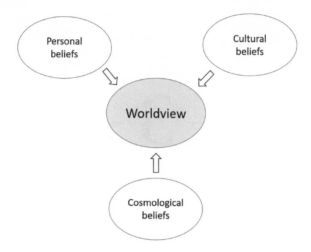

Figure 3.1: The three components of a worldview

Table 3.1: The contexts and time frames of the three human belief systems

Belief system	Context	Time frame
Cosmological	Transcendent	Life
Cultural	Social	Day to day
Personal	Emotional	Moment to moment

Cosmological belief systems

A cosmological belief system defines our place in the universe: it explains the origin and structure of our material world, our relationship to other dimensions of existence and, most importantly, how we should conduct and align ourselves with whomever or whatever we consider to be the divine creator/provider so that we can get our needs met in this life and the next.

Unlike the other cosmological belief systems, the scientific cosmology only describes the origin and structure of our material world. There is no divine creator/provider in science and there are no other dimensions of existence. From the scientific standpoint, when we die, that's the end of it. For this reason, I refer to science as a non-transcendent cosmology: there is no room for God, the soul or other dimensions of existence in science.

Cultural belief systems

A cultural belief system defines how we relate to other members of our (ethnic) community, and how we should conduct ourselves in that community in order to get our needs met on a day-to-day basis. This belief system is based on the collective history of the group.

Personal belief systems

A personal belief system defines how we believe we should react or respond to what is happening to us moment to moment so we can get our personal needs met. This belief system will always reflect the priorities of the stage of psychological development we have reached and the unmet needs we still have from previous stages of psychological development that we have not yet mastered. The needs and tasks associated with each stage of psychological development and the approximate age range when each stage of development normally occurs are shown in Table 3.2.

Table 3.2: The needs and tasks associated with the seven stages of psychological development

Stage of development	Age range	Need	Task
Serving	60+ years	To be of service to those we meet.	Contributing to the well-being of humanity.
Integrating	50–59 years	To make a difference in our world.	Connecting with others in loving relationships.
Self-actualizing	40–49 years	To find meaning and purpose.	Expressing our unique gifts and talents.
Individuating	25–39 years	To discover who we really are.	Being free to operate with autonomy.
Differentiating	8–24 years	To feel a sense of self-worth.	Being respected and recognized.
Conforming	3–7 years	To feel safe, protected and loved.	Experiencing a sense of belonging.
Surviving	0–2 years	To stay alive and thrive.	Being in control of our environment.

The seven stages of personal development occur in consecutive order. Each stage of personal development provides a foundation for the subsequent stage. We cannot jump stages, but from time to time we may experience higher *states* of consciousness, especially after we have moved beyond the individuating stage of development. It takes a lifetime to pass through all of the seven stages of development.

The first three stages of development operate on a biological time scale: they are determined by the physical development of our brains and bodies, and the associated mental development of our minds from the moment of conception to our early twenties. This is the period where we are attempting to learn how to satisfy and master our survival, safety and security needs.

Most people never reach the individuating stage of psychological development because:

- They live inside government regimes that restrict freedom of expression.
- They are poor and spend all their time focusing on their survival, safety and security needs.
- Their parental programming and cultural conditioning were such that they developed a set of fear-based beliefs about being able to satisfy their survival, safety and security needs that keep them anchored in the levels of consciousness that correspond to the first three stages of development.

Repeated painful experiences of not getting our deficiency needs met (survival, safety and security) when we are young get 'hard-wired' into our brain as synaptic connections and into our mind as fear-based beliefs. The strongest beliefs are those with the most well-developed synaptic connections. Consequently, if we constantly failed to get our needs met when we were young, we will have formed limiting beliefs that may haunt us for the rest of our life. We must build new synaptic connections, more positive beliefs, if we want to overcome our limiting beliefs.

Normally, the level of consciousness we operate from will correspond to the stage of development we have reached. However, when our mind interprets a current experience as potentially threatening – when we feel challenged about getting our survival, safety or security needs met, we will most likely drop down to one of the first three levels of consciousness. This does not mean we are moving to a lower stage of development. It simply means that we are moving to a level of consciousness where we are facing similar issues to those we had when we were at that earlier stage of development.

Prior to the advent of democracy very few people had the possibility of moving beyond the differentiating stage of psychological development. Those who had the possibility of individuating were the children of the elites or those born to wealthy parents.

Here is a brief overview of each of the seven stages of psychological development.

Surviving

The task at the surviving stage of development is to stay alive and thrive by being in control of our environment.

The surviving stage begins at conception. For the first three months of life, the growth of the embryo is controlled by our species mind – our DNA[21] programming. The species mind guides the development of the embryo into a foetus and creates a functioning body mind (reptilian brain) by the end of the first trimester of gestation.

The primary focus of the body mind is to keep the body functioning – staying alive. It does this by regulating the workings of the body's internal organs, thereby creating stability. Because of our species programming, the body mind instinctively knows how to manage the body's homeostatic functioning, and once the baby is born, it knows how to suckle and knows how to cry if it feels discomforting sensations.

Although the body mind knows how to react to the discomforts it feels, such as hunger, thirst, being too hot or too cold, it doesn't know how to alleviate the sensations it is experiencing. If the baby's reactions (grimacing, crying, etc.) to discomforting sensations result in the discomfort going away, it feels in control of its world. If, on the other hand, its reactions go unnoticed or are ignored, it becomes increasingly distressed; it becomes

---

[21] See Glossary for a definition of DNA.

fearful about its ability to get its needs met. If the primary caregivers of the baby are not vigilant, or if the baby is abused, left alone for long periods of time or abandoned, the baby will form subconscious limiting beliefs that the world is an unsafe place and that it is not loved.

If, on the other hand, the primary caregivers of the baby are attentive to its needs and are watchful and responsive to signs of discomfort, then the baby will grow up feeling in control of its environment and the world it lives in is a safe place.

At the survival stage of development, love is experienced through the satisfaction of our physiological needs. This is when the body mind experiences stability. The body mind experiences instability – a lack of love – when it feels abandoned and uncared for; when it feels a sense of separation.

Conforming

The task at the conforming stage of development is to feel safe and protected by experiencing a sense of belonging.

Towards the end of the surviving stage of development, the infant becomes mobile and learns to communicate verbally. This is when the emotional mind (limbic brain), which has been developing in the background, becomes the dominant social interface with the world. The focus of the emotional mind is on safety and protection. The body mind goes on functioning as the physical interface with the world.

At the beginning of the conforming stage of development, the child may resort to temper tantrums to get its needs met. The young infant has not yet learned how to separate itself from its needs. Neither has it learned that the people it depends on for its survival and safety may have competing needs. If the primary caregivers give in to the child's temper tantrums, the child quickly learns that behaving 'badly' is a good strategy for getting its needs met. When this happens, the primary caregivers' lives become intolerable – they become totally ruled by the children.

If the child's primary caregivers are attentive to the child's needs, if it is raised in a caring, loving environment where it feels safe and protected, then the child will grow up without any fear of forming relationships and will readily conform to society's norms of behaviour.

If, on the other hand, the child's primary caregivers are unresponsive to the child's needs or abuse and punish the child, then the child will grow up to be fearful of forming relationships and will tend not to conform to society norms of behaviour.

At the conforming stage of development, love is experienced through the satisfaction of our safety and protection needs. This is when the emotional mind experiences stability. The emotional mind experiences instability – a lack of love – when its safety and protection needs are not met; when it believes that it is not worthy of love.

Differentiating

The task at the differentiating stage of development is to feel a sense of self-worth by being respected and recognized by our community.

Around the age of seven or eight, the rational mind (the neocortex), which has been developing in the background, takes over from the emotional mind as the conscious interface with the world. The emotional mind goes on operating as the social interface with the world, and the body mind goes on operating as our physical interface with the world.

When the child becomes a teenager, it starts to explore the world outside its family environment. To satisfy their security needs, teenagers must find a way of being recognized and respected – feeling seen by the group they identify with. They must prove that they are worthy of belonging to the group. There are three ways that teenagers get their recognition needs met.

By displays of status (coolness): This means having the latest gadgets or the most fashionable hairstyles or clothes. This is the route that teenagers usually take for getting their recognition needs met by their peer group. Naturally, this requires access to money, which they must earn or obtain from their parents. I refer to this as the differentiating (1) stage of psychological development.

By displays of knowledge and learning: This means becoming a good student and being smart. This is the route that teenagers usually take for getting their recognition needs met from their parents or the authority figures in their lives. I refer to this as the differentiating (2) stage of psychological development.

By displays of beauty or physical strength: This means showing you are strong or powerful; or it may mean being beautiful or sexy. It may mean adorning your body with tattoos or metal piercings. This is usually the route that teenagers take for getting their recognition needs met from the gangs or cliques they belong to, or from potential partners. I refer to this as the differentiating (3) stage of psychological development.

Which path or mixture of paths teenagers take to get their recognition and respect needs met depends to a large extent on the relationship they have with their parents. If teenagers have a good relationship with their parents, they will naturally feel recognized and appreciated; when they grow up they will tend to adopt the worldview of their parents. If teenagers have a poor relationship with their parents, then they may turn to an authority figure or a peer group to get their recognition needs met. In this case, they will tend to adopt the worldview of the authority figure or the peer group to which they belong.

At the differentiating stage of development, love is experienced through the satisfaction of our security needs – being recognized, acknowledged and seen. This is when the rational mind experiences stability. The rational mind experiences instability – a lack of love – when its recognition needs are not met.

Individuating

The task of the individuating stage of development is to discover who we really are by being free to operate with autonomy.

Around the mid-twenties, we begin to feel the need for autonomy and freedom – to break the chains of dependency that keep us tied to the parental and cultural framework of our existence. We are finished with being dependent on our parents and our community for the satisfaction of our deficiency needs; we are seeking independence. We want to become responsible and accountable for every aspect of our life; we want to explore our own beliefs and embrace our own values; not the values and beliefs of our parents or the community in which we were raised.

For those who are fortunate enough to have been brought up by self-actualized parents, and to have lived in a community or culture where freedom and independence are celebrated, where higher education is easily available, where men and women are treated equally, and where people are encouraged from a young age to express their needs and think for themselves, it will be relatively easy to move through the individuating stage of psychological development; that is, as long as they can find work that enables them to make a living – work that gives them autonomy.

Many people find it difficult to extract themselves from the influence of their parents or the community in which they were raised, even when they are financially independent, because they are still looking for the love and respect from their parents that they never got when they were young.

Others, such as those who live in authoritarian communities or repressive regimes, may be afraid to express themselves: they fear being punished or don't want to be locked up for speaking their truth. Thus, if we were brought up by controlling parents, if we live in an authoritarian regime, if we are discriminated against because of our gender, sexual orientation, religion or race, and we have fears about being able to meet our deficiency needs, we are likely to have difficulties moving through the individuating stage of development. Our fears will keep us anchored in the lower levels of consciousness that align with the first three stages of development.

Self-actualizing

The task at the self-actualizing stage of development is to find meaning and purpose by expressing our unique gifts and talents.

If we successfully master the individuating stage of development, around the time we reach our forties, sometimes a little earlier and sometimes a little later, we will feel a desire to express our unique gifts and talents: we will be wanting to find a meaning and purpose to our life.

Uncovering our sense of purpose not only brings vitality, it also sparks our creativity. We become more intuitive and spend more time in a state of flow – being present to what we are doing and feeling committed and passionate about our work.

For all adults, mastering the self-actualizing stage of development can be challenging if our vocation or calling offers less security than the job, profession or career we chose or trained for earlier in life. We may feel scared or uncomfortable about moving in a new direction that does not pay the rent or the mortgage or finance our children's education but does bring meaning and purpose to our life. Therefore, it is important at this stage of development to master our survival fears.

It is also important, especially for women, to put their self-expression needs first. Women in their forties often have a partner, children and aging parents that have needs. They 'naturally' tend to prioritise the needs of these people rather than their own needs.

If we deny our self-expression to take care of our family's needs, or we deny our self-expression because we are afraid we cannot survive, we will eventually become depressed and may become sick. Knowing we can survive *and* take care of our needs gives us the confidence to explore our self-expression.

Integrating

The task at the integrating stage of development is to make a difference in the world by connecting with others in loving relationships.

If we were successful in traversing the individuating stage and found our sense of purpose at the self-actualizing stage, when we reach our fifties, we will want to use our gifts and talents to make a difference in the world. To do this, we will need to form caring relationships with those we want to help and those we want to collaborate with to leverage our impact in the world. Connecting with others who share our passion or calling and with those who will be the beneficiaries of our gifts and talents is essential for mastering this stage of development.

To connect with and support others, we will need to tap into our emotional and social intelligence and exercise our empathy skills. We will need to feel what others are feeling if we are truly going to help them.

Knowing we can handle our relationship needs – that we are lovable and can love others – gives us the confidence we need to successfully manage the integrating stage of development. In addition, we must shift from operating independently to operating interdependently.

Some people get so wrapped up in their 'work' at the self-actualizing stage that they are unable to make the shift to the integrating stage. They get lost in their creativity, focusing only on their self-expression, rather than the larger contribution they could make if they were able to connect and collaborate with others. Working with others in service to the universal good is more likely to bring a sense of fulfilment than working on our own at this stage of our life.

Serving

The task at the serving stage of development is to be of service to those we meet by contributing to their well-being.

The last stage of development follows naturally from the integrating stage. This is the serving stage of development. This stage of development usually begins in our early sixties, sometimes a little earlier, sometimes a little later. The focus of this stage of development is on selfless service to the community we identify with. We are feeling a desire to contribute to the common good. Having a healthy sense of self-esteem and self-confidence will enable us to make our gifts and talents available to those who need them.

It does not matter how big or small our contribution, what is important is that we make a difference in the lives of others. Alleviating suffering, caring for the disadvantaged and building a more loving society are some of the activities we may want to explore at this stage of our life. On the other hand, our contribution may be simply being kind to those we meet or caring for the life of another soul.

As we enter the serving stage of development, we will often find ourself becoming more introspective and reflective – looking for ways to deepen our sense of connection to our soul and beyond our soul to the deeper levels of our being – connecting to whatever we consider to be the divine. We may become a keeper of wisdom, an elder of the community or a person to whom younger people turn for guidance or mentoring.

As we make progress with this stage of development, we will uncover new levels of compassion in our life. We will experience feelings of well-being and fulfilment that we never experienced before. We will begin to see how connected we all are; how, by serving others, we are serving our larger identity. At this level of consciousness, giving becomes the same as receiving. We realize that, by giving to others, we are giving to another aspect of ourself.

Richard Barrett

Dominant belief systems

The influence of the three belief systems – personal, cultural and cosmological – on each worldview is shown in Table 3.3.

The worldview of Clan Awareness is dominated by cosmological beliefs. The worldview of Tribe Awareness is dominated by cultural beliefs and cosmological beliefs. Personal beliefs only have a weak influence on the worldview of Tribe Awareness. The ego is not yet fully formed in Tribe Awareness. If it is present, it is kept under control for the sake of harmony in the tribe.

Personal beliefs, cultural beliefs and cosmological beliefs strongly influence the worldviews of State Awareness, Nation Awareness and Wealth Awareness. Personal beliefs are particularly influential in the worldview of State Awareness. Cosmological beliefs are particularly influential in the worldview of Nation Awareness. The influence of cultural beliefs is moderated in the worldview of Wealth Awareness. The (male) ego is unleashed in State Awareness. It is slightly moderated by the influence of religion in the worldview of Nation Awareness and by the desire to make money collaborating with others in the worldview of Wealth Awareness.

Cosmological beliefs are the main influence in the worldviews of People Awareness and Humanity Awareness. The influence of personal beliefs begins to wane in People Awareness and practically disappears in Humanity Awareness. The (male) ego is tamed in People Awareness by the need for gender equality and racial equality. Cultural beliefs have only a weak influence in People Awareness and no influence in the worldview of Humanity Awareness when people adopt a transnational identity.

Table 3.3: The dominant belief systems in each worldview

	Worldview	Personal beliefs	Cosmological beliefs	Cultural beliefs
7	Humanity Awareness	Weak influence	Strong influence (Soul awareness)	No influence
6	People Awareness	Moderate influence	Strong influence (Spirituality)	Weak Influence
5	Wealth Awareness	Strong influence	Strong influence (Science)	Moderate influence

4	Nation Awareness	Strong influence	Strong influence (Religion)	Strong influence
3	State Awareness	Strong influence	Strong influence (Pantheism)	Strong influence
2	Tribe Awareness	Weak influence	Strong influence (Ancestor worship)	Strong influence
1	Clan Awareness	No influence	Strong influence (Nature spirits)	No influence

Not everyone has the freedom to change their worldview

People living in the worldviews of Clan Awareness, Tribe Awareness, State Awareness and Nation Awareness rarely change their worldview. They are born into a way of being that dominates every aspect of their lives.

People living in the worldviews of Clan Awareness and Tribe Awareness are rarely exposed to other worldviews. People living in the worldview of State Awareness are not free to change their worldview because they live in repressive regimes. In the worldview of Nation Awareness, only the rich (the elites) or those who can lift themselves out of poverty have the possibility of changing their worldview. They have this possibility because they are living in (flawed) democracies.

The people living in the worldview of Wealth Awareness who learn to master their deficiency needs can choose, if they so desire, to explore other worldviews, because they live in (full) democracies.

Everyone living in the worldview of People Awareness has the possibility of changing their worldview because they live in (full) democracies and their deficiency needs are taken care of through welfare programmes managed by the State.

Worldviews and stages of psychological development

If you live in a democratic regime, the worldview in your nation will reflect the dominant stage of psychological development of the masses. If, on the other hand, you live in an authoritarian regime, the worldview in your nation will reflect the stage of psychological development of the leader.

The dominant worldview in a democratic regime evolves or regresses in alignment with the fluctuation in the level of consciousness of the majority. In an authoritarian regime, the dominant worldview evolves or regresses in alignment with the fluctuation in the level of consciousness of the leader.

No matter what stage of psychological development the majority are at in a democratic regime, if people feel their livelihoods, safety or security are under threat, they will shift to a lower level of consciousness. They will become more clannish, tribalistic, racist or nationalistic.

The same is true for the leader of an authoritarian regime. If he (it is usually a male) feels his authority is under threat, he will become more ruthless, tyrannical and totalitarian and the regime will become more repressive.

The shift to a new worldview in a democratic nation is generated by a shift in the stage of psychological development of the majority, and the shift to a new worldview in an authoritarian regime is generated by a shift in the stage of psychological development of the leader.

The correspondence between stages of psychological development and worldviews is shown in Table 3.4.

Table 3.4: Worldviews and stages of psychological development

Worldview		Focus of worldview	Stage of development	Need
7	Humanity Awareness	Self-expression through creativity.	Self-actualizing	To find meaning and purpose.
6	People Awareness	Freedom through equality and accountability.	Individuating	To discover who we really are.
5	Wealth Awareness	Security through status and influence.	Differentiating 1	To feel a sense of self-worth.
4	Nation Awareness	Security through authority and education.	Differentiating 2	To feel a sense of self-worth.
3	State Awareness	Security through power and strength.	Differentiating 3	To feel a sense of self-worth.
2	Tribe Awareness	Safety through loyalty and belonging.	Conforming	To feel safe, protected and loved.
1	Clan Awareness	Survival through sharing and reciprocity.	Surviving	To stay alive and thrive.

With one exception, there is a direct correspondence between worldviews and the stages of psychological development. The one exception is the three worldviews that align with the differentiating stage of personal development.

The worldview of Clan Awareness corresponds to the surviving stage of psychological development. The worldview of Tribe Awareness corresponds to the conforming stage of psychological development, and the worldviews of State Awareness, Nation Awareness and Wealth Awareness correspond to the three different forms of the differentiating stage of psychological development described earlier in this chapter – State Awareness focuses on personal security through power and strength; Nation Awareness focuses on personal security through authority and education; and Wealth Awareness focuses on personal security through wealth and status.

Thereafter, there is a one-to-one correspondence between the stages of psychological development and worldviews; the individuating stage of psychological development corresponds to People Awareness, and the self-actualizing stage of psychological development corresponds to Humanity Awareness.

Summary

Here are the main points of this chapter.

1. There are three components to a worldview – a cosmological belief system, a cultural belief system and a personal belief system.

2. A cosmological belief system defines our place in the universe: it explains the origin and structure of our material world, our relationship to other dimensions of existence and, most importantly, how to conduct and align ourselves with whomever or whatever we consider to be the divine creator/provider so that we can get our needs met in this life and the next.

3. A cultural belief system defines how we relate to other members of our (ethnic) community, and how we should conduct ourselves in that community in order to get our needs met on a day-to-day basis.

4. A personal belief system defines how we believe we should react or respond to what is happening to us moment to moment so we can get our personal needs met.

5. A personal belief system reflects the priorities of the stage of psychological development we have reached and the unmet needs we have from stages of psychological development we have passed through but have not yet mastered.

6. Each worldview is dominated by one, two or all of the three belief systems.

7. Not everyone has the freedom to change their worldview.

8. People living in the worldviews of Clan Awareness, Tribe Awareness, State Awareness and Nation Awareness rarely change their worldview.

9. In the worldview of Nation Awareness, only the rich (the elites) or those who can lift themselves out of poverty have the possibility of changing their worldview.

10. The people living in the worldview of Wealth Awareness who learn to master their deficiency needs can choose, if they so desire, to explore other worldviews.

11. Everyone living in the worldview of People Awareness has the possibility of changing their worldview.

12. If you live in a democratic regime, the worldview in your nation will reflect the dominant stage of psychological development of the masses.

13. If you live in an authoritarian regime, the worldview in your nation will reflect the stage of psychological development of the leader.

14. A shift to a new worldview in a democratic nation is generated by a shift in the stage of psychological development of the majority.

15. A shift to a new worldview in an authoritarian regime is generated by a shift in the stage of psychological development of the leader.

4

WORLDVIEWS

Worldviews evolve in response to changes in social life conditions: changes in social life conditions are triggered by changes in human psychological development. In other words, when new stages of human psychological development emerge, social life conditions change, and a new worldview emerges.

Each shift to a higher stage of psychological development has the effect of increasing the size of our in-group and decreasing the size of our out-group. As we reach the highest stages of psychological development all separation dissolves: we achieve a sense of unity awareness. At some point in our future, we will recognize that human evolution was all about healing our belief in separation.

When a new worldview emerges, it affects every aspect of people's lives – gender relations, governance systems, social hierarchies, justice systems, child-rearing practices, education systems, health care, spiritual/religious practices, and so on. The following section provides a brief description of the worldviews that have emerged over the past 200,000 years.

I explain the historical origins of each worldview, how the worldview shows up today, the cosmology associated with the worldview and the alignment of the worldview with the stages of human psychological development. I also describe the principle behavioural characteristics of each worldview.

Clan Awareness: Survival through sharing and reciprocity

Origins

I refer to the first worldview – survival through sharing and reciprocity – as Clan Awareness. If we assume that *Homo sapiens* first appeared on the evolutionary scene about 200,000 years ago, then 95% of the life of our species has been spent in the worldview of Clan Awareness. Every specimen of *Homo sapiens* born earlier than 12,000 years ago lived in the worldview of Clan Awareness

During this early period of human history people lived in small nomadic or semi-nomadic bands comprised of 20 to 30 close relatives. They survived by hunting and gathering. They had very few possessions – mainly the tools they needed for survival. Each clan kept to itself but formed mutually supportive relationships with neighbouring clans. The practice of reciprocity, particularly the sharing of food, was one of the ways clans helped each other to survive. Warfare was unknown. Both sexes participated in decision-making according to their experience, knowledge and skills. Most decision-making was instinctive.

Leadership was situational. Men and women performed different tasks commensurate with their physical strength and their childbearing or child-rearing duties. While men focused on hunting, women focused on gathering. Men learned the ways of animals and women learned the use of plants for nutrition and healing.

There were no formal rules in the worldview of Clan Awareness, but there were common understandings about three important topics: the spheres of activity of men and women, the support that should be given to kin, and the order in which food should be distributed. Violation of these understandings caused embarrassment. Behaviours were controlled through social pressure, teasing and ridicule. There was no sense of personal ownership and no real sense of territoriality in the worldview of Clan Awareness.

How the worldview of Clan Awareness shows up today

There are very few people today who operate from the worldview of Clan Awareness. They mostly live in the remote jungles of the Amazon, Papua New Guinea and the Aboriginal communities of Australia. Their way of life has hardly changed in thousands of years.

The cosmology of Clan Awareness

Hunter/gatherers regard their physical environment as their home: the Earth is their divine mother; the world they live in is their classroom, and nature is their teacher. Nature spirits are everywhere. All things are connected, there is no separation – life and death are a continuum. When people die, they simply move out of the physical world into the spirit world.

Shamanistic practices focus on the health and well-being of the souls of clan members. The role of the shaman is to effect changes in the spirit world that result in the manifestation of changes in the physical world. In other words, the shaman acts as messenger between the spirit world and the human world. Fear-based thinking is rife in Clan Awareness: powerful nature spirits have to be appeased in order to survive.

Correspondence with the stages of development

The worldview of Clan Awareness corresponds to the surviving stage of psychological development. At this stage of development, the foetus, and later the baby, live in a world without separation; whatever they sense is taken to be an extension of themselves. For them everything is connected. All decision-making is reactive and instinctive. The young child is strongly influenced by the survival needs of its body. The baby, like the members of a clan, cannot survive without kin-based sharing.

Behavioural characteristics

The principal behavioural markers of the worldview of Clan Awareness are:

- Respect for all living creatures and plants
- Respect for Earth spirits
- Life and death on the same continuum
- Roles of males and females are defined by nature
- Very little sense of a separate self
- Sharing of resources for survival
- Practice of reciprocity.

The transition to Tribe Awareness

The transition to the worldview of Tribe Awareness from the worldview of Clan Awareness occurred because of two factors: the need to assure an all-year-round supply of food (food security) and an increased understanding of how to cultivate plants and domesticate animals. Nowadays, the worldview of Clan Awareness is found only in isolated self-sustaining, remote communities that have very little contact with the outside world.

Tribe Awareness: Safety through belonging and loyalty

Origins

I refer to the second worldview – safety through belonging and loyalty – as Tribe Awareness. This worldview first appeared around 12,000 years ago, when ethnically similar clans began to form rural communities. People living in Tribe Awareness survive through horticulture and animal husbandry. Some tribes are still nomadic.

In the worldview of Tribe Awareness, people identified with an ethnic group of several hundred thousand people. They also strongly identified with the territory they relied on to provide food for their survival.

Each tribe had its own language, rituals and body adornments. Collective aggression in this worldview was primarily limited to inter-tribe rivalries, which mainly showed up as skirmishes and raiding. Protecting the group's food stores, animals and territory from incursions from other tribes was essential for survival. Without the protection of the tribe, people stood little chance of survival.

A worldview based on safety through belonging and loyalty required that everyone conformed to the rules of the tribe. Possessions did not belong to the individual; everything belonged to the tribe.

Ceremonies and tribal rites of passage strengthened and reinforced people's connection to the tribe. No one could stand out and be different: strong egos were suppressed. People who broke the unwritten rules of the tribe were reprimanded or punished through public shaming. An apology and reparation were required before forgiveness was granted. The ultimate punishment, for those who refused to live by the rules of the tribe, was banishment. The status of women was equal to that of men. Elders were respected since they were regarded as the keepers of the tribal wisdom.

The leaders of communities that operated from the worldview of Tribe Awareness were known as Big Men or Chiefs. A big man was an influential individual who was skilled in persuasion. He provided his followers with protection in return for gifts (usually food), which were then redistributed to members of the tribe in banquets and seasonal festivities. This sharing served two functions: it kept members of the tribe loyal and it consolidated his position as the big man.

The term 'chief' was usually reserved for the leader of a large tribe that was stratified by social rank and maintained a permanent group of warriors paid for by some form of taxation administered by the henchmen of the chief. The chief displayed his wealth and power through his dress and way of living: he lived in a big house and had many wives.

Whereas in the worldview of Clan Awareness there was no sense of separation, in the worldview of Tribe Awareness, separation began to show up in the form of ethnicity and territoriality. You could trust people from your tribe, but you could not trust people from other tribes. People from other tribes were considered less than human. Therefore, in some tribal cultures, but not all, it was considered permissible to torture, maim or kill members of other tribes.

How the worldview of Tribe Awareness shows up today

The worldview of Tribe Awareness can still be found in large parts of Sub-Saharan Africa, in North and South America, the Caribbean and parts of Oceania. We also see the influence of the worldview of Tribe Awareness among indigenous peoples of the world, such as the Sámi in Finland and the Indian tribes of North America, as well as among people who live in ethnically defined regions such as the Catalans of Northern Spain and the Scottish and Welsh nationalists in the UK. In all cases these peoples are attempting to establish an independent self-governing territory to preserve their ethnicity – their unique cultural heritage and their language.

We can also find aspects of the worldview of Tribe Awareness showing up in dress codes, body adornments, hair styles and the use of rituals to differentiate one subgroup from another, such as the followers of sports teams, teenage gangs and spiritual cults.

The cosmology of Tribe Awareness

People living in Tribe Awareness, like those living in Clan Awareness, have a strong association with the spirit world. However, because of the shift from survival through sharing and reciprocity, to safety through belonging and loyalty, people living in the worldview of Tribe Awareness hold their ancestors as well as nature spirits in high regard.

Those living in the worldview of Tribe Awareness believe that after death they go to the spirit world, and because of this they believe their ancestors can intercede with the gods on their behalf. Keeping the spirits of their ancestors happy is seen as a way of assuring good fortune.

Superstition, taboos and rituals are an important aspect of the cosmology of Tribe Awareness. Shamanic and voodoo practices have a strong influence in the worldview of Tribe Awareness. Shamans not only know about healing, using natural medicines, they also know how to mix potions to cast or ward off magic spells and keep evil spirits away.

Correspondence with the conforming stage of development

Young children realize that to keep safe they must conform to the desires of their parents and the community in which they live. Safety depends on belonging, loyalty and staying close to your kin. They begin to recognize that they are living in a world of separation. They begin to develop a separate sense of 'I'. This realization leads to the formation of the psychic entity we call the ego. The child's nascent ego is often suppressed by the parents for the sake of harmony in the family, in the same way that egos are suppressed in the tribe.

Behavioural characteristics

The principal behavioural markers of the worldview of Tribe Awareness are:

- Respect for the rules of the tribe
- Respect for elders
- Big chief or council of elders makes decisions
- Respect for ancestors
- Displays of ego are suppressed
- Males and females fulfil natural roles
- Spells are used to ward off evil spirits
- Sharing of resources within the tribe
- Tribal territory.

The transition to State Awareness

Originally the transition from the worldview of Tribe Awareness to the worldview of State Awareness occurred because of mass migrations caused by the desertification of lands in the Sahara and East Asia regions at the end of the last Ice Age. However, in the past few centuries, the transition from the worldview of Tribe Awareness to the worldview of State Awareness has been driven by colonization, particularly in Africa, Asia and the Americas.

Consequently, all former tribal territories now form part of nation states. Some nation states are highly influenced by Tribe Awareness, others less so and some not at all.

State Awareness: Security through power and strength

Origins

I refer to the third worldview – security through power and strength – as State Awareness. This worldview first appeared around 5,000 years ago.[22] During the era of this worldview villages grew into towns, towns grew into cities and cities were fortified to protect the citizens. States ranged in size from several hundred thousand to several million citizens. Statehood – the State in which we were born and raised – is the primary differentiator of identity in the worldview of State Awareness.

People survived by trading, farming and animal husbandry. As the wealth of the city states grew, they formed permanent armies. To pay for the upkeep of the armies, citizens were required to pay taxes.

The concept of honour and shame became firmly established during the worldview of State Awareness. Preserving and defending family honour and avoiding family shame are significant aspects of this worldview.

Justice in State Awareness was extremely unfair. The punishment of transgressions for those in the upper strata of the hierarchies of power was always less severe than for those in the lower strata. If the aggressor had a lower status than the victim, the punishment was more severe; if the

---

[22] Steve Taylor, *The Fall: The Insanity of the Ego in Human History and The Dawning of a New Era* (New York: Winchester Books), 2005.

aggressor had a higher status than the victim, the punishment was less severe.

Justice was administered through physical mutilation of the body. An eye for an eye and a tooth for a tooth were considered normal in the administration of justice in the worldview of State Awareness. Death and maiming were considered suitable penalties for many infractions. To demonstrate the leader's power, punishments were administered in public and drew large crowds. Watching men fight each other to the death or being caged up with wild animals were regarded as spectator sports.

Populations were stratified into hierarchies of power (landowners), knowledge (priests) and wealth (traders). The most powerful – those who could raise the largest army – ruled. At the bottom of the hierarchy were women, servants and slaves. Women were regarded as the personal property of the father or husband and could be treated in whatever way the father or husband decided – basically women had no rights and could not hold property.

Health and healing in State Awareness focused on the use of traditional natural medicines and sacrifices to the gods – both animals and humans.

Around 5,000 years ago, the leaders of city states started building empires: they invaded other states, plundered their riches and slaughtered their people. Those they did not slaughter – mostly women – they captured and made into slaves to be sold in their home state to the highest bidder.

From roughly 3,000 BCE to the 6th century AD, over 47 empires were created, most of which lasted for only two or three centuries. However, some, like the Roman Empire and the Chola Dynasty in India, continued for more than 1,500 years. Over the next 1,500 years (from the 6th century to modern times) a further 135 empires were created. Some of these empires, particularly those created from the 7th century to the 15th century, were driven from the worldview of Nation Awareness (the spread of monotheistic religions), and others from the 16th century to the 19th century were driven from the worldview of Wealth Awareness (establishment of colonies for commercial trade).

How the worldview of State Awareness shows up today

In the worldview of State Awareness, leaders have absolute power; they are feared by those around them and they consider themselves above the law.

If citizens' loyalty to the leader is questioned, they can be locked up for a very long time or expect some form of immediate retribution – torture or death. Fear is rampant in nations operating from the worldview of State Awareness, and caution is everywhere.

Leaders never feel safe. There is always someone in the wings waiting to grab power. For this reason, leaders in the worldview of State Awareness are extremely wary of those around them: there is intrigue and plotting everywhere. No one can be trusted, not even the members of the leader's inner circle. Only the most powerful, the most fear-inducing and the most scheming leaders survive for significant periods.

Leaders who operate from the worldview of State Awareness demand loyalty and require constant praise and adoration – they need their egos stroked. They want what they want, when they want it, and you had better beware if you are unable to deliver it or if you cross them in any way. Corruption is rife in the worldview of State Awareness.

Leaders who operate from the worldview of State Awareness are usually men and, depending on their religion, either have several wives and many offspring or a succession of trophy wives. In the worldview of State Awareness women are subservient to the needs of men. They are little better than servants or slaves and are often treated as sexual objects.

Leaders in the worldview of State Awareness take pride in displays of military strength and accomplishment. They need such demonstrations to feed their self-esteem: they want to feel powerful and they need to show off their strength. They may even resort to displays of perceived manhood or by making public appearances with beautiful women. They like to father numerous male children. Female children are less welcome.

Leaders operating from the worldview of State Awareness will lie, cheat and manipulate to become top dog. Corruption and bribery are everywhere. This is the worldview of despots and dictators and all those who use fear to manipulate others to gain power. The leaders of State Awareness nations use secret police to monitor citizen activities: hundreds and thousands of people can easily disappear, never to be heard of again. When necessary they use the military to quell dissent and demonstrations. Consequently, citizens are afraid to demonstrate against the regime.

Discrimination is everywhere in the worldview of State Awareness. The worldview of State Awareness spawned white and black supremacists, as well as the Ku Klux Klan and Neo-Nazi political movements. Homophobia is rife: people who are homosexual, lesbian, transgender, bisexual or transsexual are not tolerated. If they are discovered, they are severely punished.

Many aspects of the worldview of State Awareness can be found in the Mafia, in street gangs and in networks of drug barons. These groups embrace the concept of machismo – exaggerated forms of masculinity.

The right to bear arms is strongly defended in the worldview of State Awareness, as is the killing and taming of wild animals and the mistreatment of domestic animals. Sports that inflict pain on another human being, such as boxing, or creatures, such as bullfighting, dogfighting and cockfighting, are part and parcel of the worldview of State Awareness.

(In the Atlas of World Consciousness,[23] I have split the worldview of State Awareness into three categories. The difference between the categories reflects the influence of the worldview of Tribe Awareness. In State Awareness 1 there is no influence of the worldview of Tribe Awareness. In State Awareness 2 there is a moderate influence of the worldview of Tribe Awareness. In State Awareness 3 there is a strong influence of the worldview of Tribe Awareness.) [24]

The cosmology of State Awareness

There was a significant shift in cosmology with the advent of State Awareness, from reverence for the spirits of ancestors to reverence for a pantheon of gods; each god being responsible for a specific aspect of human life. In Roman times, some of the gods included Mars, the God of War, Minerva, the Goddess of Wisdom, and Neptune, the God of the Sea. Everything imaginable, including all the forces of nature, had a god or goddess in charge. Animal and human sacrifices were used to appease the gods. Polytheism is still practised today in Chinese traditional religion, Hinduism and Shintoism. Modern-day nations operating from the worldview of State Awareness tend to embrace a variety of cosmologies – both traditional religions and global religions such as Christianity and Islam.

---

[23] https://www.barrettacademy.com/atlas-of-consciousness
[24] See Chapter 7.

Correspondence with the differentiating stage of development

The worldview of State Awareness corresponds to the differentiating (3) stage of psychological development – a focus on personal recognition through displays of power and physical strength, or beauty and sexiness. When children and teenagers are neglected or abused by their parents, they may resort to bullying to get their self-esteem needs met. Because of these early life experiences, they choose to be recognized through the exercise of power. They are trying to meet their unmet needs from childhood. They seek revenge for anything they believe to be an affront. As adults they tend to become manipulative, aggressive and misogynistic. They are easily consumed by rage.

Behavioural characteristics

The principal behavioural markers of the worldview of State Awareness are:

- Rules defined by powerful elites
- Impulsive decision-making
- Hierarchies of power
- Honour and shame
- Women treated as sexual objects
- Rape is rarely punished
- Sports that involve violence or death
- Justice administered by physical mutilation or death
- Elites are rarely punished
- Torture is acceptable
- Cruelty to people and animals.

The transition to Nation Awareness

Originally the transition from the worldview of State Awareness to the worldview of Nation Awareness occurred because the rivalry among leaders made the governance of the state almost impossible to manage. Nation Awareness brought stability to this chaos by creating monarchies with lines of succession and elevating the importance of religion to the state level. Nowadays, international political pressure and commercial sanctions are used to 'persuade' nations to move from the worldview of State Awareness to the worldview of Nation Awareness – from authoritarian regimes to flawed democracies.

Nation Awareness: Security through authority and education

Origins

I refer to the fourth worldview – security through authority and education – as Nation Awareness. Nations formed when states coalesced into larger territories through political alliances and/or the subjugation of ethnic minorities and appropriation of their lands by force.

The worldview of Nation Awareness brought stability, order and discipline to the governance of nations. Laws, rules and codes of conduct were established based on moral authority. Administrative bureaucracies were created to collect taxes and manage the State. Stability of leadership was achieved by the establishment of family dynasties. Kings and emperors became both political and spiritual leaders – they ruled through divine right. Everyone worshipped the same god. Organized religion served to provide an additional bond between people of different ethnic origin living in the same nation. People who embraced a religion that was not sanctioned by the State were often discriminated against and frequently persecuted.

Whereas in the worldview of State Awareness elites dominated through power and strength, in the worldview of Nation Awareness elites dominated through political and religious authority. They used this authority to amass personal fortunes

As far as women were concerned, the era of Nation Awareness began in the worst possible way. The male-dominated religious institutions exerted their power over women by labelling anyone who was suspected of evil or malicious behaviours as a witch. Women healers and shamans were particularly targeted. It is estimated that more than 200,000 women (witches) were put to death in the 16th, 17th and 18th centuries in Europe.

The elites ruled the masses, and the masses served their needs. The masses paid homage to their lords. In return the lords took care of the survival and safety needs of their vassals and slaves. This was the era of feudalism.

If you were one of the masses, it was difficult to improve your status. Serving your lord or master, distinguishing yourself in battle or becoming a religious cleric were some of the avenues open to you to improve your position in society. The more loyal or righteous you became, the more you were recognized as being a trusted servant.

Under the worldview of Nation Awareness, the idea of justice was modified to reflect equality in the eyes of God. In the early years of Nation Awareness accused persons proved their innocence by submitting to a physical ordeal, such as walking across burning coals or being doused in freezing water. If it was God's will that they survived they were considered innocent. The concepts of guilt and innocence, and right and wrong, became codified during the worldview of Nation Awareness.

Major crimes were punishable by violent death – being burned alive or hung, drawn and quartered. Minor offences were dealt with by public shaming – placing criminals in public stocks where citizens threw refuse at them.

Citizens were divided into classes. The upper classes were represented by the monarch, his court of advisors, major landowners and religious leaders. The middle classes were represented by wealthy merchants, minor landowners and clerics. The lower classes were represented by serfs, slaves and labourers.

How the worldview of Nation Awareness shows up today

Public and private organizations in the worldview of Nation Awareness are governed though hierarchies of authority – typical examples include the civil service, the military and organized religions. People can only advance through sacrifice, self-discipline and loyalty. The pathway to recognition involves decades of service with a promise of a pension at the end. A central tenet of the worldview of Nation Awareness is sacrifice now for rewards later. Awards and decorations are reserved for those who have supported the leader in some personal way or have shown outstanding service to the nation. In this worldview, religious affiliation is important, and it can play a significant role in the formation of political alliances.

Leaders consider it admissible to use the machinery of government to satisfy their personal desires. They meddle in the affairs of State. They use their influence to grant favours to those who are loyal or supporters who wield financial influence. There is a high level of corruption in Nation Awareness because the leaders believe they can operate outside the law. Leaders operating from the worldview of Nation Awareness frequently seek ways to change the laws to allow them to stay in power for longer periods. They make grand occasions into lavish spectacles. They love to show off.

The mechanisms of justice in the worldview of Nation Awareness are extremely bureaucratic and tedious and tend to favour the elites. Homicide and treason are usually punishable by death. Other serious crimes are punishable by long periods of incarceration.

In the worldview of Nation Awareness the mixing of social classes is frowned upon, as is the union in marriage of men and women from different ethnic or religious groups. Belonging to the 'right' ethnic and religious group is extremely important. Belonging to the 'wrong' group can jeopardize safety. People are expected to conform to accepted male/female sexual roles. Those who are homosexual, lesbian, bisexual or transgender may be tolerated but in most social circles they will be excluded.

In the worldview of Nation Awareness women are regarded as second-class citizens and have much less freedom than men. While women are not totally subservient to the needs of men, they are limited in the roles they can perform. They are often barred from clubs and groups dominated by men. Nation Awareness is above all the worldview of conservatism and religious intolerance. Currently there 23 nations operating from the worldview of Nation Awareness.[25]

---

[25] See Chapter 7.

The cosmology of Nation Awareness

In the year AD 312 emperor Constantine the Great of Rome had a dream about the God of the Christians the night before he went into an important battle. He won the battle and thereafter led the conversion of the Roman people to Christianity. This event was one of several that led to a shift from polytheism to monotheism. Whereas the cosmology in the worldview of State Awareness was based on a pantheon of gods, the cosmology in the worldview of Nation Awareness was based on one God.

Several new monotheistic religions[26] appeared during this period of history – Christianity and Islam being the most well known and the most expansive. This was the era of religious warfare. Armies were used to protect and expand religious affiliations. The concept of a 'Holy War' originates from this period when Christian crusaders attempted to recapture the Holy Land from the Muslims.

Monotheistic religions teach that service to God in this life will be rewarded in the next life. Suffering and sacrifice are regarded as the pathway to righteousness and everlasting life. Consequently, identification with a religion is extremely important in this worldview. Moreover, people who do not identify with the State religion, particularly Christianity, could be considered a heathen.

Health and healing in the worldview of Nation Awareness is strongly focused on prayer. The body is regarded as an instrument of God. Its purpose is to do God's work. The natural impulses of the body are regarded as evil – the body must be punished for sexual thoughts.

Correspondence with the differentiating stage of development

The worldview of Nation Awareness corresponds to the differentiating (2) stage of psychological development – a focus on recognition through authority and education. If teenagers are cared for and recognized for their achievements by their primary caregivers, instead of seeking recognition through power, they may seek recognition through authority – focusing on their studies to gain more respect from their primary caregivers and teachers and any other authority figures in their lives.

---

[26] The earliest monotheistic religion was Judaism, which arose many centuries earlier during the era of State Awareness.

When parents or others do not take enough care of their teenager's needs – do not acknowledge them for their achievements – teenagers may turn to a religious authority figure to get the recognition they are seeking. This may cause them to strengthen their relationship to their religion and their service to God. In the wrong hands, such teenagers can be radicalized to become extremists.

Behavioural characteristics

The principal behavioural markers of the worldview of Nation Awareness are:

- One true God
- Rules based on moral conduct
- Hierarchies based on seniority/loyalty
- Sacrifice now for rewards later
- Bureaucracies bring order
- Justice administered through physical punishments
- Elites manipulate government to get their needs met
- Women not respected
- Torture is acceptable.

The transition to Wealth Awareness

Originally the transition from the worldview of Nation Awareness to the worldview of Wealth Awareness occurred because of public pressure for freedom of worship and pressure from the wealthy to gain more influence in the making of public policy.

Nowadays, the transition to Wealth Awareness is not only driven by the wealthy; it has also been driven by the masses – those who are seeking to satisfy their survival, safety and security needs by increasing their personal income. Everyone wants more money, because money gives you influence and status. The worldview of Wealth Awareness is very attractive to people who have been repressed most of their lives or teenagers who are aware, through the internet, of what the lives of other teenagers are like in nations that operate from the worldview of Wealth Awareness.

The worldview of Wealth Awareness is almost always accompanied by a transition to full democracy.

Wealth Awareness: Security through status and influence

Origins

I refer to the fifth worldview – security through status and influence – as Wealth Awareness. This worldview led to the segregation of people into communities stratified by income, and Gross National Income per capita (GNI) became the defining measure of progress.

One of the key characteristics of the worldview of Wealth Awareness is the separation of Church and State. Secularism had arrived. The idea of natural justice (by God), which was present in Nation Awareness, was replaced by the idea of rational justice (by the people) administered by high-ranking elites.

The worldview of Wealth Awareness had its origins in the late 15th and early 16th centuries when the most powerful nations of Europe began to dispatch their navies to explore distant lands. The purpose of these expeditionary forces was wealth creation through empire building. The Portuguese, Spanish, French, Dutch and British competed with each other to colonize the Americas, the Caribbean, Africa and the East Indies to build trading empires.

In the worldview of Wealth Awareness, the governance structures of nations began to shift from the absolute power of kings, queens or religious leaders to constitutional monarchies. Over time monarchs gradually began to give up their powers to elected representatives of the people. For the most part these were men – people from the upper classes of society, important landowners or recognized public figures. During the era of the worldview of Wealth Awareness, the power of the aristocracy began to wane as the concept of democracy began to take root.

The first democracies to appear were two-party systems – one party representing the conservatives, who supported the monarchy, and the other party representing all those opposed to the monarchy. Later, one party came to represent the elites trying to cling to their privileges and power, and one party came to represent the working classes seeking to get a fairer share of the wealth they were creating through their labours.

During the era of Wealth Awareness, the justice system was significantly revamped. For example, in the UK, the number of offences that demanded the death penalty was reduced from over 200 to about five. It was rare that court proceedings lasted more than a few days. Once a sentence had been passed, punishment was instantaneous. Executions by hanging began to be carried out privately in prisons rather than being public spectacles.

The system of justice in the worldview of Wealth Awareness punished people's 'souls'.[27] Incarceration became the primary mode of punishment. The more serious the crime, the longer the incarceration. In the worldview of Wealth Awareness, torture was considered an appropriate method of extracting the truth in crimes of treason.

Once the worldview of Wealth Awareness became established, people were able to travel more. There was a growing diversity of ethnic populations settling in the former colonial nations. For example, the UK took in people from the West Indies, Pakistan, India and East Africa. France took in people from West, North and Sub-Saharan Africa as well as Vietnam. The Netherlands took in people from Indonesia, Spain took in people from South America, and Portugal took in people from Brazil and Mozambique. Consequently, there was more tolerance of people of different ethnic origins, especially if they could contribute to the economy.

---

[27] Michel Foucault, *Discipline and Punish: The Birth of the Prison* (London: Penguin Books), 1977.

Richard Barrett

How the worldview of Wealth Awareness shows up today

Governance systems in the worldview of Wealth Awareness tend to be polarized (two main parties), combative and based on the principle of winner takes all. Voters align themselves with the political party that reflects the needs of their subgroup – for example, the owners of industry and business versus the workers, the rich versus the poor.

In the worldview of Wealth Awareness the rich and powerful try to influence political decision-making through bribery. Corruption is tolerated if it remains in the shadows.

The poor and the disadvantaged, and the environment, seldom win out in nations dominated by the worldview of Wealth Awareness. Making money is paramount. The gap between the rich and poor consistently grows wider. The poor get left behind and inequality is constantly rising. The elites do not seem to care, and self-interest is everywhere, not just in business, but also in politics.

The focus of education in the worldview of Wealth Awareness is to prepare people to compete in the world of work. Reading, writing, arithmetic and science are prioritized in schools. The languages and arts are underfunded. Many young people, once they have finished school, sign up for universities to get a Master's in Business Administration. For them, this is considered the passport to wealth. Everyone is looking to become rich.

One of the most disturbing impacts of the worldview of Wealth Awareness is the loss of social capital: a breakdown in neighbourliness and connectedness. Municipal planning agencies segregate people into housing areas based on income. Even old people are segregated into specialized homes, some catering for the rich and some catering for the poor. Families socialize less often, and friends meet less frequently; old people feel lonely and young people struggle to get a start in their lives; everywhere there is an increase in stress and mental disorders.

Although the status of women is significantly improved in the worldview of Wealth Awareness, they continue to be discriminated against. Women's work is not valued as highly as men; they are not paid the same salary as men in similar positions or with similar qualifications. Women frequently come up against a glass ceiling. In business they are effectively barred from the upper echelons of management, which is very much regarded as the preserve of men. The only way women can be successful in business and politics is to behave like men. Most women give up. They prefer to value their health and family over the stress of competing in a system that is rigged against them. Very little support is provided for women during pregnancy and the first year after the birth of a child.

What were formerly religious holidays (as observed in Nation Awareness) have become *bank* holidays in Wealth Awareness: instead of celebrating religious festivals by name, national holidays are simply reminders that money is not available because the banks are closed.

Health and healing in the worldview of Wealth Awareness is scientifically based. The body is treated like a machine and psychological problems are treated by drugs or behavioural therapy.

Currently, there are seven nations operating from the worldview of Wealth Awareness.[28]

The cosmology of Wealth Awareness

During the worldview of Wealth Awareness, science replaced religion as the dominant cosmology. Healing through medicine, rather than through prayer, became the norm. Consequently, in the worldview of Wealth Awareness the cosmology of religion based on one 'true' God was replaced by the cosmology of science. In science there is no god – no divine creator/provider, no soul, no other dimensions of existence, and therefore no life after death. The concept of Darwinian meaninglessness – evolution based on random mutations – became accepted as the foundational theory of evolution.[29]

Whereas all previous cosmologies could be classified as transcendent – the extension of consciousness into other dimensions of existence – science was non-transcendent. Atheism became popular. This shift in cosmology significantly affected academia, particularly the humanities and more specifically the domains of philosophy and psychology. The soul as a dimension of psychology was gradually replaced by a focus on behaviours.

---

[28] See Chapter 7.
[29] Richard Barrett, *The Evolutionary Human: How Darwin Got it Wrong* (London: Fulfilling Books), 2018.

Correspondence with the differentiating stage of psychological development

The worldview of Wealth Awareness corresponds to the differentiating (1) stage of psychological development – a focus on recognition through wealth and knowledge. For the non-elites living in this worldview, becoming business 'savvy' is the most direct pathway to wealth. Intelligence and being smart are highly valued, as are success and fame. Competition is the norm. Winning means everything, because it provides status and influence.

Behavioural characteristics

The principal behavioural markers of the worldview of Wealth Awareness are as follows:

- Two-party democracies
- Inequality of incomes and wealth
- Freedom of expression up to a point
- Hierarchies based on wealth and knowledge
- Solving problems through scientific reductionism
- Justice administered through imprisonment
- Women not treated equally
- Torture admissible for treason or crimes against the State
- Corruption is tolerated.

The transition to People Awareness

Originally the transition from the worldview of Wealth Awareness to the worldview of People Awareness occurred because of demonstrations by women to have an equal voice in the governance of the nation. Nowadays, the transition from Wealth Awareness to People Awareness is being driven by citizens who want their governments to end discrimination in all its forms, eliminate income inequalities and provide social welfare and safety nets for all so that everyone can satisfy their survival, safety and security needs.

People Awareness: Freedom through equality and accountability

Origins

I refer to the sixth worldview – freedom through equality and accountability – as People Awareness. The first significant sign of this worldview was the French Revolution. Further signs showed up in the 19th century with an increasing interest in humanitarian ideas and reforms such as the abolition of slavery. Around the beginning of the 20th century women were given the vote and a few decades later they could stand for election.

The worldview of People Awareness represented a major transformation in our collective psychological development. Central to this worldview was the concept of inclusivity through equality, and the 'demonization' of privilege – all the aspects of elitism that were present in State Awareness, National Awareness and Wealth Awareness. The worldview of People Awareness went a long way towards taming the male ego but reducing the gender gap is still a work in progress in some nations operating from the worldview of People Awareness today; in others it is well advanced.

The influence of the aristocracy and wealthy elites that was present in the worldview of Wealth Awareness began to wane. Class systems began to dissolve, and universal education became the norm. At a geopolitical level, the former colonies of European nations were granted independence and given equal status in the United Nations.

Through the influence of People Awareness, increasing recognition was given to the rights of indigenous peoples, and nations became more willing to accept refugees who were being oppressed in nations operating from State Awareness. Nations operating from the worldview of People Awareness were more generous in sharing their wealth with less fortunate nations than the nations operating from Wealth Awareness.

How the worldview of People Awareness shows up today

The focus of the worldview of People Awareness is freedom through equality and accountability. People Awareness attempts to correct the inequalities between the elites (the rich) and the masses (the poor) by focusing on social welfare programmes that give emphasis to satisfying citizens' survival, safety and security (deficiency) needs, thereby giving everyone the opportunity to focus on their individuation and self-actualization (growth) needs.

Governments in nations operating from the worldview of People Awareness are usually made up of political coalitions, with members of parliament elected through proportional representation. Compared with the worldview of Wealth Awareness the political parties are much less polarized. To a large extent all parties in nations operating from the worldview of People Awareness have the same central focus – creating freedom and equality through social welfare programmes, restraining the adverse impacts of free market economics and promoting conscious capitalism. In the worldview of People Awareness progress is measured through Gross National Happiness (GNH) per capita, rather than Gross National Product (GNP) or Gross National Income (GNI) per capita.

In this worldview, political correctness – the avoidance of language or actions that exclude, marginalize or insult minorities or groups of people who are disadvantaged or different – is the essential condition for proper relations. Everyone's voice and everyone's aspirations are considered important. Conflicts are avoided, and dialogue is used in resolving disputes. Societies operating from People Awareness solve problems by working things out together to discover what is best for the common good. Consensus is important because harmony is valued.

Gender equality and racial equality is regarded as important in People Awareness. There is a strong focus on the needs of the family: a long leave of absence for parents during the first year of life of a child, free kindergarten attendance, shared male and female participation in childcare, an equitable distribution of labour at home and a better work–life balance for both women and men. As a result of all these policies, there are more women who are economically active in nations that operate from the worldview of People Awareness.

As far as justice is concerned, instead of punishment being regarded as retribution, in the worldview of People Awareness it is regarded as an opportunity to focus on the rehabilitation of wrongdoers – helping people who have broken the law to reintegrate into society. Capital punishment has been abolished in nations operating from the worldview of People Awareness.

There is no racial, religious or ethnic discrimination in nations operating from the worldview of People Awareness. Significant attention is given to the protection of animals – domestic and wild.

In the worldview of People Awareness, there is a shift in emphasis in education from reading, writing and arithmetic to emotional intelligence and relationship management.

Health and healing in the worldview of People Awareness is strongly orientated towards alternative, non-invasive natural medicine and psychotherapeutic therapies that focus on the mind–body linkage.

The cosmology of People Awareness

People Awareness heralded a major cosmological shift. Whereas in the worldview of Nation Awareness we worshipped an external god, and in the worldview of Wealth Awareness we became atheists, in the worldview of People Awareness we built a relationship with our own personal god – we embraced spirituality.

Spirituality unites people from different faiths by focusing on the values that people share rather than the beliefs that separate them. In addition to promoting equal treatment of people of different religions, People Awareness promotes equal treatment of people of different genders, people of different sexual orientations and people of different ethnicities. There are no barriers to sexual unions in People Awareness. Despite the objections of male religious clerics (mostly operating from Nation Awareness), same-gender marriages are legal and women have gradually been accepted into the priesthood.

The principal issue that arises with spirituality is that it belongs to a worldview that is only one step removed from the worldview of Wealth Awareness. Consequently, spirituality is often hijacked by well-educated gurus seeking fame and fortune. They use their knowledge of the spiritual world to make money through the vehicle of the self-help movement. The self-helpers are usually people from the more advanced countries who have met their deficiency needs and are looking to meet their growth needs.

Correspondence with the individuating stage of development

The worldview of People Awareness corresponds to the individuating stage of personal development – a focus on freedom and autonomy. At this stage of development, we begin to discover who we are outside our parental and cultural conditioning. We start to let go of our dependency on others and institutions to meet our deficiency needs. We stop being a victim and a complainer; we accept the situation we find ourselves in and take action to create the life we want. This takes courage because we must become responsible and accountable for our life.

Behavioural characteristics

The principal behavioural markers of the worldview of People Awareness are:

- Democracy through multi-party coalitions
- Focus on social welfare
- Elitism not tolerated
- Redistribution of income to raise the level of well-being for all people
- Women and men regarded as equals
- Consensus and open dialogues
- Focus on emotional intelligence
- No capital punishment
- Support for the underprivileged and disenfranchised
- No discrimination in any form
- Focus on health prevention and alternative healing modalities.

The transition to Humanity Awareness

The transition from the worldview of People Awareness to the worldview of Humanity Awareness will occur when the people in every nation act together to force their governments to address cross-border global issues of climate change, people trafficking, international crime, the observance of human rights and the elimination of global poverty. Humanity Awareness will introduce new forms of internet-based democracy that allow people of all ages (stages of psychological development) to participate in policymaking. Certain aspects of this new worldview are now appearing in some communities and nations in various parts of the world.

Humanity Awareness: Self-expression through the exploration of personal creativity

What Humanity Awareness will look like

I refer to the seventh worldview that is now emerging – self-expression through the exploration of personal creativity – as Humanity Awareness. The focus of Humanity Awareness is finding meaning and purpose through the exploration of our natural gifts and talents.

In Humanity Awareness we assume a transnational identity; we recognize that we are all members of the human race – we identify with humanity. Not only are there no ethnic, religious or gender divisions in Humanity Awareness, there are also no territorial boundaries. We all share the same home – the planet Earth.

In the worldview of Humanity Awareness, the approach to solving problems is holistic and systemic. We focus our efforts on system-wide changes. We are not blinkered by our beliefs, as people have been in the preceding worldviews. We seek answers to the questions that are facing humanity through deep dialogue, intuitive insights and processes that invite our collective intelligence – processes that involve all concerned parties and align with our universal 'soul' values.

In addition to improving social welfare, Humanity Awareness also focuses on psychological welfare. Whereas social welfare solved the problems associated with meeting our deficiency needs, psychological welfare solves the problems associated with meeting our growth needs – moving through and beyond the individuating stage of psychological development to the self-actualizing stage of psychological development.

Instead of measuring happiness, the focus now is on measuring well-being. Well-being is a more important indicator than happiness: well-being is the feeling we get when we satisfy the needs of the stage of psychological development we are at. Other measures of human progress in the worldview of Humanity Awareness will focus on improving empathy, kindness and compassion and decreasing suicide and homicide rates.

Unlike previous worldviews, the worldview of Humanity Awareness recognizes and appreciates the 'verticality' of societal development – it understands the evolutionary perspective. Those operating from this worldview understand that people at different stages of psychological development have different needs and can operate from different worldviews. People operating from the earlier worldviews are unable to do this because they look at the world only through the myopic belief structures of their own worldviews. They live in societal flatland – they can only interpret and judge what is going on from the beliefs of their worldview. People operating from the worldview of Humanity Awareness see other worldviews not through the lens of competing belief structures but through the lens of competing value priorities.

In the worldview of Humanity Awareness, the evolution of human consciousness is seen as a work in progress. Chaos and change are accepted as the natural order of things. The difficulties that we face are regarded as opportunities for learning, rather than problems to be solved.

People operating from the worldview of Humanity Awareness may experience anxieties about the future, but they are not fearful. They trust in their collective intelligence and knowledge and their innate creativity to resolve all issues.

Respect and recognition in Humanity Awareness are earned; they are not dependent on power, authority or wealth; leadership is situational – it is based on a person's competence and creativity.

Justice in Humanity Awareness recognizes that we make mistakes due to our childhood conditioning. Rehabilitation is handled though psychotherapeutic support (the reprogramming of our limiting beliefs) and self-knowledge – understanding our true nature and purpose in life.

In Humanity Awareness we find a focus on values-based education, meditation and psychological growth. Children are taught how to fully express their unique gifts and talents, connect with others in meaningful relationships and contribute to the well-being of their community. They are taught how to be the best for the world, rather than how to be the best in the world.

Humanity Awareness heralds a new form of democracy; not dominated by power, authority and status-hungry elites, but by citizens working together collaboratively to find solutions that focus on the good of the whole. Different age groups are represented in governance structures. Decision-making is decentralized to the appropriate regional or local level.

To tackle issues such as the pollution of the global commons, global warming and international crime, new and improved global governance structures are developed based on national representation at a regional level and regional representation at a global level.[30] The structures and the decision-making processes in the United Nations are completely overhauled.

Health and healing in the worldview of Humanity Awareness focus on ego–soul alignment. The body is seen as an energy field – the vehicle of the soul in the material dimension of existence. When the energy field is healthy – aligned with the motivations of the soul – the body is healthy; when it is not, it gets sick.[31] Health is improved by releasing anxiety and fear and embracing love and joy.

---

[30] Richard Barrett, *Love, Fear and the Destiny of Nations* (Bath: Fulfilling Books), 2011.

[31] Richard Barrett, *A New Psychology of Human Well-being: An Exploration of the Influence of Ego-Soul Dynamics on Mental and Physical Health* (London: Fulfilling Books), 2016.

Whereas there are many individuals around the world beginning to embrace Humanity Awareness, there are no nations operating from this worldview. There are some nations that are exploring policies which align with the worldview of Humanity Awareness.

The cosmology of Humanity Awareness

In Humanity Awareness, people of different ethnicity, nationality and race share an overarching cosmology that unifies the belief systems of spirituality, science and psychology in an energetic framework of understanding, where every human being is seen as an individuated aspect of the universal energy field – as a soul experiencing three-dimensional material reality in a physical body.

At this level of awareness, it is understood that every person on the planet shares the same level of identity, and at the deepest level of their being they share the same humanitarian values. There is a common understanding that when I give to you, I am giving to another aspect of myself. There is no discrimination in Humanity Awareness.

Correspondence with the self-actualizing stage of development

The worldview of Humanity Awareness corresponds to the self-actualizing stage of personal development – a focus on internal cohesion (ego–soul alignment) and external cohesion (living in harmony with others). People who embrace the worldview of Humanity Awareness want to bond with other people in group structures that care about the future of humanity.

At this stage of psychological development, we fully embrace the values of inclusion, openness, fairness, tolerance and transparency. Instead of making decisions based on our beliefs, we make decisions based on our values. Our values become our internal guidance system for making all decisions. The focus of the worldview of Humanity Awareness is on becoming whole.

Behavioural characteristics

The principal behavioural markers of the worldview of Humanity Awareness are:

- New forms of governance involving all age groups
- New forms of global cooperation
- Everyone regarded as equal and important
- Focus on energy healing
- Focus on psychological welfare
- Values-based education
- Focus on competence and creativity
- Global redistribution of income to meet everyone's deficiency needs.

The transition to Earth Awareness

The transition from the worldview of Humanity Awareness to the worldview of Earth Awareness will occur when the people of the world collectively recognize the need to arrest the deterioration in the quality of the natural environment and focus on the amelioration of the Earth's life-support systems. Certain aspects of the worldview of Earth Awareness are already appearing in some communities in different parts of the world.

Earth Awareness: Making a difference through connection and empathy

What Earth Awareness will look like

People operating from the worldview of Earth Awareness understand the nature of holism. They see the embedded nature of things: they see individuals embedded in families, which in turn are embedded in communities. They see communities and organizations embedded in nations, which in turn are embedded in the living organism we call Earth. They see the interconnectedness of all things. They look at the world and see the interplay of forces and energies. They understand how all the other worldviews operate and integrate.

Whereas the task in the worldview of Humanity Awareness was to bond with ourselves – fully align our ego with our soul and live in harmony with others, the task in the worldview of Earth Awareness is to live in harmony with the planet. People who embrace the worldview of Earth Awareness want to bond with other people in group structures that care about the future of the Earth. They want to safeguard their physical home. We become a tribe of souls caring for all other souls and caring for the soul of the planet.

Our task in Earth Awareness is to balance our collective energies (the energy field of humanity) so we are in tune with the energy field of the Earth. To make this happen we must work where the energies are least balanced – where there is most fear and where there is most pollution – in nations where people are struggling to meet their deficiency needs, where they have not yet developed their full self-awareness and misuse or deplete the Earth's natural resources for personal or commercial gain.

At this stage of collective development, we are each called upon to integrate our energy field with the energy field of humanity, and for the energy field of humanity to integrate with the energy field of the Earth. This impulse is already showing up in the drive towards sustainable environmental and ecological development at the planetary level. In this sense, the UN Sustainable Development Goals provide a framework for manifesting Humanity and Earth Awareness.

The cosmology of Earth Awareness

In the worldview of Earth Awareness, the energetic connection to other souls and the soul of the Earth is deeply felt. We recognize that the energy field of our body is part of the energy field of the Earth. The health of our body depends on the health of the Earth.

At a personal level we become the servant of our soul.[32] We let go of any fear-based attachments. We are guided in all our actions by our soul's inspiration. All our personal needs are met before we are aware we have them. Thoughts are shared without speaking.

Correspondence with the integrating stage of development

The worldview of Earth Awareness corresponds to the integrating stage of personal development – a focus on connecting and cooperating with others in unconditional loving relationships so we can use our gifts and talents to make a difference in the world. We feel a deep sense of empathy for humanity in general and the Earth in particular.

Behavioural characteristics

The potential behavioural markers of the worldview of Earth Awareness are:

- Focus on the impact of decisions on future generations
- Focus on sustainable development
- Energy-based medicine
- High levels of empathy
- Alignment with the energy field of the Earth.

The transition to Unity Awareness

The transition from the worldview of Earth Awareness to the worldview of Unity Awareness will occur when the people of the world recognize the need to improve the life conditions for all living entities, thereby halting and reversing what has become known as the sixth extinction – the modern man-made extinction of species. Certain aspects of this new worldview are already appearing in some communities and parts of the world.

---

[32] Richard Barrett, *What My Soul Told Me* (Bath: Fulfilling Books), 2012.

Unity Awareness: Caring for the world through service and compassion

What Unity Awareness will look like

At this level of awareness, we recognize that we are one with all life forms and with the Earth itself. All living organisms on the planet are interconnected in an energetic web of life. Everything, including the human species, is an individuated aspect of the Gaia[33] energy field – every living thing is dependent on the energy field of the Earth for its continued existence. Consciousness is everywhere. There is no longer any separation. We can transcend our material awareness and see the world we live in through the energetic eyes of unity consciousness.

We return to a more enlightened form of the undifferentiated wholeness we experienced in the cosmology of Clan Awareness. We learn how to influence our physical world from the quantum level of existence. We understand that our collective beliefs create our collective reality, and personal beliefs create our personal reality. We are the co-creators of the world we experience.

At a personal level, we immerse ourselves in the experience of being. There is no focus on past or future and there is a complete absence of separation. Subject and object merge into one. We live in a state of non-duality. It is difficult to say much more about Unity Awareness, because it cannot be described, it can only be felt.

---

[33] Gaia refers to the Earth as a self-regulation complex system that includes all life forms.

The cosmology of Unity Awareness

In the worldview of Unity Awareness, we become one with our soul. There is a distinct difference between being the servant of our soul (Earth Awareness) and becoming one with our soul. When our ego serves our soul, we give up our freedom; when our ego becomes one with our soul, we surrender our existence – a part of us that has served us well has to die. We will know this part of us is dead when we recognize we no longer have needs and we no longer have fears. When we become focused in present-moment awareness and our intuition and inspiration guide everything we do.

Correspondence with the serving stage of development

The worldview of Unity Awareness corresponds to the serving stage of personal development – a focus on contributing our gifts and talents for the well-being of humanity and the planet. It is about serving those we meet through kindness and compassion.

Behavioural characteristics

The potential behavioural markers of the worldview of Unity Awareness are:

- High levels of compassion for all life forms
- Focus on energetic flourishing
- Focus on ecological justice
- Focus on non-duality.

Summary

Here are the main points of this chapter.

1. When new stages of human psychological development emerge, social life conditions change, and a new worldview emerges.
2. When a new worldview emerges, it affects every aspect of our lives – gender relations, governance systems, social hierarchies,

81

justice systems, child-rearing practices, education systems, health care, spiritual/religious practices, and so on.

3. The focus of the worldview of Clan Awareness is on survival through sharing and reciprocity.
4. The focus of the worldview of Tribe Awareness is on safety through belonging and loyalty.
5. The focus of the worldview of State Awareness is on security through power and strength.
6. The focus of the worldview of Nation Awareness is on security through authority and education.
7. The focus of the worldview of Wealth Awareness is on security through status and influence.
8. The focus of the worldview of People Awareness is on freedom through equality and accountability.
9. The focus of the worldview of Humanity Awareness is on self-expression through the exploration of personal creativity.
10. The focus of the worldview of Earth Awareness is on making a difference through connection and empathy.
11. The focus of the worldview of Unity Awareness is on caring for the world through service and compassion.

5

THE EVOLUTION AND
REGRESSION OF WORLDVIEWS

Having identified the fundamental role that the evolution of the stages of psychological development play in creating new worldviews, and having described the characteristics of each worldview, I would now like to explore how worldviews evolve and regress.

Evolutionary intelligence

In the *Evolutionary Human*,[34] I suggested that evolution was never about species, it was always about consciousness. At the heart of this new theory is the concept of evolutionary intelligence.

'Evolutionary intelligence is the ability of an entity to adapt to changes in its environment, so it can thrive and prosper. If an entity is unable to maintain its internal stability and external equilibrium it will struggle to function and will eventually disintegrate or decompose into its component parts. This is true for all entities, from atoms, to molecules, to cells, to organisms, to creatures, including *Homo sapiens* and all human group structures such as clans, communities, tribes and nations.'[35]

When we examine the evolution of life on Earth, we notice two types of adaptation: physical adaptation and psychological adaptation. As far as living creatures are concerned, prior to the appearance of *Homo sapiens,* these

---

[34] Richard Barrett, *The Evolutionary Human* (Bath: Fulfilling Books), 2018.
[35] Ibid. p. 1.

two types of adaptation progressed in parallel. Physical adaptation led to species evolution, and species evolution was accompanied by psychological evolution – an expansion of awareness, conscious and intelligence.

However, once *Homo sapiens* arrived on the scene, evolution stopped being about physical adaptation and became all about psychological adaptation. Each new stage of personal psychological development led to a new stage of collective psychological development (worldview), and each new stage of collective psychological development (worldview) created social changes that fostered a new stage of personal psychological development – a continuing evolutionary spiral of interaction between personal psychological development and collective psychological development.

The key to understanding evolutionary intelligence is that it only kicks in when an entity is confronted with a threat to its existence that it has never experienced before. If an entity has experienced a similar threat before, then it will have a memory of how it successfully tackled that threat previously, and that memory will click in to determine its actions. When an entity is faced with an existential threat it hasn't experienced before, it must rely on its evolutionary intelligence to find a solution. If it doesn't find a solution, it will cease to exist.

The first response of an entity (the first algorithm[36] of evolutionary intelligence) is to try to overcome the threat by becoming stronger, more powerful and more resilient. A very male approach to solving problems.

If the first algorithm doesn't work, if the threat has not gone away, then the second algorithm clicks in. The second algorithm consists of bonding with similar others who are facing the same threat to share resources and create a stronger front against the threat. If the second algorithm fails to overcome the threat, then the third algorithm clicks in. The third algorithm consists of dissimilar groups that are facing the same threat cooperating with each other to overcome the threat. The second and third algorithms are more in line with the female approach to solving problems.

The theory of evolutionary intelligence shows us not only how important bonding and cooperation strategies are in overcoming a threat, but also how important it is for entities to be able to shift to a higher level of identity/awareness in order to overcome a threat, even to the point of cooperating with dissimilar others. However, perhaps the most important

---

[36] See Glossary for a definition of algorithm.

learning is the role that fear plays in triggering evolutionary intelligence. Existential fear is the trigger of evolutionary intelligence.

The evolution of worldviews is an example of evolutionary intelligence in action. Each new worldview led to an expansion of identity/awareness. Existential problems were solved by a shift to a higher stage of psychological development that was more inclusive and less discriminatory – algorithms two and three in action; bonding and cooperation to form a higher-order entity. Each shift to a higher-order entity reduced the level of fear.

Fear and democracy

In *Love, Fear and the Destiny of Nations*[37] I developed a way of measuring the level of fear that people experience in a nation by combining the culture work of Geerte Hofstede and the Economist Intelligence Unit's Democracy Index. Figure 5.1 shows the relationship between the level of fear in a nation and the level of democracy.[38]

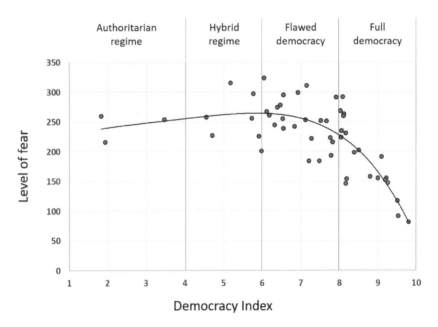

Figure 5.1: Level of fear vs. Democracy Index

---

[37] Richard Barrett, *What My Soul Told Me* (Bath: Fulfilling Books), 2012.
[38] Richard Barrett, *Love, Fear and the Destiny of Nations* (Bath: Fulfilling Books), 2010, p. 115.

It is noticeable in Figure 5.1 that the level of fear in a nation begins to decline when the Democracy Index reaches 6.0 – the beginning of the level of flawed democracies. It continues to decline as the Democracy Index approaches 8.0 – as the level of democracy increases towards full democracy. Thereafter the level of fear declines rapidly as the level of full democracy increases. This leads me to the conclusion that the level of fear people feel in their nation is inversely proportional to the level of democracy.

The level of democracy in a nation is also linked to the level of consciousness of a nation. Figure 5.2 shows a plot of the level of democracy in 145 nations compared with the level of consciousness of those nations. (I explain how I calculated the consciousness of nations in Part 2 of this book.)

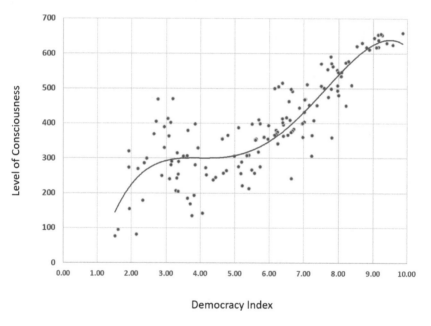

Figure 5.2: Plot of level of consciousness vs.
Democracy Index in 145 nations

Based on these correlations between the level of fear and the level of democracy, and the level of democracy and the level consciousness, we can conclude the level of consciousness of a nation is limited by the presence of fear in people's lives. Therefore, the higher the level of consciousness a nation can attain, the less fear in their lives people can attain, the happier they will feel.

Since most human fears arise from our inability to meet our deficiency needs, it follows that the more we are enabled to meet our deficiency needs, the less fearful we are; and the less fearful we are, the happier and more conscious we become.

Not surprisingly, therefore, there is a strong relationship between happiness and consciousness. Figure 5.3 plots the level of happiness against the level of consciousness in 145 nations.

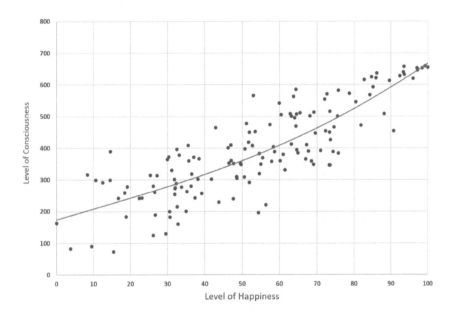

Figure 5.3: Plot of level of consciousness vs.
level of happiness in 145 nations

To close the loop Figure 5.4 shows a plot of the level of democracy against the level of happiness in 145 nations.

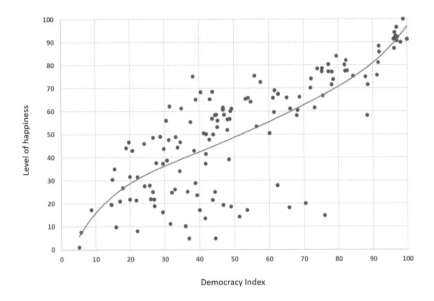

Figure 5.4: Plot of the level of happiness vs.
level of democracy in 145 nations

Although the relationship between happiness and democracy is not strong at the lower levels of democracy (authoritarian and hybrid regimes), it becomes much stronger in the realm of flawed and full democracies.

The data presented in Figures 5.1, 5.2, 5.3 and 5.4 clearly shows that the level of democracy, the level of happiness and the level of consciousness are linked to the level of fear in a nation, and the level of fear in a nation is linked to the ability of citizens to meet their deficiency needs.

Thus, we find, as I will show later, the most advanced democratic nations not only support people in meeting their deficiency needs, they also support people in meeting their growth needs (see Table 6.11). They don't just provide social welfare for their people; they also provide psychological welfare. (I will explore this idea in more detail in the last two chapters of the book.)

Upwards shifts in consciousness

Based on this reasoning, it becomes obvious that upward shifts in consciousness occur in democratic regimes when governments change their policies so that people can gratify their unmet psychological needs. Upward shifts in consciousness occur in authoritarian regimes when the leader embraces a new stage of development.

The most important triggering events that humans have experienced that led to the creation of a new worldview – a shift to a new level of collective psychological development – are described in Table 2.2 in Chapter 2.

A brief summary of the problems these triggering events highlighted and the solutions that the subsequent worldview provided are shown in Table 5.1. The table should be read from the bottom upwards.

Table 5.1: Problems that led to the emergence of new worldviews and how the new worldview solved them

From … to …	Problems of existence in …	Solution provided …
From People Awareness to Humanity Awareness	PEOPLE AWARENESS Global issues of climate change, human rights, people trafficking, international crime and lack of agility in decision-making.	HUMANITY AWARENESS Systemic and integral decision-making to promote self-expression and the harmonization of well-being of all peoples of the world.
From Wealth Awareness to People Awareness	WEALTH AWARENESS Lack of social safety nets for the poor and disadvantaged, gender discrimination, and the influence of corporate interests on policymaking.	PEOPLE AWARENESS Elimination of all forms of discrimination and the reduction of inequality by the creation of social welfare programmes for all citizens.
From Nation Awareness to Wealth Awareness	NATION AWARENESS Oppression of masses by landowners and discrimination against religious and ethnic minorities.	WORLD WEALTH AWARENESS Freedom of worship and acceptance of democratic governance and integration of ethnic minorities.
From State Awareness to Nation Awareness	STATE AWARENESS Intense rivalry among leaders for power and control of the State and its territory.	NATION AWARENESS Creation of order through the formation of kingdoms and the worship of one God.
From Tribe Awareness to State Awareness	TRIBE AWARENESS Territorial disputes brought on by population growth.	STATE AWARENESS Creation of armies to protect and expand territories.
From Clan Awareness to Tribe Awareness	CLAN AWARENESS Survival difficulties due to food shortages at certain times of the year.	TRIBE AWARENESS Farming, horticulture and animal husbandry in a tribal territory.

Downward shifts in consciousness

Downwards shifts in consciousness occur in democratic regimes when a significant number of people struggle to get their needs met – when they experience hardship or adversity on a continuing basis. In order to feel safer and more secure, they regress to a lower level of identity/ awareness (worldview) where they feel closer to 'kin' and less exposed to existential risks. This is what is currently happening in the US and what is influencing politics in the UK regarding Brexit. Such shifts always result in an increase in discrimination as people become more conservative and more discriminatory.

Downward shifts in consciousness in authoritarian regimes occur when there is a threat to the leader's authority – an unsuccessful rebellion or coup d'état. In such situations, the leader will introduce more repressive policies (with the backing of the police or the army), which trigger a shift towards a lower-order worldview.

In both authoritarian and democratic regimes, an external threat, such as displays of aggression from a neighbouring nation, will always cause a downward shift in consciousness towards a lower-order worldview and can cause an increase in discrimination.

Summary

Here are the main points of this chapter.

1. Evolution was never really about species; it was always about consciousness.
2. Evolutionary intelligence is the ability of an entity to adapt to changes in its environment, so it can thrive and prosper.
3. Evolutionary intelligence only kicks in when an entity is confronted with a threat to its existence that it has never experienced before.
4. Existential fear is the trigger of evolutionary intelligence.
5. The level of democracy in a nation is inversely proportional to the level of fear.
6. The level of fear in a nation limits the level of consciousness a nation can attain.

7. The most advanced democratic nations not only support people in meeting their deficiency needs, they also support people in meeting their growth needs.

8. They don't just provide social welfare; they also provide psychological welfare.

9. Upward shifts in consciousness occur in democratic regimes when governments change their policies so that people can gratify their unmet psychological needs.

10. Upward shifts in consciousness occur in authoritarian regimes when the leader embraces a new stage of development.

11. Downward shifts in consciousness occur in democratic regimes when people struggle to get their needs met inside the current worldview.

12. Downward shifts in consciousness in authoritarian regimes occur when there is a threat to the leader's authority – an unsuccessful rebellion or coup d'état.

13. In both authoritarian and democratic regimes, an external threat, such as displays of aggression from a neighbouring nation, will always cause a downward shift in consciousness towards a lower-order worldview.

PART 2

THE GLOBAL CONSCIOUSNESS INDICATOR

The second part of the book describes the creation and application of the Global Consciousness Indicator® (GCI) for nations. In Chapter 6, I describe how the GCI was created, and how it has been used to measure the consciousness (well-being) of 145 nations. In Chapter 7, I make the link between GCI scores and worldviews. I show how nations have evolved or regressed in consciousness by comparing their GCI scores for 2014, 2016 and 2018.

In Chapter 8, I compare the GCI scores and worldviews of member nations of the EU to discover the values fault-lines between nations. In Chapter 9, I compare the GCI scores for the five Nordic nations operating from the worldview of People Awareness. In Chapter 10, I compare the GCI scores for the four other nations operating from the worldview of People Awareness in 2018. In Chapter 11, I compare the GCI scores of the five Nordic and the four other nations operating from the worldview of People Awareness in 2018. I also compare the GCI scores of Norway and Sweden, New Zealand and Australia, Canada and the US, and Ireland and the UK.

In Chapter 12, I discuss what has been done in the Nordic nations to support the psychological development of young adults and the application of such an approach in other countries. In Chapter 13, I explore the rationale for a shift in focus from social welfare (in the worldview of People Awareness) to psychological welfare (in the worldview of Humanity Awareness).

In Chapter 14, the final chapter, I provide a detailed overview of what a nation would look like if it was living from the worldview of Humanity Awareness. I conclude with a call to action.

6

THE CONSCIOUSNESS OF NATIONS

Since I began mapping the values of nations in 2001, I have often wondered which are the most conscious nations on the planet. Sixteen years later I found a way of answering this question by creating the GCI.

The GCI is a barometer of consciousness for measuring the level of well-being experienced by the citizens of a nation. The GCI is based on the Barrett Seven Levels of Consciousness Model*, which in turn is based on an expanded version of Maslow's Hierarchy of Needs.[39]

There are many types of global indicators for measuring and comparing nations: each indicator focuses on a specific aspect of societal development – such as the Health Index, Peace Index, Education Index, Democracy Index, Gender Gap – but there is nothing measuring the whole; nothing that measures the overall level of well-being in a nation. The GCI is an attempt to rectify this situation.

Most of the current global indicators look at what is happening in a nation through a single lens. Each lens represents one aspect of a level of consciousness. For example, the Health Index focuses on an aspect of the survival level of consciousness; the Peace Index focuses on an aspect of the relationship level of consciousness; the Education Index focuses on an aspect of the self-esteem level of consciousness; the Democracy Index and the Gender Gap focus on two aspects of the transformation level of consciousness; etc.

---

[39] Chapter 1 provides a detailed explanation of the construction of the Seven Levels of Consciousness Model.

The GCI was constructed by allocating two, three or four global indicators, such as those mentioned above, to each of the seven levels of consciousness – 17 global indicators in all (see Figure 6.1). The indicators used are all well tried and tested.[40] The big advantage of the GCI is that it provides a single score that represents the level of well-being of the people of a nation.

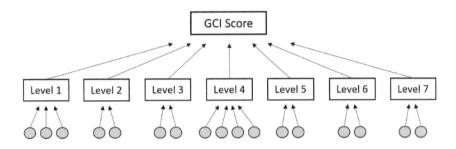

Figure 6.1: The construction of the GCI for a nation

The scores for the 17 global indicators were normalized, and the normalized scores for the indicators at each level of consciousness were averaged to obtain a score for each level of consciousness (out of 100). The average scores for the seven levels of consciousness were added together to obtain an overall GCI score (out of 700) for the nation. The GCI scores in 2018 range from 659 for Norway to 77 for Afghanistan.

It should be recognized that the GCI model does not provide by any means a perfect measure of every level of consciousness. Some levels are better represented by the indicators than others. Also, some of the 17 indicators cover similar topics, which may result in an element of double counting. However, overall the GCI is a reasonably good representation of the Seven Levels of Consciousness Model.

The focus of each level of consciousness and the number and types of indicators used at each level of consciousness are shown in Table 6.1.

---

[40] A list of the seventeen indicators used in the GCI model is provided in Annex 2.

Table 6.1: The number and types of indicators at each level of consciousness

Focus of each level of consciousness		Types and (number) of indicators
7	Satisfying citizens' needs for stability, well-being and happiness.	Strength, stability and legitimacy of the State, and level of happiness of the people. (2)
6	Satisfying citizens' needs for environmental quality and environmental preservation.	Health and quality of the natural environment, and quality of preservation efforts. (2)
5	Satisfying citizens' needs for inclusion, fairness, openness, tolerance and transparency.	Strength of personal relationships, social network support and civic participation (social cohesion), and foundations and opportunities for social progress. (2)
4	Satisfying citizens' needs for freedom, equality and accountability.	Legal rights, individual freedoms and social tolerance, level of democracy, press freedom, and gender equality. (4)
3	Satisfying citizens' needs for education, and a supportive, business environment.	Access to and quality of education, and business infrastructure, support to entrepreneurs and labour market flexibility. (2)
2	Satisfying citizens' needs for safety, protection and peace.	Societal safety and security, and the level of militarization and peace/violence. (2)
1	Satisfying citizens' needs for health care and economic performance.	Level of corruption, physical and mental health infrastructure and economic performance. (3)

The evolution of world consciousness

Based on data from 145 nations, the average GCI score for the world in 2018 was 444. World consciousness increased from 435 to 448 (2.79%) between 2014 and 2016 and decreased from 448 to 444 (0.75%) between 2016 and 2018 (see Table 6.2).

Table 6.2: World consciousness (average GCI score for 145 nations)

	2014	2016	2018
	435	448	444
% Increase		2.79	−0.75

As you will discover in the next chapter, a GCI score of 444 corresponds to the worldview of State Awareness 1,[41] a worldview of flawed democracies where ego-driven leaders seek to cling to power, where corruption is rife, where women are disenfranchised and people of different religions and ethnicities are discriminated against. Nations with scores around 444 in 2018 included Bulgaria, Qatar, Trinidad and Tobago, Greece and Argentina.

World GCI scores by level of consciousness

The average world GCI scores for 2014, 2016 and 2018 by level of consciousness are shown in Table 6.3.[42] Row 5 shows the change in GCI score over the four-year period from 2014 to 2018, and row 6 shows this change expressed as a percentage. The largest improvement is shown in bold and underlined; the second and third-largest improvements are underlined. The scores at each level are out of 100.

Table 6.3: World GCI scores by level of consciousness 2014, 2016 and 2018

Year	Level 1	Level 2	Level 3	Level 4	Level 5	Level 6	Level 7
2014	60.94	70.05	64.31	58.28	66.69	56.10	59.09
2016	63.71	70.40	65.65	59.58	65.16	61.01	62.11
2018	63.40	68.07	64.46	59.67	69.83	57.16	61.67
Change	2.46	–1.98	0.15	1.39	3.14	1.06	2.58
%	4.03%	–2.82%	0.24%	2.8%	**4.70%**	1.89%	4.36%

The most significant increases during the period 2014 to 2018 occurred at three levels of consciousness: Level 5 – satisfying citizens' needs for inclusion, fairness, openness, tolerance and transparency; Level 7 – satisfying citizens' needs for stability, well-being and happiness; and Level 1 – satisfying citizens' needs for health care and economic performance.

Of the two global indicators that make up the Level 5 consciousness, 94% of the improvement was due to an increase in social cohesion, and only 6% was due to an increase in social progress. Of the two indicators

---

[41] See Table 7.5.

[42] A full listing of the GCI scores for 145 nations for 2014, 2016 and 2018 can be found at www.aahv.gcr.

that make up the Level 7 consciousness, 90% of the improvement was due to an increase in the strength, stability and legitimacy of nations and only 10% was due to an increase in happiness. Of the three indicators that make up the Level 1 consciousness, 96% of the improvement was due to better economic performance.

The largest increases among the 17 indicators were in economic performance (+9.08), social cohesion (+4.82) and the strength, stability and legitimacy of nations (+4.13).

The only level of consciousness that showed a decrease was Level 2 – satisfying citizens' needs for safety, protection and peace. Of the two indicators that make up Level 2 consciousness, 56% of the decrease was due to an increase in violence and 44% was due to a decrease in the level of personal safety.

World GCI scores by region

The average GCI scores by region are shown in Table 6.4. The number of nations in each region is shown in brackets in column 1. Column 5 shows the overall change in GCI score between 2014 and 2018, and column 6 shows this change expressed as a percentage. The largest improvement is shown in bold and underlined; the second-largest improvement is underlined. The scores are out of 700.

Table 6.4: World GCI scores by region

Regions	2014	2016	2018	Change	%
Africa (37)	302	350	358	56	**18.46%**
Americas (24)	481	500	484	3	0.62%
Asia (23)	369	363	352	–17	–4.64%
Australasia (2)	644	646	640	–4	–0.62%
Europe (40)	511	512	513	2	0.38%
MENA (19)	305	315	318	13	4.30%
World	435	448	444	9	2.02%

Note: MENA = Middle East and North Africa

The region with the highest GCI score in 2018 was Australasia (New

99

Zealand and Australia) with an average overall GCI score of 640. Europe was the second highest with an average overall GCI score of 513. The lowest-scoring region was MENA with an average overall GCI score of 318.

The largest improvement was in the Africa region (+18.46%). The second-largest improvement was in the MENA region (+4.30%). The largest decrease was in the Asia region (−4.64%). There was very little change in the other regions.

The key issues in each region

The average GCI scores by region and levels of consciousness for 2018 are shown in Table 6.5. The lowest-scoring level of consciousness in each region is shown in bold and underlined. The second-lowest scoring level of consciousness is shown underlined.

The primary issue in the world is Level 6 consciousness – satisfying citizens' needs for environmental quality and environmental preservation (57.16). This is also the primary issue in all regions except Africa and MENA, where it is the most important secondary issue.

The most important secondary issue in the world is Level 4 consciousness – satisfying citizens' needs for freedom, equality and accountability. This is the primary issue in the MENA region. The primary issue in the Africa region is Level 7 consciousness – the strength, stability and legitimacy of the State and the happiness of the people.

Table 6.5: GCI scores by region and level of consciousness in 2018

Regions	Level 1	Level 2	Level 3	Level 4	Level 5	Level 6	Level 7	Score
Africa (37)	46.82	61.73	48.47	58.15	57.77	<u>43.61</u>	**<u>41.44</u>**	358
Americas (24)	<u>65.99</u>	69.29	68.25	72.72	73.30	**<u>63.45</u>**	71.00	484
Asia (23)	55.52	57.26	57.15	<u>42.16</u>	54.35	**<u>38.81</u>**	46.98	352
Australasia (2)	<u>89.31</u>	91.17	93.42	89.57	98.79	**<u>82.93</u>**	94.91	640
Europe (40)	71.55	79.45	74.36	71.56	75.92	**<u>69.51</u>**	<u>71.02</u>	513
MENA (19)	51.19	49.56	45.12	**<u>23.83</u>**	58.84	<u>44.67</u>	44.69	318
World	63.40	68.07	64.46	<u>59.67</u>	69.83	**<u>57.16</u>**	61.67	444

National consciousness

The most conscious nations

The nations with the highest GCI scores in 2014, 2016 and 2018 are shown in Table 6.6. Nine of the same nations were in the top ten every year. These included the five Nordic nations – Denmark, Finland, Iceland, Norway and Sweden – plus New Zealand, Australia, Switzerland and Canada. The most consistent performer was New Zealand, which ranked in the top two every year. The Netherlands dropped out of the top ten in 2016 and Ireland came into the top ten.

Table 6.6: The world's most conscious nations

Ranking	2014		2016		2018	
	Nation	Score	Nation	Score	Nation	Score
1	Switzerland	658	New Zealand	659	Norway	659
2	New Zealand	651	Finland	657	New Zealand	656
3	Denmark	648	Norway	650	Finland	654
4	Finland	646	Iceland	649	Denmark	652
5	Norway	646	Switzerland	649	Switzerland	651
6	Sweden	643	Denmark	648	Iceland	645
7	Iceland	639	Sweden	642	Sweden	638
8	Australia	636	Australia	633	Ireland	631
9	Canada	631	Canada	631	Canada	630
10	Netherlands	626	Ireland	621	Australia	624

Nations that are consistently improving in consciousness

Sixty nations consistently improved their consciousness from 2014 to 2016 and 2016 to 2018. Eight of the top ten consistent improvers were in West Africa (see Table 6.7). The other two top ten consistent improvers were Kyrgyzstan and Romania.

Table 6.7: World's top ten consistent improvers in consciousness

Nation	2014	2016	2018	Increase	Percentage
Guinea	184	200	245	61	33.33%
Togo	193	227	241	48	24.87%
Côte d'Ivoire	210	241	250	40	19.31%
Nigeria	218	225	256	38	17.43%
Sierra Leone	231	247	267	36	15.65%
Kyrgyzstan	316	363	365	49	15.65%
Romania	408	451	467	59	14.58%
Comoros	243	252	274	31	12.76%
Mali	198	202	221	23	11.64%
Senegal	288	302	318	30	10.42%

What's been improving?

There was no consistent pattern to the improvements in the top ten nations between 2014 and 2018. Here are the topics that account for the biggest changes in the three most consistent improvers.

Guinea
The improvements in consciousness in Guinea have come about primarily from an increase in health care (49.53 points) and secondly from an increase in economic performance (28.31 points). Other areas of improvement have been in gender equality (18.80 points) and the preservation of the environment (18.12 points).

Togo
The improvements in consciousness in Togo have come about from an increase in gender equality (33.15 points), an increase in social cohesion (23.79 points) and an improvement in economic performance (22.16 points).

Côte d'Ivoire
The improvements in consciousness in Côte d'Ivoire have come about from an increase in personal safety (15.13 points), an increase in social cohesion (14.52 points), an improvement in economic performance (13.48 points)

and an increase in the strength, stability and legitimacy of the State (12.47 points).

Nations that are consistently decreasing in consciousness

Only ten nations consistently decreased their consciousness from 2014 to 2016 and 2016 to 2018. These nations are shown in Table 6.8. The nations with the most significant decrease – more than 2% – are Turkey (–6.85%), Saudi Arabia (–6.25%), Gabon (–5.90%), Thailand (–5.26%) and Mauritania (–3.20%). All the remainder show a decrease of less than 2%. There are three Western nations among those that are consistently decreasing – Australia, Austria and Sweden.

Table 6.8: World's consistent decliners in consciousness

Nation	2014	2016	2018	Decrease	Percentage
Turkey	354	346	330	–24	–6.85
Saudi Arabia	384	364	360	–24	–6.25
Gabon	271	267	255	–16	–5.90
Thailand	399	392	378	–21	–5.26
Mauritania	191	191	185	–6	–3.20
Australia	636	633	624	–12	–1.83
Chile	508	507	500	–8	–1.63
Austria	619	615	612	–7	–1.16
Laos	283	281	280	–3	–1.02
Sweden	643	642	638	–4	–0.69

What's been decreasing

There is no consistent pattern to the decreases in consciousness. Here are the topics that account for the biggest changes in the three most consistent decliners.

Turkey
The decline in consciousness in Turkey has come about mainly from a decrease in press freedom (–30.57 points) and an increase in violence (–17.93 points). Other factors include a decrease in the quality of the

environment (–10.37 points) and a decrease in environmental preservation (–10.13 points). There has been a significant increase in social cohesion (+13.74 points) and economic performance (+10.33 points).

Gabon

The decline in consciousness in Gabon has come about mainly from a decrease in press freedom (–12.58 points), a decrease in environmental preservation (–11.31 points), an increase in corruption (–9.13points), and a decrease in personal safety (–8.59 points). There has been a significant improvement in economic performance (+17.92 points).

Saudi *Arabia*

The decline in consciousness has come about mainly from a decrease in environmental preservation (–19.58 points), an increase in violence (–16.52 points) and a decrease in personal safety (–14.23 points). There has been a significant improvement in personal freedom (+9.16 points).

Full spectrum consciousness

Full spectrum* consciousness[43] is a term I coined more than two decades ago for an individual or organization that can operate successfully from all seven levels of consciousness. Such people and organizations are quite rare.

As far as nations are concerned, I have defined a full spectrum consciousness nation as one that enables its citizens to meet their deficiency needs (Levels 1, 2 and 3),[44] their transformation needs (Level 4)[45] and their growth needs (Levels 5, 6 and 7).[46]

In this section, I explore which nations are the best at satisfying each

---

[43] See Glossary for a definition of full spectrum.
[44] Deficiency needs refer to our basic survival, safety and security needs. Once we have satisfied these needs, we no longer pay them much attention.
[45] Transformation needs refer to our freedom, autonomy and independence needs. Once we have satisfied these needs, we can begin to focus on our growth needs.
[46] Growth needs refer to our self-actualization, making a difference and service needs. It is only when we can satisfy these needs that we begin to feel a sense of fulfilment in our lives.

of these categories of needs, and which nations are the best at satisfying all these needs – the full spectrum nations.

The best nations for satisfying citizens' deficiency needs

The nations with the highest scores for satisfying citizens' deficiency needs (Levels 1, 2 and 3) in 2014, 2016 and 2018 are shown in Table 6.9. Eight of the nations listed were in the top ten in each year. They include four of the five Nordic nations in 2014, and all five Nordic nations in 2016 and 2018. In addition, Switzerland, Singapore, New Zealand and Hong Kong appeared in the top ten every year. The Netherlands dropped out of the top ten and Norway came into the top ten in 2016.

Table 6.9: The best nations for satisfying citizens' deficiency needs

	2014		2016		2018	
Ranking	Nation	Score	Nation	Score	Nation	Score
1	Switzerland	96.02	Switzerland	95.42	Singapore	95.80
2	New Zealand	94.85	Singapore	94.91	Switzerland	93.91
3	Singapore	94.83	New Zealand	94.55	New Zealand	93.73
4	Denmark	94.11	Denmark	93.75	Denmark	93.07
5	Finland	93.77	Finland	93.02	Norway	92.42
6	Sweden	93.02	Sweden	91.89	Finland	92.38
7	Hong Kong	93.00	Hong Kong	91.77	Hong Kong	91.85
8	Canada	91.70	Norway	91.17	Sweden	90.96
9	Australia	91.49	Iceland	90.85	Iceland	90.96
10	Netherlands	91.28	Canada	90.83	Canada	90.92

The best nations for satisfying citizens' transformation needs

The nations with the highest scores at Level 4 consciousness are shown in Table 6.10. These are the nations with the highest levels of freedom and equality. The five Nordic nations plus New Zealand, Canada, Ireland and the Netherlands appear in the top ten every year. Switzerland dropped out of the top ten in 2018 and Luxembourg came into the top ten.

Table 6.10: The best nations for satisfying citizens' transformation needs

Ranking	2014		2016		2018	
	Nation	Score	Nation	Score	Nation	Score
1	Iceland	97.81	Iceland	98.08	Iceland	97.46
2	Norway	95.49	Norway	95.80	Norway	97.10
3	Sweden	94.14	Finland	94.32	Sweden	94.56
4	Finland	92.03	Sweden	92.86	New Zealand	93.60
5	New Zealand	91.26	New Zealand	91.05	Finland	93.48
6	Denmark	90.35	Ireland	90.81	Ireland	91.97
7	Netherlands	89.39	Netherlands	87.37	Canada	91.52
8	Canada	88.31	Switzerland	87.09	Denmark	88.88
9	Ireland	87.50	Canada	87.04	Netherlands	88.05
10	Switzerland	87.39	Denmark	86.33	Luxembourg	85.65

The best nations for satisfying citizens' growth needs

The nations with the highest score for satisfying citizens' growth needs (Levels 5, 6 and 7) are shown in Table 6.11. The five Nordic nations plus Switzerland, Australia and New Zealand appear in the top ten each year. Austria and Canada dropped out of the top ten in 2016 and Ireland and Luxembourg came into the top ten.

Table 6.11: The best nations for satisfying citizens' growth needs

Ranking	2014		2016		2018	
	Nation	Score	Nation	Score	Nation	Score
1	Switzerland	94.07	New Zealand	94.70	Switzerland	94.87
2	Norway	92.44	Finland	94.53	Norway	94.81
3	Australia	91.96	Norway	93.57	Denmark	94.77
4	Denmark	91.83	Denmark	93.40	Finland	94.48
5	New Zealand	91.75	Iceland	92.80	New Zealand	93.64
6	Finland	91.04	Australia	92.62	Iceland	91.54
7	Iceland	90.29	Switzerland	91.81	Australia	90.78
8	Austria	89.87	Sweden	91.22	Ireland	90.56
9	Sweden	89.86	Canada	90.61	Luxembourg	90.29
10	Canada	89.15	Austria	88.60	Sweden	90.28

Full spectrum nations

There are only six nations that can be regarded as full spectrum nations – in the top ten of the best nations for satisfying citizens' deficiency, transformation and growth needs. These are Denmark, Finland, Iceland, Norway, Sweden and New Zealand (see Table 6.12).

Table 6:12: Full spectrum nations

	Deficiency needs Levels 1, 2 and 3		Transformation needs Level 4		Growth needs Levels 5, 6 and 7	
Ranking	Nation	Score	Nation	Score	Nation	Score
1	Singapore	95.80	Iceland	97.46	Switzerland	94.87
2	Switzerland	93.91	Norway	97.10	Norway	94.81
3	New Zealand	93.73	Sweden	94.56	Denmark	94.77
4	Denmark	93.07	New Zealand	93.60	Finland	94.48
5	Norway	92.42	Finland	93.48	New Zealand	93.64
6	Finland	92.38	Ireland	91.97	Iceland	91.54
7	Hong Kong	91.85	Canada	91.52	Australia	90.78
8	Sweden	90.96	Denmark	88.88	Ireland	90.56
9	Iceland	90.96	Netherlands	88.05	Luxembourg	90.29
10	Canada	90.92	Luxembourg	85.65	Sweden	90.28

In 2018 Singapore was the #1 nation at satisfying citizens' deficiency needs but ranked #79 at satisfying citizens' transformation needs and #25 at satisfying citizens' growth needs. The low ranking for transformation needs is because Singapore is a flawed democracy. The low ranking for growth needs is because of Singapore's low score in the quality of its environment.

Switzerland ranked #1 at satisfying citizens' growth needs and #2 at satisfying citizens' deficiency needs but ranked #14 at satisfying citizens' transformation needs. The lower ranking for transformation needs is because of Switzerland's low score in individual freedom, tolerance and gender equality.

Hong Kong ranked #7 at satisfying citizens' deficiency needs but ranked #55 at satisfying citizens' transformation needs and #67 at satisfying citizens' growth needs. The lower ranking for transformation needs is because Hong Kong is a flawed democracy. The lower ranking for growth needs is because of Hong Kong's low score in the quality of its environment.

Canada ranked #7 at satisfying citizens' transformation needs and #10 at satisfying citizens' deficiency needs but ranked #14 at satisfying citizens' growth needs. The lower ranking for growth needs is because of Canada's low score in caring for the environment.

Ireland ranked #6 at satisfying citizens' transformation needs and #9 at satisfying citizens' growth needs but ranked #12 at satisfying citizens' deficiency needs. The lower ranking for deficiency needs is due to Ireland's low score in health care.

Australia ranked #7 at satisfying citizens' growth needs but ranked #11 at satisfying citizens' transformation needs and #14 at satisfying citizens' deficiency needs. The lower ranking for transformation needs is due to Australia's low score in gender equality. The lower ranking for deficiency needs is due to Australia's low score in economic performance and personal safety.

The Netherlands ranked #9 at satisfying citizens' transformation needs but ranked #11 at satisfying citizens' deficiency needs and #15 at satisfying citizens' growth needs. The lower ranking for deficiency needs is due to the Netherlands' low score in the level of peace. The lower ranking for growth needs is due to the Netherlands' low score in the quality of its environment.

Luxembourg ranked #9 at satisfying citizens' growth needs and #10 at satisfying citizens' transformation needs but ranked #18 at satisfying citizens' deficiency needs. The lower ranking for deficiency needs is due to Luxembourg's low score in education and providing a supportive business environment.

The most consciousness nations by level of consciousness

The nations most focused on satisfying citizens' needs for health care and economic performance

The nations with the highest GCI scores at Level 1 consciousness are shown in Table 6.13. Singapore and Switzerland are the clear winners. Together they rank either #1 or #2 in every year. The five Nordic nations (except Iceland in 2016) plus New Zealand, Luxembourg and the Netherlands all show up in the top ten for every year. Iceland dropped out of the top ten in 2016 and Germany came into the top ten. Iceland came back into the top ten in 2018 and Germany dropped out.

Table 6.13: The top ten nations for satisfying citizens' Level 1 needs

	2014		2016		2018	
Ranking	Nation	Score	Nation	Score	Nation	Score
1	Singapore	96.41	Singapore	97.37	Singapore	98.15
2	Switzerland	96.05	Switzerland	96.52	Switzerland	96.13
3	Sweden	95.58	New Zealand	95.39	Luxembourg	94.93
4	New Zealand	94.87	Luxembourg	95.19	Sweden	94.89
5	Denmark	93.20	Sweden	95.13	Denmark	94.24
6	Luxembourg	93.08	Denmark	93.42	Norway	93.25
7	Norway	91.61	Norway	93.16	New Zealand	92.86
8	Finland	91.36	Finland	92.01	Netherlands	92.29
9	Netherlands	91.16	Netherlands	91.88	Iceland	91.94
10	Iceland	90.59	Germany	90.95	Finland	91.81

The nations most focused on satisfying citizens' needs for safety, protection and peace

The nations with the highest GCI scores at Level 2 consciousness are shown in Table 6.14. Hong Kong, Iceland, Denmark and Austria score highly at this level of consciousness every year. New Zealand, Malta and Japan also show up in the top ten every year.

Norway, which ranked #21 in 2018, and Finland, which ranked #14, do not make the top ten in any year, and Sweden is notably absent in both 2016 (#11) and 2018 (#17). Switzerland dropped out of the top ten in 2018 and Ireland came into the top ten. Luxembourg came into the top ten in 2016 and remained there in 2018.

Table 6.14: The top ten nations for satisfying citizens' Level 2 needs

Ranking	2014 Nation	Score	2016 Nation	Score	2018 Nation	Score
1	Hong Kong	100.00	Iceland	99.34	Hong Kong	98.28
2	Denmark	99.28	Denmark	97.28	Iceland	98.18
3	Austria	98.86	Austria	96.43	Malta	97.43
4	Iceland	97.84	Luxembourg	96.35	Luxembourg	95.36
5	Switzerland	97.69	Hong Kong	95.89	Austria	94.89
6	Malta	96.97	New Zealand	94.44	Japan	93.66
7	Japan	96.39	Malta	94.36	Singapore	93.57
8	Finland	95.14	Switzerland	94.34	New Zealand	93.51
9	New Zealand	95.08	Japan	94.25	Denmark	93.16
10	Sweden	95.00	Singapore	92.79	Ireland	92.79

The nations most focused on satisfying citizens' needs for education and a supportive business environment

The nations with the highest GCI scores at Level 3 consciousness are shown in Table 6.15. The United States, Singapore, Switzerland, Finland and New Zealand score highly at this level of consciousness every year. Other countries that show up in the top ten every year include the UK, Australia and Canada.

Norway came into the top ten in 2016 and remained there in 2018. The Netherlands dropped out of the top ten in 2016 and Hong Kong dropped out of the top ten in 2018.

Table 6.15: The top ten nations for satisfying citizens' Level 3 needs

Ranking	2014 Nation	Score	2016 Nation	Score	2018 Nation	Score
1	United States	97.09	United States	96.53	United States	97.06
2	Singapore	96.29	Switzerland	95.41	Singapore	95.68

3	Australia	95.02	Finland	95.10	Finland	95.65
4	Finland	94.81	U. Kingdom	94.96	New Zealand	94.82
5	New Zealand	94.60	Singapore	94.57	Switzerland	93.96
6	Switzerland	94.32	Australia	94.50	Canada	93.13
7	Canada	94.19	New Zealand	93.82	U. Kingdom	92.77
8	U. Kingdom	93.80	Canada	93.07	Norway	92.52
9	Hong Kong	92.88	Hong Kong	91.90	Australia	92.02
10	Netherlands	91.33	Norway	90.68	Denmark	91.79

The nations most focused on satisfying citizens' needs for freedom, equality and accountability

The nations with the highest scores at Level 4 consciousness are shown in Table 6.16.[47] The five Nordic nations plus New Zealand, Canada, Ireland and the Netherlands appear in the top ten every year. Switzerland dropped out of the top ten in 2018 and Luxembourg came into the top ten.

Table 6.16: The nations most focused on satisfying citizens' Level 4 needs

	2014		2016		2018	
Ranking	Nation	Score	Nation	Score	Nation	Score
1	Iceland	97.81	Iceland	98.08	Iceland	97.46
2	Norway	95.49	Norway	95.80	Norway	97.10
3	Sweden	94.14	Finland	94.32	Sweden	94.56
4	Finland	92.03	Sweden	92.86	New Zealand	93.60
5	New Zealand	91.26	New Zealand	91.05	Finland	93.48
6	Denmark	90.35	Ireland	90.81	Ireland	91.97
7	Netherlands	89.39	Netherlands	87.37	Canada	91.52
8	Canada	88.31	Switzerland	87.09	Denmark	88.88
9	Ireland	87.50	Canada	87.04	Netherlands	88.05
10	Switzerland	87.39	Denmark	86.33	Luxembourg	85.65

---

[47] This is the same as Table 6.10.

The nations most focused on satisfying citizens' needs for inclusion, fairness, openness, tolerance and transparency

The nations with the highest GCI scores at Level 5 consciousness are shown in Table 6.17. These are the best at satisfying citizens' social cohesion and social progress needs. Iceland, Denmark, Norway, New Zealand, Canada, Ireland and Australia show up in the top ten every year. Switzerland and the Netherlands dropped out of the top ten in 2016 and came back in 2018. The United States dropped out of the top ten in 2018. Germany and Finland jumped into the top ten in 2016 and dropped out in 2018. The UK jumped into the top ten in 2018.

Table 6.17: The top ten nations for satisfying citizens' Level 5 needs

Ranking	2014		2016		2018	
	Nation	Score	Nation	Score	Nation	Score
1	New Zealand	98.73	New Zealand	98.50	Norway	99.41
2	Iceland	97.30	Australia	96.12	New Zealand	99.11
3	Canada	97.22	Canada	94.55	Iceland	98.82
4	United States	96.84	Iceland	94.11	Australia	98.47
5	Denmark	96.39	Norway	94.02	Denmark	98.46
6	Australia	95.77	Denmark	92.72	Ireland	96.34
7	Ireland	95.59	United States	91.65	Netherlands	95.76
8	Norway	94.79	Finland	91.12	U. Kingdom	95.66
9	Netherlands	94.42	Germany	90.48	Canada	94.10
10	Switzerland	93.54	Ireland	89.79	Switzerland	93.96

The nations most focused on satisfying citizens' needs for environmental quality and environmental preservation

The nations with the highest GCI scores at Level 6 consciousness are shown in Table 6.19. This is the most volatile level of consciousness with different nations jumping in and out of the top ten in all years. The UK, Luxembourg, New Zealand, Austria and Sweden show up in the top ten every year. Norway dropped out of the top ten in 2016 and came back in again in 2018. Slovenia dropped out of the top ten in 2018. Estonia jumped into the top ten in 2016 and out again in 2018. France jumped into the top ten in 2016 and stayed in the top ten in 2018.

Table 6.19: The top ten nations for satisfying citizens' Level 6 needs

	2014		2016		2018	
Ranking	Nation	Score	Nation	Score	Nation	Score
1	Luxembourg	92.35	Slovenia	98.41	Switzerland	93.11
2	Slovenia	91.88	Finland	93.69	U. Kingdom	92.11
3	Switzerland	91.64	U. Kingdom	90.94	France	91.93
4	Australia	87.86	Luxembourg	90.67	Finland	89.89
5	U. Kingdom	87.14	Sweden	90.31	Luxembourg	89.28
6	Germany	86.38	Estonia	90.14	Denmark	88.01
7	Austria	85.96	New Zealand	89.74	New Zealand	86.73
8	Norway	85.26	France	89.32	Austria	86.58
9	New Zealand	84.42	Denmark	88.98	Sweden	86.50
10	Sweden	84.28	Austria	88.38	Norway	86.00

The nations most focused on satisfying citizens' needs for stability, well-being and happiness

The nations with the highest GCI scores at Level 7 consciousness are shown in Table 6.20. The same nations appear in the top ten every year. They include the five Nordic nations plus Switzerland, Canada, the Netherlands, Australia and New Zealand.

Table 6.20: The top ten nations for satisfying citizens' Level 7 needs

	2014		2016		2018	
Ranking	Nation	Score	Nation	Score	Nation	Score
1	Denmark	97.77	Finland	98.78	Finland	100.00
2	Norway	97.26	Norway	98.74	Norway	99.03
3	Switzerland	97.05	Switzerland	98.54	Denmark	97.84
4	Finland	96.80	Denmark	98.51	Switzerland	97.53
5	Sweden	96.29	Iceland	97.71	Iceland	97.05
6	Canada	93.00	Canada	96.60	Canada	95.18
7	Netherlands	92.71	New Zealand	95.85	New Zealand	95.09
8	Iceland	92.53	Australia	95.78	Sweden	94.88
9	Australia	92.26	Sweden	95.65	Australia	94.74
10	New Zealand	92.10	Netherlands	93.34	Netherlands	93.89

Having used the GCI scores to identify the most conscious nations in the world in this chapter, I am going to use the GCI scores to explore the differences in consciousness between worldviews in the next chapter.

Summary

Here are the main points of this chapter.

1. The GCI is a barometer of consciousness that measures the well-being of citizens of a nation.
2. The GCI is based on the Barrett Seven Levels of Consciousness Model". The Seven Levels Model is based on an expanded version of Maslow's Hierarchy of Needs.
3. The overall GCI score for a nation is calculated using 17 global indicators.
4. The world GCI score is based on the results for 145 nations.
5. The world GCI score increased by 2.79% between 2014 and 2016 and decreased by 0.75% between 2016 and 2018.
6. The most significant increases in consciousness during the period 2014 to 2018 occurred at three levels of consciousness: Level 5 – satisfying citizens' needs for inclusion, fairness, openness, tolerance and transparency; Level 7 – satisfying citizens' needs for stability, well-being and happiness; and Level 1 – satisfying citizens' needs for health care and economic performance.
7. The only level of consciousness that showed a decrease was Level 2 consciousness – satisfying citizens' needs for safety, protection and peace.
8. The lowest level of consciousness in the world is Level 6 – satisfying citizens' needs for environmental quality and environmental preservation.
9. The second-lowest level of consciousness in the world is Level 4 – satisfying citizens' needs for freedom, equality and accountability.
10. The region with the highest GCI score in 2018 was Australasia (New Zealand and Australia) with an average overall GCI score of 640. Europe was the second highest with an average overall

GCI score of 513. The lowest-scoring region was MENA with an average overall GCI score of 318.

11. The largest improvement was in in the Africa region (+18.46%). The second-largest improvement was in the MENA region (+4.30%). The largest decrease was in the Asia region (–4.64%). There was very little change in the other regions.

12. Sixty nations consistently improved their consciousness from 2014 to 2016 and 2016 to 2018. Eight of the top ten consistent improvers were in West Africa.

13. Ten nations consistently decreased their consciousness from 2014 to 2016 and 2016 to 2018. The nations with the most significant decreases were Turkey, Saudi Arabia, Gabon, Thailand and Mauritania.

14. There are only six nations that can be regarded as full spectrum nations – Denmark, Finland, Iceland, Norway, Sweden and New Zealand.

7

WORLDVIEWS AND CONSCIOUSNESS

In the last chapter, I used the GCI scores to compare the consciousness of regions and nations. In this chapter, I use the GCI scores to compare worldviews. To make the link between the GCI scores and worldviews I had to establish a table of correspondence (see Table 7.1). The number of nations operating from each worldview in 2018 is shown in the third column of Table 7.1.

Table 7.1: Correspondence of worldviews with GCI scores

Worldview	GCI score	Number of nations
Humanity Awareness	Above 680	0
People Awareness	630–679	9
Wealth Awareness	580–629	7
Nation Awareness	480–579	22
State Awareness 1	380–479	34
State Awareness 2	280–379	41
State Awareness 3	Below 280	32

Since there are more than 100 nations operating from State Awareness, I have divided this worldview into three levels. The main difference between the three levels is the degree to which a nation is influenced by the worldview of Tribe Awareness.[48] I will be referring to nations where

---

[48] Although there are no nations operating directly from Tribe Awareness, many nations are influenced by this worldview. In the worldview of State Awareness 3 there are many communities where Tribe Awareness is the dominant worldview.

there is very little or no influence of Tribe Awareness as operating from State Awareness 1. Nations where there is a moderate influence of Tribe Awareness I will be referring to as operating from State Awareness 2. Nations where there is marked influence of Tribe Awareness I will be referring to as State Awareness 3.

Worldviews by nation

The allocation of nations to worldviews is shown in Table 7.2. Nations are listed in the order of their GCI scores in 2018.[49] The nations that are listed first in a worldview show some of the characteristics of the succeeding worldview. Conversely, nations that are listed last in each worldview show some of the characteristics of the preceding worldview.

For example, although France and Slovenia are operating from the worldview of Nation Awareness they both embrace some policies that are close to those found in Wealth Awareness, and although Austria and Belgium are operating from the worldview of Wealth Awareness they both embrace some policies that are close to those found in Nation Awareness.

Table 7.2: Worldviews of nations in 2018

Worldview	GCI Score	Nations
People Awareness	Above 630	Norway, New Zealand, Finland, Denmark, Switzerland, Iceland, Sweden, Ireland, Canada.
Wealth Awareness	580–629	Australia, Netherlands, Luxembourg, Germany, United Kingdom, Austria, Belgium.
Nation Awareness	480–579	France, Slovenia, Malta, United States of America, Singapore, Japan, Spain, Portugal, Czech Republic, Estonia, Costa Rica, Uruguay, Slovakia, Italy, Cyprus, Hong Kong. Lithuania, Chile, Poland, South Korea, Mauritius, Latvia.

[49] A full listing of nations by GCI score and worldviews for 2014, 2016 and 2018 can be found at https://www.barrettacademy.com/gci-reports

State Awareness 1	380–479	Israel, United Arab Emirates, Hungary, Panama, Croatia, Romania, Malaysia, Bulgaria, Qatar, Trinidad and Tobago, Greece, Argentina, Jamaica, Montenegro, Kuwait, Serbia, Peru, Colombia, Suriname, Brazil, Mongolia, Indonesia, Belize, Mexico, Bahrain, Dominican Republic, Albania, Ecuador, Paraguay, Oman, Namibia, Belarus, Kazakhstan, Philippines.
State Awareness 2	280–379	Sri Lanka, Thailand, Nicaragua, Guyana, Bolivia, Botswana, Guatemala, Georgia, Kyrgyzstan, Ghana, South Africa, Moldova, Saudi Arabia, El Salvador, Honduras, Jordan, Armenia, Tunisia, China, Morocco, Vietnam, Russia, Zambia, Turkey, Lebanon, Senegal, Algeria, Azerbaijan, Nepal, India, Kenya, Ukraine, Iran, Tanzania, Tajikistan, Rwanda, Malawi, Cambodia, Liberia, Bangladesh, Laos.
State Awareness 3	Below 279	Burkina Faso, Egypt, Comoros, Benin, Lesotho, Sierra Leone, Uganda, Mozambique, Djibouti, Nigeria, Gabon, Madagascar, Côte d'Ivoire, Guinea, Zimbabwe, Cameroon, Togo, Libya, Mali, Pakistan, Congo, Ethiopia, Niger, Mauritania, Angola, Iraq, Burundi, Chad, Sudan, Yemen, Central African Republic, Afghanistan.

Worldviews by region

The distribution of worldviews by region is shown in Table 7.3. Currently, New Zealand is the only nation in Australasia operating from People Awareness. Australia dropped down from People Awareness to Wealth Awareness in 2018 mainly due to its poor score at Level 6 consciousness – satisfying citizens' needs for environmental quality and environmental preservation.

Europe is the most diverse region with five different worldviews. Asia is the second most diverse region, with four different worldviews. Currently, the only nations operating from Wealth Awareness are found in Europe and Australasia. The US, which was operating from Wealth Awareness in 2016, dropped down to Nation Awareness in 2018.

All African nations except two are operating from State Awareness 2 and 3. The only African nation operating from Nation Awareness is Mauritius, and the only African nation operating from State Awareness 1 is Namibia. All nations in the MENA region operate from State Awareness 1, State Awareness 2 or State Awareness 3.

Table 7.3: The distribution of worldviews by region[50]

Regions	PA	WA	NA	SA1	SA2	SA3	Number
Australasia	1	1	-	-	-	-	2
Europe	7	6	13	9	5	-	40
Americas	1	-	4	13	6	-	24
Asia	-	-	4	5	12	2	23
Africa	-	-	1	1	10	25	37
MENA	-	-	-	6	8	5	19
Total	9	7	22	34	41	32	145

Worldviews by specific indicators

The following tables show the distribution of worldviews by seven of what I regard as some of the most important of the 17 global indicators:

- Economic performance
- Level of democracy
- Gender equality
- Corruption
- Social cohesion
- Strength, stability and legitimacy of the State
- Level of happiness.

Worldviews and economic performance

The distribution of worldviews by level of economic performance is shown in Table 7.4. All nations operating from the worldview of People Awareness, except Canada, are in the top category of economic performance. All nations operating from Wealth Awareness, except Belgium and Australia, are also in the top category.

[50] Throughout the rest of the book PA refers to People Awareness, WA refers to Wealth Awareness, NA refers to Nation Awareness and SA refers to State Awareness.

Most nations operating from Nation Awareness are in the second category of economic performance. Singapore, the US, Malta and Japan are in the top category, and Lithuania and Latvia are in the third category. Two nations operating from State Awareness 1 are in the top category – Bahrain and the UAE.

Most nations operating from State Awareness 1 are in the second or third category. One nation – Namibia – is in the fourth category. Most nations operating from State Awareness 2 are in the third category. Most nations operating from State Awareness 3 are in the fourth category.

Table 7.4: Worldviews by level of economic performance

Economy	PA	WA	NA	SA1	SA2	SA3	Number
75+	8	5	4	2	-	-	19
65.00–74.99	1	2	16	9	6	-	34
55.00–64.99	-	-	2	22	28	8	60
45.00–54.99	-	-	-	1	6	21	28
<45.00	-	-	-	-	1	3	4
Total	9	7	22	34	41	32	145

Worldviews and level of democracy

The distribution of worldviews by level of democracy is shown in Table 7.5. All nations operating from the worldview of People Awareness and all nations operating from Wealth Awareness, except Belgium, are full democracies. Belgium is a flawed democracy.

The six nations operating from Nation Awareness are full democracies – Australia, the Netherlands, Luxembourg, Germany, the UK and Austria. Most of the remainder operating from the worldview of Nation Awareness are flawed democracies except Poland, Singapore and Hong Kong, which are hybrid regimes.

Most nations operating from the worldview of State Awareness 1 are flawed democracies. Most nations operating from the worldview of State Awareness 2 are hybrid regimes. Most nations operating from the worldview of State Awareness 3 are authoritarian regimes.

Table 7.5: Worldviews by levels of democracy

Democracy	PA	WA	NA	SA1	SA2	SA3	Total
Full	9	6	6	-	-	-	21
Flawed	-	1	13	24	8	1	47
Hybrid	-	-	3	2	20	10	35
Authoritarian	-	-	-	8	13	21	42
Total	9	7	22	34	41	32	145

Worldviews and gender equality

The distribution of worldviews by gender equality is shown in Table 7.6. Five nations operating from the worldview of People Awareness are in the highest category of gender equality. These are Iceland, Norway, Sweden, Finland and New Zealand. Two nations operating from State Awareness 2 are also in the highest category – Nicaragua and Rwanda.

Four nations operating from the worldview of People Awareness are in the second category of gender equality – Ireland, Denmark, Canada and Switzerland. Two nations operating from the worldview of Wealth Awareness are also in the second category – Germany and the UK.

There are three nations operating from the worldview of Nation Awareness in the second category of gender equality – Slovenia, France and Latvia; three nations operating from the worldview of State Awareness 1 – Philippines, Namibia and Bulgaria; and one nation operating from State Awareness 2 – South Africa.

Five nations operating from the worldview of Wealth Awareness are in the third category of gender equality – the Netherlands, Belgium, Australia, Austria and Luxembourg. Most nations operating from the worldview of Nation Awareness and State Awareness 1 are in the third category of gender equality.

Most nations operating from the worldview of State Awareness 2 are in the third and fourth categories of gender equality. Nations operating from the worldview of State Awareness 3 are equally split between the second, third, fourth and fifth categories of gender equality.

Table 7.6: Worldviews by gender equality

Gender Gap	PA	WA	NA	SA1	SA2	SA3	Total
0.800+	5	-	-	-	2	-	7
0.750–0.799	4	2	3	3	1	-	13
0.700–0.749	-	5	11	17	11	5	49
0.650–0.699	-	-	7	8	16	6	37
0.600–0.649	-	-	-	5	6	7	18
<0.600	-	-	-	-	3	6	9
Total	9	7	21	33	39	24	133

Note: Data not available for 12 nations.

Worldviews and corruption

The inverse distribution of worldviews by level of corruption (the most honest) is shown in Table 7.7. Seven nations operating from the worldview of People Awareness are in the highest category of honesty. Iceland and Ireland are in the second category. Four nations operating from the worldview of Wealth Awareness – the Netherlands, Luxembourg, the UK and Germany – are also in the highest category of honesty, along with one nation operating from Nation Awareness – Singapore.

Three nations operating from the worldview of Wealth Awareness are in the second category – Australia, Austria and Belgium. Apart from Singapore, all the other nations operating from the worldview of Nation Awareness are in the second and third categories of honesty.

Three nations operating from the worldview of State Awareness 1 – UAE, Qatar and Israel – and one nation operating from the worldview of State Awareness 2 – Botswana – are also in the second category.

Most nations operating from the worldviews of State Awareness 1 and State Awareness 2 are in the third and fourth categories. Most nations operating from the worldview of State Awareness 3 are in the fourth and fifth categories of honesty.

Table 7.7: Worldviews by honesty (inverse of level of corruption)

Honesty	PA	WA	NA	SA1	SA2	SA3	Total
80+	7	4	1	-	-	-	12

60–79	2	3	10	3	1	-	19
40–59		-	11	15	11	2	39
20–39				15	29	20	64
<20			-	-	-	9	9
Total	9	7	22	33	41	31	143

Note: Data not available for two nations.

Worldviews and social cohesion

The distribution of worldviews by level of social cohesion is shown in Table 7.8. Eight nations operating from the worldview of People Awareness are in the highest category of social cohesion. One nation – Sweden – is in the second category. Six nations operating from the worldview of Wealth Awareness are also in the highest category. One nation – Belgium – is in the second category.

Four nations operating from the worldview of Nation Awareness – US, Malta, Singapore and Slovenia – and two nations operating from the worldview of State Awareness 1 – Indonesia and Bahrain – are also in the highest category. Twelve nations operating from the worldview of Nation Awareness are in the second category, and six nations are in the third category – Czech Republic, Poland, South Korea, Lithuania, Japan and Latvia.

Sixteen nations operating from the worldview of State Awareness 1 are in the second category, and 16 nations are in the third category. Fifteen nations operating from the worldview of State Awareness 2 are in the second category, and 26 nations are in the third category. Most nations operating from the worldview of State Awareness 3 are in the third category. The least cohesive nation is Afghanistan. It is in the last category.

Table 7.8: Worldviews by level of social cohesion

Social Cohesion	PA	WA	NA	SA1	SA2	SA3	Total
60+	8	6	4	2	-	-	20
50–59	1	1	12	16	15	5	50
40–49	-	-	6	16	26	20	68
30–39	-	-	-	-	-	6	6
<30	-	-	-	-	-	1	1
Total	9	7	22	34	41	32	145

Worldviews and strength, stability and legitimacy of the State

The distribution of worldviews by level of strength, stability and legitimacy of the State is shown in Table 7.9. All nine nations operating from the worldview of People Awareness, five operating from Wealth Awareness – Australia, Luxembourg, Germany, the Netherlands and Austria – and one operating from Nation Awareness – Portugal – are in the first category of strength, stability and legitimacy.

Two nations operating from the worldview of Wealth Awareness – Belgium and the UK – 19 nations operating from the worldview of Nation Awareness and two nations operating from the worldview of State Awareness 1 – UAE and Qatar – are in the second category. One nation operating from the worldview of Nation Awareness is in the third category – Cyprus. Most nations operating from the worldview of State Awareness 1 are in the third and fourth categories. Most nations operating from the worldview of State Awareness 2 are in the fourth category, and most nations operating from the worldview of State Awareness 3 are in the fifth category.

Table 7.9: Worldviews by strength, stability and legitimacy of the State

Stability	PA	WA	NA	SA1	SA2	SA3	Total
90+	9	5	1	-	-	-	15
70–89	-	2	19	2	-	-	23
50–69	-	-	1	19	1	-	21
30–49	-	-	-	13	33	6	52
<30	-	-	-	-	7	26	33
Total	9	7	21	34	41	32	144

Note: Data not available for one nation.

Worldviews and level of happiness

The distribution of worldviews by level of happiness is shown in Table 7.10. Eight nations operating from the worldview of People Awareness are in the first category of happiness. One nation – Ireland – falls into the second category.

Three nations operating from the worldview of Wealth Awareness are also in the first category of happiness – the Netherlands, Australia and

Austria. The other four – Germany, Belgium, Luxembourg and the UK – are in the second category. One nation operating from the worldview of Nation Awareness – Costa Rica – and one nation operating from the worldview of State Awareness 1 – Israel – are in the highest category of happiness.

Almost all nations operating from the worldview of Nation Awareness and State Awareness 1 are in the second and third categories of happiness. Most nations operating from the worldview of State Awareness 2 are in the third and fourth categories of happiness. Most nations operating from the worldview of State Awareness 3 are in the fourth and fifth categories of happiness.

Table 7.10: Worldviews by happiness

Happiness	PA	WA	NA	SA1	SA2	SA3	Total
7.00+	8	3	1	1	-	-	13
6.00–6.99	1	4	11	13	5	-	34
5.00–5.99	-	-	9	17	14	-	40
4.00–4.99	-	-	-	3	16	17	36
<4.00	-	-	-	-	5	10	15
Total	9	7	21	34	40	27	138

Note: Data not available for seven nations.

As one might expect, the distribution of worldviews by these seven global indicators shows that the nations with the highest GCI scores are concentrated at the top of each of the categories and the nations with the lowest GCI scores are concentrated at the bottom of each of the categories.

GCI scores by worldview in 2014, 2016 and 2018

The world GCI scores by worldview in 2014, 2016 and 2018 are shown in Table 7.11. The largest sustained improvement in consciousness between 2014 and 2018 occurred in the nations operating from the worldview of State Awareness 2 – an improvement of 7.62%. The largest sustained decrease in consciousness occurred in nations operating from the worldview of State Awareness 3 – a decrease of 6.15%. There was also a decrease in consciousness in the nations operating from State Awareness 1 – a decrease of 3.62%. There was very little change (±1.5%) in the average GCI scores for the worldviews of People, Wealth and Nation Awareness between 2014 and 2016.

Table 7.11: Evolution of world GCI scores by worldview

Worldview	2014	2016	2018	Change	%
People Awareness	640	642	644	4	0.62
Wealth Awareness	610	598	619	9	1.40
Nation Awareness	524	510	520	–4	–0.77
State Awareness 1	431	413	416	–16	–3.62
State Awareness 2	315	338	339	24	7.62
State Awareness 3	197	196	185	–12	–6.15

Similarities and key differences between worldviews

In order to determine the similarities and key differences between adjacent worldviews, I calculated the average score for every level of consciousness in each worldview and compared the results. In the following tables, the levels of consciousness that are most aligned between worldviews are shown in italics. The most misaligned levels of consciousness are in bold.

Comparison between People Awareness and Wealth Awareness

The average score for all nations operating from the worldview of People Awareness is 646 and the average score for all nations operating from the worldview of Wealth Awareness is 615 – 31 points difference (see Table 7.12). Levels of consciousness 6, 5 and 1 are most aligned and levels of consciousness 4, 7 and 3 are least aligned.

Table 7.12: Comparison of People Awareness with Wealth Awareness

Worldviews	Level 1	Level 2	Level 3	Level 4	Level 5	Level 6	Level 7	Score
PA (9)	92.23	92.36	91.20	92.63	95.91	85.54	96.42	646
WA (7)	89.36	89.01	86.12	84.34	93.05	83.47	89.47	615
Difference	*–2.87*	*–3.35*	**–5.08**	**–8.29**	*–2.86*	*–2.07*	**–6.95**	–31

The most aligned of the 17 indicators between People Awareness and Wealth Awareness are the level of health care at Level 1 consciousness, the level of social progress at Level 5 consciousness and the quality of the environment at Level 6 consciousness.

The least aligned of the 17 indicators between People Awareness and Wealth Awareness by a large margin is the level of gender equality at Level 4 consciousness. The level of democracy at Level 4 consciousness, the level of happiness at Level 7 consciousness and a supportive business environment at Level 3 consciousness are also misaligned but to a much lesser extent than gender equality.

Comparison between Wealth Awareness and Nation Awareness

The average score for all nations operating from the worldview of Wealth Awareness is 615 and the average score for all nations operating from the worldview of Nation Awareness is 529 – 86 points difference (see Table 7.13). The level of consciousness that is most aligned is Level 2. All other levels of consciousness are misaligned. The most misaligned are Levels 7, 5 and 6.

Table 7.13: Comparison of Wealth Awareness with Nation Awareness

Worldviews	Level 1	Level 2	Level 3	Level 4	Level 5	Level 6	Level 7	Score
WA (7)	89.36	89.01	86.12	84.34	93.05	83.47	89.47	615
NA (22)	75.59	82.83	75.78	73.87	78.01	69.46	73.01	529
Difference	–13.77	*–6.18*	–10.34	–10.47	**–15.04**	**–14.01**	**–16.46**	–86

The most aligned of the 17 indicators between Wealth Awareness and Nation Awareness are the level of peace and the level of safety at Level 2 consciousness.

The least aligned of the 17 indicators between Wealth Awareness and Nation Awareness are the level of social cohesion at Level 5 consciousness, the level of corruption at Level 1 consciousness and the level of happiness at Level 7 consciousness.

Richard Barrett

Comparison between Nation Awareness and State Awareness 1

The average score for all nations operating from the worldview of Nation Awareness is 529 and the average score for all nations operating from the worldview of State Awareness 1 is 421 – 108 points difference (see Table 7.14). None of the levels of consciousness are aligned. The most misaligned are Levels 4, 1 and 2.

Table 7.14: Comparison of Nation Awareness with State Awareness 1

Worldviews	Level 1	Level 2	Level 3	Level 4	Level 5	Level 6	Level 7	Score
NA (22)	75.59	82.83	75.78	73.87	78.01	69.46	73.01	529
SA 1 (34)	58.06	66.01	60.86	55.62	65.30	57.36	58.00	421
Difference	**-17.53**	**-16.82**	-14.92	**-18.25**	*-12.71*	*-12.10*	-15.01	-108

The least aligned of the 17 indicators between Nation Awareness and State Awareness 1 are the level of honesty (corruption) at Level 1 consciousness, the level of press freedom, the level of democracy and the level of freedom of the people at Level 4 consciousness and the strength, stability and legitimacy of the State at Level 7 consciousness.

Comparison between State Awareness 1 and State Awareness 2

The average score for all nations operating from the worldview of State Awareness 1 is 421 and the average score for all nations operating from the worldview of State Awareness 2 is 336 – 85 points difference (see Table 7.15). None of the levels of consciousness are aligned. The most misaligned are Levels 7, 6 and 4.

Table 7.15: Comparison of State Awareness 1 with State Awareness 2

Worldviews	Level 1	Level 2	Level 3	Level 4	Level 5	Level 6	Level 7	Score
SA 1 (34)	58.06	66.01	60.86	55.62	65.30	57.36	58.00	421
SA 2 (41)	47.75	57.57	50.95	43.12	53.80	42.04	40.21	336
Difference	-10.31	*-8.44*	-9.91	**-12.50**	-11.50	**-15.32**	**-17.79**	-85

The least aligned of the 17 indicators between State Awareness 1 and State Awareness 2 are the level of happiness of the people and the strength, stability and legitimacy of the State at Level 7 consciousness, the level of press freedom at Level 4 consciousness and the level of quality and preservation of the environment at Level 6 consciousness.

Comparison between State Awareness 2 and State Awareness 3

The average score for all nations operating from the worldview of State Awareness 2 is 336 and the average score for all nations operating from the worldview of State Awareness 3 is 215 – 121 points difference (see Table 7.16). None of the levels of consciousness are aligned. The most misaligned are Levels 3, 1 and 5.

Table 7.16: Comparison of State Awareness 2 with State Awareness 3

Worldviews	Level 1	Level 2	Level 3	Level 4	Level 5	Level 6	Level 7	Score
SA 2 (41)	47.75	57.57	50.95	43.12	53.80	42.04	40.21	336
SA 3 (32)	28.38	43.23	25.03	30.07	36.26	27.46	25.00	215
Difference	**-19.37**	-14.34	**-25.92**	*-13.05*	**-17.54**	-14.58	-15.21	-121

The least aligned of the 17 indicators between State Awareness 2 and State Awareness 3 are the level of education at Level 3 consciousness, the level of social progress at Level 5 consciousness and the level of health care at Level 1 consciousness.

Key factors in transitioning between worldviews

Based on the results of the above analysis, the key transition factors between adjacent worldviews are summarized in Table 7.17. The factors listed are the issues that nations need to focus on to transition from one worldview to the next.

Table 7.17: Key transition factors between worldviews

From	To	Key transition conditions
Wealth Awareness	People Awareness	Increase in gender equality, democracy, social welfare and level of support for business.

Nation Awareness	Wealth Awareness	Increase in social cohesion, decrease in corruption and increase in happiness.
State Awareness 1	Nation Awareness	Decrease in corruption, increase in press freedom, democracy, personal freedom and the strength, stability and legitimacy of the State.
State Awareness 2	State Awareness 1	Increase in happiness, strength, stability and legitimacy of the State, press freedom, and the quality and preservation of the environment.
State Awareness 3	State Awareness 2	Increase in education, social progress and health care.

By far the largest differentiator between nations operating from the worldview of People Awareness and Wealth Awareness is gender equality. The largest differentiators between nations operating from the worldview of Wealth Awareness and Nation Awareness are the level of social cohesion, the level of corruption and the level of happiness.

The largest differentiators between nations operating from the worldview of Nation Awareness and State Awareness 1 are the level of corruption, the level of press freedom, the level of democracy, the level of personal freedom and the strength, stability and legitimacy of the State. The largest differentiators between nations operating from the worldview of State Awareness 1 and State Awareness 2 are the level of happiness, the level of strength, stability and legitimacy of the State, the level of press freedom and the quality and level of preservation of the environment. The largest differentiators between nations operating from the worldview of State Awareness 2 and State Awareness 3 are the level of education, the level of social progress and the level of health care.

Summary

Here are the main points of this chapter.

1. In 2018 there were nine nations operating from the worldview of People Awareness, seven nations operating from the worldview of Wealth Awareness, 22 nations operating from the worldview of Nation Awareness and over 100 nations operating from different levels of State Awareness.

2. New Zealand is the only nation in Australasia operating from People Awareness. Australia dropped down from People Awareness to Wealth Awareness in 2018.

3. Europe is the most diverse region in terms of worldviews, with five different worldviews. Asia is the second most diverse region, with four different worldviews.

4. Currently, the only nations operating from Wealth Awareness are found in Australasia and Europe.

5. All African nations except two are operating from State Awareness 2 and 3.

6. All nations in the MENA region operate from State Awareness 1, 2 or 3.

7. The largest differentiator between nations operating from the worldviews of People Awareness and Wealth Awareness is gender equality.

8. The largest differentiators between nations operating from the worldviews of Wealth Awareness and Nation Awareness are the level of social cohesion, the level of corruption and the level of happiness.

9. The largest differentiators between nations operating from the worldview of Nation Awareness and State Awareness 1 are the level of corruption, the level of press freedom, the level of democracy, the level of personal freedom and the strength, stability and legitimacy of the State.

10. The largest differentiators between nations operating from the worldview of State Awareness 1 and State Awareness 2 are the level of happiness, the level of strength, stability and legitimacy of the State, the level of press freedom and the quality and level of preservation of the environment.

11. The largest differentiators between nations operating from the worldview of State Awareness 2 and State Awareness 3 are the level of education, the level of social progress and the level of health care.

8

HOW UNIFIED IS THE EUROPEAN UNION?

The EU is a political and economic union that was created in 1993 by the Treaty of Maastricht. The EU has an estimated population of 513 million people and currently comprises 28 member states. The EU has a single internal market and a standardized internal system of laws that apply to all member states. EU policies aim to ensure the free movement of people, goods, services and capital within an internal market. A monetary union based on the Euro came into force in 2002 comprising 19 EU member states.

The EU maintains permanent diplomatic missions throughout the world and is represented at the United Nations, the World Trade Organization, the G7 and the G20. Because of its global influence, the EU has been described as an emerging superpower, along with the US, China and potentially India.

The EU operates through a system of supranational independent institutions and inter-governmental negotiated decisions by the member states. Important institutions of the EU include the European Commission, the Council of the European Union, the European Council, the Court of Justice of the European Union, and the European Central Bank. The European Parliament is elected every five years by EU citizens.

Origins of the EU

The EU came into being as a natural development of the European Economic Community (EEC), which was created in 1957 by the Treaty of Rome. One of the main reasons for creating the EEC was to develop strong economic ties between the nations of Europe in the hope that this would lessen the possibility of a third World War.

The EEC had six founding members – Belgium, France, Italy, Luxembourg, the Netherlands and West Germany. Sixteen years later, in 1973, Denmark, Ireland and the UK joined the EEC. Greece joined in 1981, and Portugal and Spain joined in 1986. Thus, when the EU was created in 1993, there were 12 founding members.

Austria, Finland and Sweden joined the EU in 1994. Cyprus, Czech Republic, Estonia, Hungary, Latvia, Lithuania, Malta, Poland, Slovakia and Slovenia joined in 2004, Bulgaria and Romania joined in 2007 and Croatia joined in 2013. The stages of expansion of the EEC and the EU are shown in Table 8.1.

Table 8.1: Stages of expansion of the EEC and the EU

Grouping	Stages of expansion	Nations	Number of members
European Economic Community	Stage 1: 1957	Belgium, France, Germany, Italy, Luxembourg, the Netherlands	6
	Stage 2: 1973	Denmark, Ireland and UK	9
	Stage 3: 1981	Greece	10
	Stage 4: 1986	Portugal, Spain	12
European Union	Stage 5:1994	Austria, Finland, Sweden	15
	Stage 6: 2004	Cyprus, Czech Republic, Estonia, Hungary, Latvia, Lithuania, Malta, Poland, Slovakia, Slovenia	25
	Stage 7: 2007	Bulgaria, Romania	27
	Stage 8: 2013	Croatia	28

Distribution of worldviews in the EU

The member nations of the EU currently operate from four different worldviews (see Table 8.2). In 2014 there were three nations operating from People Awareness, seven nations operating from Wealth Awareness, 11 nations operating from Nation Awareness and seven nations operating from State Awareness.

Since that time, one nation – Ireland – graduated from Wealth Awareness to People Awareness and two nations – Latvia and Lithuania – graduated from State Awareness[51] to Nation Awareness.

Table 8.2: Number of EU nations operating from different worldviews (2014, 2016 and 2018)

	People Awareness	Wealth Awareness	Nation Awareness	State Awareness
2014	3	7	11	7
2016	3	7	13	5
2018	4	6	13	5

Table 8.3 shows the dominant worldviews in each of the member states of the EU along with the GCI score in brackets and the global ranking of the nation in 2018. The most conscious nations in the EU are Finland, Denmark, Sweden and Ireland. Finland and Denmark ranked #3 and #4 in the world with GCI scores of 654 and 652. The least conscious nations in the EU were Hungary, Croatia, Romania, Bulgaria and Greece, with GCI scores ranging between 445 and 470, and rankings ranging between #41 and #49 in the world.

---

[51] Throughout this section on the European Union I am referring to State Awareness 1.

Table 8.3: GCI scores and global ranking of nations in the EU by worldview in 2018

People Awareness (PA)	Wealth Awareness (WA)	Nation Awareness (NA)	State Awareness (SA)
Finland (654), #3	Netherlands (621), #11	France (578), #17	Hungary (470), #41
Denmark (652), #4	Luxembourg 619), #12	Slovenia (573), #18	Croatia (469), #43
Sweden (638), #7	Germany (618), #13	Malta (571), #19	Romania (467), #44
	UK (618), #14	Spain (552), #23,	Bulgaria (453), #46
	Austria (612), #15,	Portugal	Greece (445), #49
	Belgium (591), #16	(547), #24	
		Czech Rep.	
		(546), #25	
		Estonia (534), #26	
		Slovakia (509), #29	
		Italy (508), #30	
		Cyprus (507), #31	
		Lithuania	
		(501), #33	
		Poland (499), #35	
		Latvia (492), #38	
4	6	13	5

Worldviews by specific indicators

The following tables show the distribution of worldviews in the member nations of the EU by seven of the most important of the 17 global indicators.

Worldviews and economic performance

The distribution of worldviews by level of economic performance are shown in Table 8.4. All nations operating from the worldview of People Awareness are in the top category of economic performance. All nations operating from Wealth Awareness, except Belgium, are also in the top category. Most nations operating from Nation Awareness are in the second category of economic performance. Malta is in the top category, and Lithuania and Latvia are in the third category. Most nations operating from State Awareness are in the third category. One nation – Hungary – is in the second category.

Richard Barrett

Table 8.4: EU: Worldviews and economic performance

Economic Performance	PA	WA	NA	SA1	Total
75+	4	5	1	-	10
65.00–74.99	-	1	10	1	12
55.00–64.99	-	-	2	4	6
Total	4	6	13	5	28

Worldviews and level of democracy

The distribution of worldviews by level of democracy is shown in Table 8.5. All nations operating from the worldview of People Awareness and all nations operating from Wealth Awareness, except Belgium, are full democracies. According to the Economic Intelligence Unit (EIU) Belgium is a flawed democracy. Two nations operating from Nation Awareness are full democracies – Malta and Spain. All other nations operating from the worldview of Nation Awareness are flawed democracies except Poland, which according to the EIU is a hybrid regime. Two nations operating from the worldview of State Awareness are flawed democracies – Greece and Bulgaria – and three are hybrid regimes – Hungary, Croatia and Romania.

Table 8.5: EU: Worldviews and levels of democracy

Democracy	PA	WA	NA	SA1	Total
Full	4	5	2	-	11
Flawed	-	1	10	2	13
Hybrid	-	-	1	3	4
Total	4	6	13	5	28

Worldviews and gender equality

The distribution of worldviews by gender equality is shown in Table 8.6. Two nations operating from the worldview of People Awareness are in the highest category of gender equality – Sweden and Finland. Ireland and Denmark are in the second category. Two nations operating from the worldview of Wealth Awareness are in the second category – Germany and

136

the UK. The other four nations operating from Wealth Awareness are in the third category – the Netherlands, Belgium, Austria and Luxembourg.

There are three nations operating from the worldview of Nation Awareness in the second category of gender equality – Slovenia, France and Latvia – and one nation operating from the worldview of State Awareness – Bulgaria.

Six nations operating from the worldview of Nation Awareness are in the third category and four nations – Czech Republic, Slovakia, Malta and Cyprus – are in the fourth category.

There are two nations operating from the worldview of State Awareness in the third category – Croatia and Romania – and two are in the fourth category – Greece and Hungary.

Table 8.6: EU: Worldviews and gender equality

Gender Gap	PA	WA	NA	SA1	Total
0.800+	2	-	-	-	2
0.750–0.799	2	2	3	1	8
0.700–0.749	-	4	6	2	12
0.650–0.699	-	-	4	2	6
Total	4	6	13	5	28

Worldviews and corruption

The inverse distribution of worldviews by level of corruption (the most honest) is shown in Table 8.7. Three nations operating from the worldview of People Awareness appear in the highest category of honesty. Ireland is in the second category. Four nations operating from the worldview of Wealth Awareness – the Netherlands, Luxembourg, the UK and Germany –are in the highest category of honesty.

Two nations operating from the worldview of Wealth Awareness are in the second category – Austria and Belgium. All nations operating from the worldview of Nation Awareness are in the second and third categories of honesty.

All five nations operating from the worldview of State Awareness are in the third category.

Table 8.7: EU: Worldviews by honesty (inverse of level of corruption)

Honesty	PA	WA	NA	SA1	Total
80+	3	4	-	-	6
60–79	1	2	5	-	9
40–59		-	8	5	13
Total	4	6	13	5	28

Worldviews and social cohesion

The distribution of worldviews by level of social cohesion is shown in Table 8.8. Three nations operating from the worldview of People Awareness have the highest scores in social cohesion. One nation – Sweden – falls into the second category. Five nations operating from the worldview of Wealth Awareness are also in the highest category. One nation – Belgium – falls into the second category. Two nations operating from the worldview of Nation Awareness – Malta and Slovenia – are also in the highest category.

Seven nations operating from the worldview of Nation Awareness are in the second category and four nations are in the third category – Czech Republic, Poland, Lithuania and Latvia. All nations operating from the worldview of State Awareness are in the third category.

Table 8.8: EU: Worldviews by level of social cohesion

Social cohesion	PA	WA	NA	SA1	Total
60+	3	5	2	-	10
50–59	1	1	7	-	9
40–49	-	-	4	5	9
Total	4	6	13	5	28

Worldviews and strength, stability and legitimacy of the State

The distribution of worldviews by level of strength, stability and legitimacy of the State is shown in Table 8.9. All four nations operating from the worldview of People Awareness, four nations operating from Wealth Awareness – Luxembourg, Germany, the Netherlands and Austria – and one nation operating from Nation Awareness – Portugal – are in the highest category of strength, stability and legitimacy.

Two nations operating from the worldview of Wealth Awareness – Belgium and the UK – and 11 nations operating from the worldview of Nation Awareness are in the second category. One nation operating from the worldview of Nation Awareness is in the third category – Cyprus – along with all nations operating from the worldview of State Awareness.

Table 8.9: EU: Worldviews by strength, stability and legitimacy of the State

Stability	PA	WA	NA	SA1	Total
90+	4	4	1	-	9
70–89	-	2	11	-	13
50–69	-	-	1	5	6
Total	4	6	13	5	28

Worldviews and levels of happiness

The distribution of worldviews by level of happiness is shown in Table 8.10. Three nations operating from the worldview of People Awareness are in the highest category of happiness. One nation – Ireland – falls into the second category. Two nations operating from the worldview of Wealth Awareness are also in the highest category of happiness – the Netherlands and Austria. The other four – Germany, Belgium, Luxembourg and the UK – are in the second category.

Seven nations operating from the worldview of Nation Awareness are in the second category and six nations are in the third category. Four nations operating from the worldview of State Awareness are in the third category and one – Bulgaria – falls into the fourth category.

Table 8.10: EU: Worldviews by happiness

Happiness	PA	WA	NA	SA1	Total
7.00+	3	2	-	-	5
6.00–6.99	1	4	7	-	12
5.00–5.99	-	-	6	4	10
4.00–4.99	-	-	-	1	1
Total	4	6	13	5	28

The distribution of worldviews by these seven important indicators shows that the nations with the most advanced worldviews in the EU are always concentrated at the top of each category, and the nations with the least advanced worldviews are always concentrated at the bottom of each category.

Consistent improvers and decliners

In this next section, I identify the member nations of the EU that are consistent improvers and consistent decliners in consciousness. The bad news is that only 12 of the 28 member nations of the EU showed a consistent improvement in consciousness in the periods 2014 to 2016 and 2016 to 2018 (see Table 8.11). The good news is that there were only two consistent decliners. Fourteen nations did not show a change in either direction.

Nations that are consistently evolving in consciousness

The only nation operating from the worldview of People Awareness that consistently improved over the two time periods was Ireland. The only nation operating from the worldview of Wealth Awareness that consistently improved was the UK. Seven of the 13 nations operating from the worldview of Nation Awareness were consistent improvers. Romania and Bulgaria were the only two nations operating from the worldview of State Awareness 1 that showed a consistent improvement.

Table 8.11: EU: Consistent improvers (2014 to 2016 and 2016 to 2018)

Worldview	Nation	2014	2016	2018	Change	%
People Awareness	Ireland	613	621	631	+18	2.9
Wealth Awareness	Luxembourg	600	618	619	+19	3.2
	UK	610	615	618	+8	1.3

	Lithuania	454	486	501	+47	10.4
	Malta	529	548	571	+42	7.9
	Portugal	525	534	547	+22	4.2
Nation Awareness	Estonia	515	530	534	+19	3.7
	Czech R.	529	540	546	+17	3.2
	Slovakia	496	499	509	+13	2.6
	France	565	571	578	+13	2.3
State Awareness 1	Romania	408	451	467	+59	14.5
	Bulgaria	417	429	453	+36	8.6

What's been improving?

Ireland
The improvements in Ireland have come about mainly from increases in economic performance (13.67 points), personal freedom (8.97 points) and quality of the environment (7.28 points).

Luxembourg
The improvements in Luxembourg have come about mainly from increases in social cohesion (a difference 22.81 points) and personal freedom (16.70 points).

UK
The improvements in the UK have come about mainly from increases in gender equality (11.71 points) and quality of the environment (7.58 points).

Lithuania
The improvements in Lithuania have come about mainly from increases in social cohesion (20.96 points), quality of the environment (12.85 points), level of happiness of the people (12.12 points), economic performance (10.57 points), gender equality (9.82) and the level of personal safety (9.59 points).

Malta
The improvements in Malta have come about mainly from increases in preservation of the environment (a difference of 18.38 points), happiness of the people (15.09 points) and quality of the environment.

Portugal
The improvements in Portugal have come about mainly from increases in economic performance (15.34 points), happiness of the people (7.48 points), strength, stability and legitimacy of the State (6.97 points), the level of social cohesion (6.67 points) and efficiency of the business environment (5.37 points).

Estonia
The improvements in Estonia have come about mainly from increases in economic performance (13.36 points) and gender equality (11.18 points). There was a significant decrease in environmental preservation (–19.73 points).

Czech Republic
The improvements in Czech Republic have come about mainly from increases in economic performance (a difference of 10.80 points), the level of happiness (10.01 points) and social cohesion (9.40 points). There was a significant decrease in environmental preservation (–23.95 points).

Slovakia
The improvements in Slovakia have come about mainly from increases in social cohesion (13.71 points) and economic performance (11.89 points).

France
The improvements in France have come about mainly from increases in preservation of the environment (18.22 points), social cohesion (13.83 points), quality of the environment (7.58 points) and gender equality (7.16 points).

Romania
The improvements in Romania have come about mainly from increases in economic performance (20.25 points), happiness (20.23 points), preservation of the environment (15.91 points), quality of the environment (11.92 points) and social cohesion (15.74 points).

Bulgaria

The improvements in Bulgaria have come about mainly from increases in economic performance (22.34 points), happiness (20.91 points) and social cohesion (16.95 points).

Nations that are consistently declining in consciousness

The two nations that consistently declined in consciousness over the periods 2014 to 2016 and 2016 to 2018 were Austria and Sweden (see Table 8.12). In both cases the overall decrease was less than 2%.

Table 8.12: EU: Consistent decliners (2014 to 2016 and 2016 to 2018)

	2014	2016	2018	Change	%
Austria	619	615	612	–7	1.1
Sweden	643	642	638	–4	0.6

What's been decreasing?

Austria

The decline in consciousness in Austria has come about mainly from an increase in violence (–6.66 points), a decrease in happiness (–3.62 points) and a decrease in social cohesion (–3.09 points). On the positive side, Austria showed a decrease in corruption (–8.48 points).

Sweden

The decline in consciousness in Sweden has come about mainly from an increase in violence (–7.69 points), a decrease in democracy (–3.38 points), a decrease in health care (–3.09 points), a decrease in personal safety (–2.80 points) and a decrease in happiness (–2.25 points). On the positive side, Sweden has shown an increase in social cohesion (+2.64 points), an increase in gender equality (+2.41 points) and increases in the preservation of the environment (+2.32 points) and the quality of the environment (+2.12 points).

Impact of stages of expansion on the overall GCI score for the EU

This section shows the evolution of the average GCI score for the EU at each stage of expansion. Since GCI data was not available for the early years of the EEC and EU, I have used GCI scores for 2018 to carry out this analysis. The results do not therefore represent the situation as it existed at each stage of expansion: they represent the current situation. The nations involved at each stage of expansion are shown in Table 8.13. The eight stages of expansion have been grouped into three phases:

- Phase A represents the stages of expansion prior to the inclusion of Greece (Stages 1 and 2).
- Phase B represents the stages of expansion that included Greece (Stage 3), Portugal and Spain (Stage 4) and Austria, Finland and Sweden (Stage 5).
- Phase C represents the stages of expansion that included 13 Central and Eastern European nations (Stages 6, 7 and 8).

Table 8.13: Phases and stages of expansion of the EU

Phases	Stages of expansion	Nations
Phase A	Stage 1: 1957	Belgium (WA), France (NA), Germany (WA), Italy (NA), Luxembourg (WA), Netherlands (WA)
	Stage 2: 1973	Denmark (PA), Ireland (PA) and UK (WA)
Phase B	Stage 3: 1981	Greece (SA)
	Stage 4: 1986	Portugal (NA), Spain (NA)
	Stage 5:1994	Austria (WA), Finland (PA) and Sweden (PA)
Phase C	Stage 6: 2004	Cyprus (NA), Czech Republic (NA), Estonia (NA), Hungary (SA), Latvia (NA), Lithuania (NA), Malta (NA), Poland (NA), Slovakia (NA), Slovenia (NA)
	Stage 7: 2007	Bulgaria (SA) and Romania (SA)
	Stage 8: 2013	Croatia (SA)

The number of nations operating from each worldview and the average GCI score for the EU at each phase and stage of expansion are shown in Table 8.14 and Figure 8.2.

Table 8.14: The number of nations operating from each worldview at each phase and stage of expansion of the EU

Phases	Stages	People Awareness	Wealth Awareness	Nation Awareness	State Awareness	Total	GCI Score
Phase A	Stage 1: 1957	-	4	2	-	6	589
	Stage 2: 1973	2	5	2	-	9	604
Phase B	Stage 3: 1981	2	5	2	1	10	588
	Stage 4: 1986	2	5	4	1	12	581
	Stage 5: 1994	4	6	4	1	15	592
Phase C	Stage 6: 2004	4	6	13	2	25	563
	Stage 7: 2007	4	6	13	4	27	556
	Stage 8: 2013	4	6	13	5	28	553

The average GCI score for the EU took a significant downward shift at the start of Phase B, from 604 to 588 (with the entry of Greece) and again at the start of Phase C from 592 to 563 (with the entry of ten Central and Eastern European nations). The downward shift continued, from 563 to 553, with the entry of Bulgaria, Romania and Croatia in Stages 7 and 8.

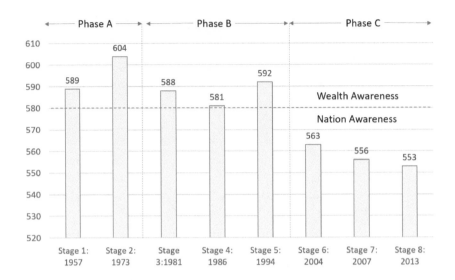

Figure 8.2: Average GCI score for the EU at
each phase and stage of expansion

The numbers of nations operating from each worldview in each of the
three phases of expansion are shown in Figure 8.3.

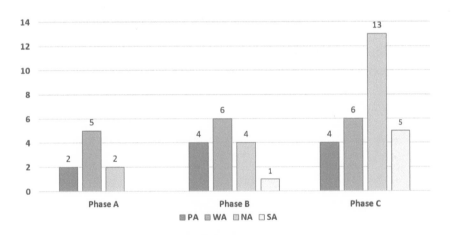

Figure 8.3: Composition of worldviews in the EU in the three phases

All the nations in Phase A were operating from People Awareness (2),
Wealth Awareness (5) or Nation Awareness (2). The average GCI score for

these nine nations was 604 – corresponding to the worldview of Wealth Awareness. Greece, which operates from the worldview of State Awareness, has the lowest GCI score of all the EU nations (445) – a difference of 159 from the average score for Phase A.

The biggest differences between Greece and the Phase A nations were social cohesion (–46.71 points), the level of corruption (–41.74 points), economic performance (–39.73 points), freedom of the people (–35.61 points), efficiency of the business environment (–31.61 points) and happiness of the people (–32.57 points).

In retrospect, I would say that from a fiscal, economic, business and social perspective Greece was not ready to join the EU. Its values and beliefs (worldview) were so different to the Stage A nations that it should probably never have been invited to become a member.

Phase B represents the stages of expansion that included Greece (Stage 3), Portugal and Spain (Stage 4) and Austria, Finland and Sweden (Stage 5). Whereas Stages 3 and 4 lowered the level of consciousness of the EU to 581, Stage 5 raised it to 592. At this point, even with Greece included, the average GCI score for the EU corresponded to the worldview of Wealth Awareness. The overall impact of Phase B was to lower the Phase A GCI score by 12 points from 604 to 592.

Phase C represents the stages of expansion that included 13 Central and Eastern European nations. The average GCI score for Stage 6 nations is 520, a difference of –84 from the average of Phase A nations. The average score for Stage 7 and 8 nations is 463, a difference of –141 from the Phase A nations.

The biggest differences between the Stage 6 nations and the Phase A nations were corruption (–24.40 points), social cohesion (–22.83 points), the happiness of the people (–17.74 points), a supportive business environment (–17.46 points), the preservation of the environment (–17.06 points) and the freedom of the people (–16.78 points).

The biggest differences between Stages 7 and 8 combined and the Phase A nations were corruption (–40.84 points), social cohesion (–35.34 points), the happiness of the people (–31.69 points), a supportive business environment (–30.29 points), the freedom of the people (–26.73 points) and the level of economic performance (–26.53 points).

The overall impact of Phase C was to lower the Phase B GCI score by 39 points from 592 to 553, and to lower the Phase A GCI score by 51 points from 604 to 553.

What conclusions can we draw from this analysis?

All the nations in Stages 1, 2, 4 and 5 of the EU expansions operate from the worldviews of People Awareness (4), Wealth Awareness (6) or Nation Awareness (4). All the nations in Stages 3, 6, 7 and 8 of the EU expansions operate from the worldviews of Nation Awareness (9) and State Awareness (5). From 2004 onwards the EU became increasingly dominated by the worldview of Nation Awareness and more strongly influenced by the worldview of State Awareness 1 (see Figure 8.3).

The nations that are least aligned with the values of the original members of the EU are those that are most deeply embedded in Nation Awareness – Slovakia, Italy, Cyprus, Lithuania, Poland and Latvia – and those embedded in State Awareness – Hungary, Croatia, Romania, Bulgaria and Greece. The nations deeply embedded in the worldview of Nation Awareness have GCI scores below 510. The nations embedded in the worldview of State Awareness have GCI scores of 470 or below.

Of these 11 nations, Slovakia, Italy, Cyprus, Lithuania, Latvia, Greece and Bulgaria operate as flawed democracies, and Poland, Hungary, Croatia and Romania operate as hybrid regimes. Eight of these nations operate from the lowest level of social cohesion (see Table 8.8). These are Poland, Hungary, Romania, Bulgaria, Lithuania, Croatia, Latvia and Greece. Italy and Slovakia have the next-to-lowest level of social cohesion. All 11 nations except Poland operate from the highest level of corruption (see Table 8.7). Poland operates from the next-to-highest level of corruption.

Six of the 11 nations operate from the lowest level of gender equality in the EU – Greece, Czech Republic, Slovakia, Malta, Cyprus and Hungary. Poland, Croatia, Romania and Italy operate at the next-to-lowest level of gender equality. Bulgaria operates at the second-highest level of gender equality.

Similarities and key differences between worldviews

There are significant differences in consciousness between the nations operating at different worldviews. The average GCI scores for the nations operating from each worldview are shown in Figure 8.4. There is a 183-point difference between the average GCI score of nations operating from the worldviews of People Awareness and State Awareness.

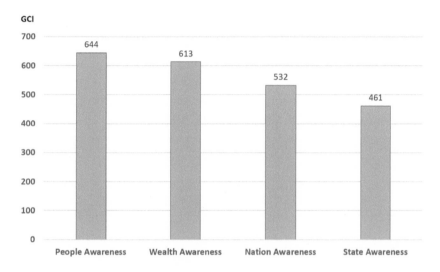

Figure 8.4: Average overall GCI scores for EU nations operating from each worldview in 2018

Values fault-lines

In order to expose the values fault-lines – the key differentiators between worldviews – I have compared the average score for each of the seven levels of consciousness for nations in each worldview. The three largest differences between adjacent worldviews are shaded. The largest difference is shown in bold and underlined and the second-largest difference is underlined in the following four tables.

Comparison between People Awareness and Wealth Awareness

The average scores for each level of consciousness for nations operating from People Awareness and Wealth Awareness are compared in Table 8.15. Approximately 69% of the difference is accounted for by three levels of consciousness – Levels 4, 7 and 3.

Of the four indicators that make up the Level 4 consciousness score, 52% of the difference can be attributed to gender equality and 27% to the level of democracy. The difference at Level 7 consciousness is equally divided between two indicators – the strength and legitimacy of the nation and the level of happiness of the people. At Level 3 consciousness, 59% of the difference can be attributed to a supportive business environment and 41% to the level of education.

Table 8.15: EU: Comparison of average scores by level of consciousness for People Awareness and Wealth Awareness 2018

Worldview	Level 1	Level 2	Level 3	Level 4	Level 5	Level 6	Level 7	Overall
P A	91.81	91.35	90.91	92.22	94.46	87.15	95.97	643.86
WA	89.96	89.04	85.14	84.15	92.15	84.20	88.59	613.22
Difference	–1.85	–2.31	–5.77	**–8.07**	–2.31	–2.95	–7.38	30.64

Comparison between Wealth Awareness and Nation Awareness

The average scores for each level of consciousness for nations operating from Wealth Awareness and Nation Awareness are compared in Table 8.16. Approximately 58% of the difference between Wealth Awareness and Nation Awareness is accounted for by three levels of consciousness – Levels 1, 7 and 5.

Of the three indicators that make up the Level 1 consciousness score, 51% of the difference can be attributed to the level of corruption and 31% can be attributed to the level of economic performance. At Level 7 consciousness, 52% of the difference can be attributed to the strength, stability and legitimacy of the State and 48% to the level of happiness of the people. At Level 5 consciousness, 75% of the difference can be attributed to the level of social cohesion.

Table 8.16: EU: Comparison of average scores by level of consciousness for Wealth Awareness and Nation Awareness in 2018

Worldview	Level 1	Level 2	Level 3	Level 4	Level 5	Level 6	Level 7	Overall
WA	89.96	89.04	85.14	84.15	92.15	84.20	88.59	613.22
NA	72.89	84.11	73.69	76.05	78.19	74.88	72.30	532.11
Difference	–17.07	–4.93	–11.45	–8.10	–13.96	–9.32	–16.29	81.11

Comparison between Nation Awareness and State Awareness 1

The average scores for each level of consciousness for nations operating from Nation Awareness and State Awareness 1 are compared in Table 8.17. Approximately 56% of the difference between nations operating from Nation Awareness and State Awareness 1 is accounted for by three levels of consciousness – Levels 1, 5 and 7. There is also a significant difference at Levels 4 and 3.

Of the three indicators that make up the Level 1 consciousness score, 45% of the difference can be attributed to the level of corruption and 35% to the level of economic performance. At Level 5 consciousness, 69% of the difference can be attributed to the level of social cohesion. At Level 7 consciousness, 55% of the difference can be attributed to the level of happiness of the people and 45% to the strength, stability and legitimacy of the State.

Table 8.17: EU: Comparison of average scores by level of consciousness for Nation Awareness and State Awareness 1 in the EU in 2018

Worldview	Level 1	Level 2	Level 3	Level 4	Level 5	Level 6	Level 7	Overall
NA	72.89	84.11	73.69	76.05	78.19	74.88	72.30	532.11
SA 1	58.56	79.36	64.72	65.30	65.44	67.61	59.70	460.70
Difference	**–14.33**	–4.75	–8.97	–10.75	<u>–12.75</u>	–7.27	–12.60	–71.41

Comparison between nations operating from People Awareness and State Awareness

To explore the largest differences in consciousness in the EU, I have compared the GCI scores for People Awareness and State Awareness 1 (see Table 8.18.) Approximately 54% of the difference is accounted for by three levels of consciousness – Levels 7, 1 and 5. There are also significant differences at Levels 4, 3 and 6.

Of the two indicators that make up the Level 7 consciousness score, 56% of the difference can be attributed to the level of happiness of the people and 44% to the strength, stability and legitimacy of the State. Of the three indicators that make up the Level 1 consciousness score, 50% of the difference can be attributed to the level of corruption and 33% can be attributed to the level of economic performance. Of the two indicators that make up the Level 5 consciousness score, 71% can be attributed to the level of social cohesion.

Table 8.18: EU: Comparison of average scores by level of consciousness for People Awareness and State Awareness in 2018

Worldview	Level 1	Level 2	Level 3	Level 4	Level 5	Level 6	Level 7	Overall
NA	72.89	84.11	73.69	76.05	78.19	74.88	72.30	532.11
SA 1	58.56	79.36	64.72	65.30	65.44	67.61	59.70	460.70
Difference	**−14.33**	−4.75	−8.97	−10.75	−12.75	−7.27	−12.60	−71.41

Summary of the key differences between worldviews in the EU

The key differences between nations operating from adjacent worldviews in the EU are shown in Table 8.19.

Table 8.19: EU: Key differences between nations operating from adjacent worldviews

Difference between…	Key differences
Wealth Awareness and People Awareness	Gender equality, level of democracy, strength, stability and legitimacy of the state and the level of happiness of the people.
Nation Awareness and Wealth Awareness	Corruption, social cohesion and the level of happiness of the people.
State Awareness 1 and Nation Awareness	Social cohesion, economic performance, freedom of the people and corruption.
People Awareness and State Awareness 1	Corruption, social cohesion and the level of happiness of the people.

Based on these comparisons of worldviews, we can conclude that the primary values fault-line between nations operating from the worldview of People Awareness and nations operating from all other worldviews in the EU is gender equality.

The primary values fault-lines between nations operating from the worldviews of People Awareness and Wealth Awareness, and those operating from the worldviews of Nation Awareness and State Awareness, are the level of corruption and the level of social cohesion.

The primary values fault-lines between nations operating from the worldviews of People Awareness, Wealth Awareness and Nation Awareness, and those operating from the worldview of State Awareness, are the level of economic performance and the level of freedom of the people.

Thus, we can identify five values fault-lines between nations operating from the four worldviews found in the EU: gender equality, level of corruption, level of social cohesion, level of economic performance and level of freedom of the people.

Why the EU is becoming less unified?

As the EU expanded, its overall GCI score decreased, particularly in the areas of gender equality, corruption, social cohesion, economic performance and freedom of the people.

The largest decreases occurred at Stages 3, 6, 7 and 8 of the EU's expansion with the entry of Greece at Stage 3, the entry of Cyprus, Czech Republic, Estonia, Hungary, Latvia, Lithuania, Malta, Poland, Slovakia and Slovenia at Stage 6, the entry of Bulgaria and Romania at Stage 7 and the entry of Croatia at Stage 8. The entry of these nations brought about a significant lowering of the EU's values and a decrease in the level of internal cohesion.

The first cracks in internal cohesion of the EU began to appear in 2009 with the Eurozone crisis: the threat to the EU of a sovereign debt default by Greece, Cyprus, Ireland, Italy, Portugal and Spain. Although the threat was contained, it put considerable strain on internal relations between the more well-managed nations and some of the less well-managed nations.

Further strains began to appear in 2015 when large numbers of migrants and asylum seekers began arriving at the borders of the EU. The difficulties that arose were around the questions of who should bear the burden of resettling these people and who should bear the burden of controlling their entry. Some member states welcomed the migrants – mostly those operating from People Awareness and Wealth Awareness; other member states were reluctant to provide homes for them; and some member states refused them – mostly those operating from State Awareness.

The migrant issue uncovered deep values fault-lines (worldview differences), not just between member nations but also within member nations, resulting in a downward shift in consciousness and a hardening of conservative worldviews in several nations.

In the UK, the immigrant issue exposed a significant values fault-line between the people embracing the worldview of Nation Awareness and those embracing the worldview of Wealth Awareness. This fault-line was instrumental in the people of the UK voting, albeit by a very narrow margin, to regain their sovereignty by leaving the EU.

The most visible outcome of the strains placed on the EU by the Eurozone crisis and the migrant issue has been a retreat from liberalism and a resurgence of populism – a shift from the values of the worldviews of People Awareness and Wealth Awareness to the ethnically and religiously defined values of the worldview of Nation Awareness. At the same time there has been a resurgence in some nations of the worldview of State Awareness – a retreat into fascism and white supremacism, and an increase in displays of homophobia and hatred of foreigners.

As a result of these deepening values fault-lines the EU is becoming increasingly unmanageable. Will it survive? The outcome is not sure. There is an increasing likelihood that the EU will split into two camps – nations with current GCI scores above 530 and nations with current GCI scores below 510 (see Table 3). This gap has increased between 2014 and 2018. On one side of this split are the nations operating from the worldviews of People Awareness, Wealth Awareness and the top half of Nation Awareness. On the other side of the split are those nations operating from the bottom half of Nation Awareness and all the nations operating from State Awareness.

Summary

Here are the main points of this chapter.

1. The member nations of the EU currently operate from four different worldviews.
2. In 2018 there were four nations operating from People Awareness, six nations operating from Wealth Awareness, 13 nations operating

from Nation Awareness and five nations operating from State Awareness.

3. The most conscious nations in the EU are Finland, Denmark, Sweden and Ireland.
4. The least conscious nations in the EU are Hungary, Croatia, Romania, Bulgaria and Greece.
5. From 2014 to 2016, and 2016 to 2018, 12 nations were consistent improvers, two were consistent decliners and 14 did not show a shift in either direction.
6. The only nation operating from the worldview of People Awareness that consistently improved between 2014 and 2016 and between 2016 and 2018 was Ireland.
7. The only nation operating from the worldview of Wealth Awareness that consistently improved between 2014 and 2016 and between 2016 and 2018 was the UK.
8. Seven of the 13 nations operating from the worldview of Nation Awareness were consistent improvers.
9. Romania and Bulgaria were the only two nations operating from the worldview of State Awareness that showed a consistent improvement.
10. The primary values fault-line between nations operating from the worldview of People Awareness and nations operating from all other worldviews in the EU is gender equality.
11. The primary values fault-lines between nations operating from the worldviews of People Awareness and Wealth Awareness and those operating from the worldviews of Nation Awareness and State Awareness are the level of corruption and the level of social cohesion.
12. The primary values fault-lines between nations operating from the worldview of People Awareness, Wealth Awareness and Nation Awareness and those operating from the worldview of State Awareness are the level of economic performance and the level of freedom of the people.
13. There are five key values fault-lines between nations operating from the four worldviews found in the EU: gender equality,

corruption, social cohesion, economic performance and freedom of the people.

14. The nations that are least aligned with the values of the original members of the EU are those that are most deeply embedded in Nation Awareness – Slovakia, Italy, Cyprus, Lithuania, Poland and Latvia and those operating from the worldview of State Awareness – Hungary, Croatia, Romania, Bulgaria and Greece.

15. As the EU expanded, the overall GCI score decreased, particularly in the arenas of gender equality, corruption, social cohesion, economic performance and freedom of the people.

16. The largest decreases in the average GCI score for the EU occurred with the entry of Greece at Stage 3, Cyprus, Czech Republic, Estonia, Hungary, Latvia, Lithuania, Malta, Poland, Slovakia and Slovenia at Stage 6, Bulgaria and Romania at Stage 7 and Croatia at Stage 8.

17. The most visible outcome of the strains placed on the EU by the Eurozone crisis and the migrant issue have been a retreat from liberalism and a resurgence of populism – a shift from the values of the worldviews of People Awareness and Wealth Awareness to the ethnically and religiously defined values of the worldview of Nation Awareness.

18. As a result of these deepening values fault-lines the EU is becoming increasingly unmanageable.

9

PEOPLE AWARENESS – NORDIC NATIONS

In this chapter and the next, I take a close look at the worldview of People Awareness – currently the cutting-edge of the evolution of human consciousness. There were nine nations operating from this worldview in 2014, 2016 and 2018. These nations are shown in Table 9.1. In each year we find the same nations, except in 2018 when Australia dropped down into Wealth Awareness and Ireland moved up from Wealth Awareness.

Table 9.1 Nations operating from People Awareness in 2014, 2016 and 2018

Rank	2014	2016	2018
1	Switzerland	New Zealand	Norway
2	New Zealand	Finland	New Zealand
3	Denmark	Norway	Finland
4	Finland	Iceland	Denmark
5	Norway	Switzerland	Switzerland
6	Sweden	Denmark	Iceland
7	Iceland	Sweden	Sweden
8	Australia	**Australia**	**Ireland**
9	Canada	Canada	Canada

This chapter focuses uniquely on the five Nordic nations – Denmark, Finland, Iceland, Norway and Sweden – and the next chapter focuses on the other nations operating from People Awareness – New Zealand, Switzerland, Canada and Ireland. My reason for separating these two groups was to identify any differences between the Nordic nations and the other nations.

Changes in the overall GCI scores in Nordic nations

The highest levels of consciousness in the world are found in the Nordic nations. Table 9.2 shows the GCI scores for Denmark, Finland, Iceland, Norway and Sweden in 2014, 2016 and 2018 and the changes that occurred between 2014 and 2018.

Norway, with an overall increase of 13 points (2%), is the only nation to show an increase in consciousness in both two-year periods. Denmark and Norway are the only nations to have increased their level of consciousness between 2016 and 2018. All the other nations showed a decrease in consciousness between 2016 and 2018.

Sweden is the only Nordic nation to show a decrease in consciousness between 2014 and 2016, and between 2016 and 2018. Finland and Iceland both showed a decrease in consciousness between 2016 and 2018 but showed an overall improvement between 2014 and 2018.

Table 9.2: Evolution of GCI scores in Nordic nations 2014, 2016 and 2018

Nation	2014	2016	2018	Change	%
Denmark	648	648	652	+4	0.6%
Finland	646	657	654	+8	1.2%
Iceland	639	649	645	+6	0.9%
Norway	646	650	659	+13	2.0%
Sweden	643	642	638	−5	−0.8%

Changes in consciousness between 2014, 2016 and 2018

The GCI scores by level of consciousness for Denmark, Finland, Iceland, Norway and Sweden in 2014, 2016 and 2018 and global rankings for each level of consciousness are shown in Tables 9.3, 9.4, 9.5, 9.6 and 9.7.

Denmark

In 2018 Denmark ranked #4 in consciousness in the world.

Significant improvements and decreases in consciousness
The largest improvement (+6.68 points) in Denmark between 2014 and 2018 was at Level 6 consciousness – satisfying citizens' needs for environmental quality and preservation.

Strengths
The main strength of Denmark is its commitment to satisfying citizens' needs for stability, well-being and happiness (Level 7 consciousness). In 2014 it ranked #3 in the world for Level 7; in 2016 it ranked #4, and in 2018 it again ranked #3.

Things that are improving but need attention
The focus on improving environmental quality and preservation (Level 6 consciousness) needs to be sustained. There was a significant improvement between 2014 and 2016 (+7.65) and then a slight drop between 2016 and 2018 (–0.97). In 2014 Denmark ranked #14 in the world at Level 6 consciousness, and in 2018 it ranked #6.

Things that are worsening and need attention
The most pressing need in Denmark is to focus on satisfying citizens' needs for safety, protection and peace (Level 2 consciousness). The situation has been progressively worsening since 2014. In 2014 and 2016 Denmark ranked #2 in the world for Level 2; in 2018 it ranked #9. The key issue is to improve the level of personal safety.

Table 9.3: Denmark: GCI scores by level of consciousness in 2014, 2016 and 2018, and global rankings in 2018

	Level 1	Level 2	Level 3	Level 4	Level 5	Level 6	Level 7	Overall
2014	93.20	99.28	89.84	90.35	96.39	81.33	97.77	648
2016	93.42	97.28	90.55	86.33	92.72	88.98	98.51	648
2018	94.24	93.16	91.79	88.88	98.46	88.01	97.84	652
Change	+1.04	**–6.12**	+1.95	–1.47	+2.07	**+6.68**	+0.07	+4
Rank	5	9	10	8	5	6	3	4

Finland

In 2018 Finland ranked #3 in consciousness in the world.

Significant improvements *and decreases in consciousness*
The largest improvement (+5.81) in Finland between 2014 and 2018 was at Level 6 consciousness – satisfying citizens' needs for environmental quality and preservation.

Strengths
The main strength of Finland is its commitment to satisfying citizens' needs for stability, well-being and happiness (Level 7 consciousness). The situation has been steadily improving since 2014. In 2014 it ranked #4 in the world for Level 7 consciousness. In 2018 it ranked #1.

Things that are improving *but need attention*
The focus on improving environmental quality and preservation (Level 6 consciousness) needs to be sustained. There was a significant improvement between 2014 and 2016 (+9.61) and then a drop between 2016 and 2018 (–3.80). In 2014 Finland ranked #11 in the world at Level 6 consciousness, and in 2018 it ranked #4.

Things that are worsening *and need attention*
The most pressing need in Finland is to focus on satisfying citizens' needs for safety, protection and peace (Level 2 consciousness). The situation has been progressively worsening since 2014. In 2014 Finland ranked #8 in the world for Level 2 consciousness; in 2016 it ranked #14, and in 2018 it ranked #18. The key issues are to improve the level of personal safety and reduce the level of violence.

Table 9.4: Finland: GCI scores by level of consciousness in 2014, 2016 and 2018, and global rankings in 2018

	Level 1	Level 2	Level 3	Level 4	Level 5	Level 6	Level 7	Overall
2014	91.36	95.14	94.81	92.03	92.22	84.08	96.80	646
2016	92.01	91.95	95.10	94.32	91.12	93.69	98.78	657
2018	91.81	89.69	95.65	93.48	93.55	89.89	100.00	654
Change	+0.45	**–5.45**	+0.84	+1.45	+1.33	**+5.81**	+3.20	+8
Rank	10	18	3	5	11	4	1	3

Iceland

In 2018 Iceland ranked #6 in consciousness in the world.

Significant improvements and decreases in consciousness
The largest improvement (+4.52) in Iceland between 2014 and 2018 was at Level 7 consciousness – satisfying citizens' needs for stability, well-being and happiness.

Strengths
The main strength of Iceland is its commitment to satisfying its citizens' needs for freedom, equality and accountability (Level 4 consciousness). It ranked #1 in the world for Level 4 consciousness in 2014, 2016 and 2018.

Things that are improving but need attention
The focus on stability, well-being and happiness (Level 7 consciousness) needs to be sustained. There was a significant improvement between 2014 and 2016 (+5.18) and then a slight drop between 2016 and 2018 (–0.66). In 2014 Iceland ranked #8 in the world at Level 7 consciousness, and in 2016 and 2018 it ranked #5.

Things that are worsening and need attention
There are two pressing needs in Iceland: to focus on satisfying citizens' needs for education and a supportive business environment (Level 3 consciousness), and to focus on citizens' needs for environmental quality and preservation (Level 6 consciousness). The situation regarding Level 3 consciousness changed little between 2014 and 2018, but Iceland's current world ranking of #17 gives cause for concern. As far as Level 6 consciousness is concerned Iceland saw a significant improvement between 2014 and 2016 (+5.52) and then a significant drop between 2016 and 2018 (–7.82). Iceland's current ranking of #17 gives cause for concern.

Table 9.5: Iceland: GCI scores by level of consciousness in 2014, 2016 and 2018, and global rankings in 2018

	Level 1	Level 2	Level 3	Level 4	Level 5	Level 6	Level 7	Overall
2014	90.59	97.84	82.36	97.81	97.30	81.06	92.53	639

2016	90.82	99.34	82.39	98.08	94.11	86.58	97.71	649
2018	91.94	98.18	82.74	97.46	98.82	78.76	97.05	645
Change	+1.35	+0.34	+0.38	−0.35	+1.52	**−2.30**	**+4.52**	+6
Rank	9	2	17	1	3	17	5	6

Norway

In 2018 Norway ranked #1 in consciousness in the world.

Significant improvements and decreases in consciousness
The largest improvement (+4.62) in Norway between 2014 and 2018 was at Level 5 – satisfying citizens' needs for inclusion, fairness, openness, tolerance and transparency.

Strengths
The main strength of Norway is its all-round positive performance; between 2014 and 2018, every level of consciousness improved. It currently ranks #1 at Level 5 consciousness; in 2014 it ranked #8 and in 2016 it ranked #5. It currently ranks #2 in the world at satisfying citizens' needs for stability, well-being and happiness (Level 7 consciousness), and satisfying citizens' needs for freedom, equality and accountability (Level 4 consciousness).

Things that need attention
There were no levels of consciousness that experienced a decrease in consciousness between 2014 and 2018. Norway currently ranks in the top ten at every level of consciousness except Level 2 – satisfying citizens' needs for safety, protection and peace, where it ranks #13.

Table 9.6: Norway: GCI scores by level of consciousness in 2014, 2016 and 2018, and global rankings in 2018

Nation	Level 1	Level 2	Level 3	Level 4	Level 5	Level 6	Level 7	Overall
2014	91.61	91.02	90.97	95.49	94.79	85.26	97.26	646
2016	93.16	89.68	90.68	95.80	94.02	87.96	98.74	650
2018	93.25	91.50	92.52	97.10	99.41	86.00	99.03	659
Change	+1.64	+0.48	+1.55	+1.61	**+4.62**	+0.74	+1.77	+13
Rank	6	13	5	2	1	10	2	1

Sweden

In 2018 Sweden ranked #7 in consciousness in the world.

Significant improvements in consciousness
The largest improvement (+2.22) in Sweden between 2014 and 2018 was at Level 6 consciousness – satisfying citizens' needs for environmental quality and preservation.

Strengths
The main strength of Sweden is its commitment to satisfying its citizens' needs for freedom, equality and accountability (Level 4 consciousness) and satisfying citizens' needs for health care and economic performance (Level 1 consciousness). It currently ranks #3 at Level 4, and #4 at Level 1. In 2014 it also ranked #3 at Level 4, and it ranked #3 at Level 1.

Things that are improving but need attention
The focus on environmental quality and preservation (Level 6 consciousness) needs to be sustained. There was a significant improvement between 2014 and 2016 (+6.03) and then a drop between 2016 and 2018 (–3.81). In 2014 Sweden ranked #10 in the world at Level 6 consciousness, in 2016 it ranked #5 and in 2018 it ranked #9.

Things that are worsening and need attention
The most pressing need in Sweden is to focus on satisfying citizens' needs for safety, protection and peace (Level 2 consciousness). There has been a steady decline in this level of consciousness since 2014. In 2014 Sweden ranked #10 in the world, in 2016 it ranked #11 and in 2018 it ranked #17. The key issues are to improve the level of personal safety and reduce the level of violence. Both these indicators have been in a sustained decline from 2014 to 2018.

Another important need is to focus on satisfying citizens' needs for inclusion, fairness, openness, tolerance and transparency (Level 5 consciousness). In 2014 Sweden ranked #16, in 2016 it ranked #14 and in 2018 it ranked #18. The key issue is to improve the level of social cohesion – strength of personal relationships, social network support and civic participation. This has been an ongoing problem for several years.

In 2014 Sweden ranked #20 for social cohesion, in 2016 it ranked #19 and in 2018 it ranked #22. Although Sweden improved by 3.78 points between 2016 and 2018, it fell in the global rankings. The issues Sweden is experiencing at Level 5 consciousness are linked to the issues it is experiencing at Level 2 consciousness.

Sweden also has a relatively low ranking at Level 3 consciousness – satisfying citizens' needs for education and a supportive business environment, for which it ranked #14 in 2014, 2016 and 2018. The key issue is creating a more supportive and efficient business environment.

Table 9.7: Sweden: GCI scores by level of consciousness in 2014, 2016 and 2018, and global rankings in 2018

Nation	Level 1	Level 2	Level 3	Level 4	Level 5	Level 6	Level 7	Overall
2014	95.58	95.00	88.48	94.14	88.99	84.28	96.29	643
2016	95.13	92.24	88.28	92.86	87.69	90.31	95.65	642
2018	94.89	89.76	88.25	94.56	89.47	86.50	94.88	638
Change	–0.69	**–5.24**	–0.23	+0.42	+0.48	**+2.22**	–1.41	–5
Rank	4	17	14	3	18	9	8	7

Overview

Among the five Nordic nations, Norway has been the most consistent improver and Sweden has been the most consistent decliner. Denmark, Iceland and Finland have a good record of maintaining their overall level of consciousness.

The largest improvement in Denmark, Finland and Sweden between 2014 and 2018 has been in satisfying citizens' needs for environmental quality and preservation (Level 6 consciousness). The largest improvement in Norway has been in satisfying citizens' needs for inclusion, fairness, openness, tolerance and transparency (Level 5 consciousness). The largest improvement in Iceland has been satisfying citizens' needs for stability, well-being and happiness (Level 7 consciousness).

The largest decreases in consciousness in Denmark, Finland and Sweden have been in satisfying citizens' needs for safety, protection and peace (Level 2 consciousness): the level of personal safety has reduced, and the level of violence has increased. The largest decrease in consciousness in Iceland has been in satisfying citizens' needs for environmental quality and preservation (Level 6 consciousness). There have been no decreases at any level of consciousness in Norway.

Denmark, Finland and Sweden are the most similar. They have shown the largest improvements in Level 6 consciousness and the largest decreases in Level 2 consciousness.

Summary

Here are the main points of this chapter.

1. Among the five Nordic nations, Norway has been the most consistent improver.
2. Denmark, Iceland and Finland have a good record of maintaining their level of consciousness.
3. Sweden has seen the most consistent decrease in consciousness.
4. The largest improvements in Denmark, Finland and Sweden between 2014 and 2018 have been in satisfying citizens' needs for environmental quality and environmental preservation (Level 6 consciousness).
5. The largest improvement in Norway has been in satisfying citizens' needs for inclusion, fairness, openness, transparency and tolerance (Level 5 consciousness).
6. The largest improvement in Iceland has been satisfying citizens' needs for stability, well-being and happiness (Level 7 consciousness).
7. The largest decreases in consciousness in Denmark, Finland and Sweden have been in satisfying citizens' needs for safety, protection and peace (Level 2 consciousness).
8. The largest decrease in consciousness in Iceland has been in satisfying citizens' needs for environmental quality and environmental preservation (Level 6 consciousness).
9. There have been no decreases at any level of consciousness in Norway.

10

PEOPLE AWARENESS – OTHER NATIONS

As mentioned at the beginning of the previous chapter, in addition to the five Nordic nations there are three other nations that have been consistently operating from the worldview of People Awareness – New Zealand, Switzerland and Canada. Ireland started operating from the worldview of People Awareness in 2018. This chapter compares the GCI scores by level of consciousness for these four nations.

Changes in the overall GCI scores in other nations

The overall GCI scores for New Zealand, Switzerland, Canada and Ireland in 2014, 2016 and 2018 and the overall change between 2014 and 2018 are shown in Table 10.1

Table 10.1: Other nations: GCI scores in 2014, 2016 and 2018

Nation	2014	2016	2018	Change
New Zealand	651	659	656	+4
Switzerland	658	649	651	-7
Canada	631	631	630	-1
Ireland	613	621	631	+18

Ireland with an overall increase in consciousness of +18 points is the only nation showing a consistent improvement from 2014 to 2016 and 2016 to 2018. New Zealand is the only other nation in addition to Ireland to have increased its level of consciousness between 2014 and 2018. Switzerland and Canada showed a decrease in consciousness between 2014 and 2018.

GCI scores by level of consciousness in 2014, 2016 and 2018

The GCI scores by level of consciousness for New Zealand, Switzerland, Canada and Ireland in 2014, 2016 and 2018 and the global rankings for each level are shown in Tables 10.2, 10.3, 10.4 and 10.5.[52]

New Zealand

In 2018 New Zealand ranked #2 in consciousness in the world.

Significant improvements in consciousness
The largest improvements (+2.99 and +2.34) between 2014 and 2018 were satisfying citizens' needs for stability, well-being and happiness (Level 7 consciousness) and satisfying citizens' needs for freedom, equality and social accountability (Level 4 consciousness).

Strengths
The main strengths of New Zealand are its commitment to satisfying citizens' needs for inclusion, fairness, openness, transparency and tolerance (Level 5 consciousness). In 2014 and 2016 New Zealand ranked #1 in the world at Level 5 consciousness; in 2018 it ranked #2.

Things that are improving but need attention
The focus on improving environmental quality and environmental preservation (Level 6 consciousness) needs to be sustained. There was a significant improvement between 2014 and 2016 (+5.32) and then a drop between 2016 and 2018 (–3.01). In 2014 New Zealand ranked #9 in the world at Level 6 consciousness and in 2016 and 2018 it ranked #7.

---

[52] Some of the tables in this section are subject to minor rounding errors.

Things that are worsening and need attention
The most pressing needs in New Zealand are at Level 1 consciousness – satisfying citizens' needs for health care and economic performance – and at Level 2 – satisfying citizens' needs for safety, protection and peace. Since 2014 there has been a drop of –2.06 points at Level 1 consciousness, and –1.57 points at Level 2 consciousness. In 2014 New Zealand ranked #4 at Level 1 consciousness in the world; in 2016 it ranked #3, and in 2018 it ranked #7. In 2014 New Zealand ranked #9 at Level 2 consciousness; in 2016 it ranked #6 and in 2018 it ranked #8.

Table 10.2: New Zealand: GCI scores by level of consciousness in 2014, 2016 and 2018, and global rankings in 2018

Nation	Level 1	Level 2	Level 3	Level 4	Level 5	Level 6	Level 7	Overall
2014	94.87	95.08	94.60	91.26	98.73	84.42	92.10	651
2016	95.39	94.44	93.82	91.05	98.50	89.74	95.85	659
2018	92.86	93.51	94.82	93.60	99.11	86.73	95.09	656
Change	**-2.06**	-1.57	+0.22	**+2.34**	+0.38	+2.31	**+2.99**	+4
Rank	7	8	4	4	2	7	7	2

Switzerland

In 2018 Switzerland ranked #5 in consciousness in the world.

Significant improvements *in consciousness*
The largest improvement (+1.47) between 2014 and 2018 was in satisfying citizens' needs for environmental quality and environmental preservation (Level 6 consciousness).

Strengths
The main strength of Switzerland is its focus on satisfying citizens' needs for stability, well-being and happiness (Level 7 consciousness). In 2018 it ranked #4 in the world at Level 7 consciousness; in 2016 and 2014 it ranked #3.

Things that are improving but need attention
The focus on satisfying citizens' needs for education, business opportunities
and productivity (Level 3 consciousness) needs to be sustained. There was
an improvement of +1.09 points between 2014 and 2016 and then a drop
of –1.45 points between 2016 and 2018.

Things that are worsening and need attention
The largest decreases in consciousness between 2014 and 2018 were at
Level 2 (–6.05) – satisfying citizens' needs for safety, protection and
peace – and at Level 4 (–2.31) – satisfying citizens' needs for freedom,
equality and social accountability. In 2014 Switzerland ranked #8 in the
world at Level 2 consciousness; in 2016 it also ranked #8; and in 2018 it
ranked #11. The key issues are personal safety and the level of violence. In
2014 Switzerland ranked #10 at Level 4 consciousness; in 2016 it ranked
#8; and in 2018 it ranked #14. The key issues are the level of freedom of
the people and the level of gender equality.

Table 10.3: Switzerland: GCI scores by level of consciousness in 2014, 2016
and 2018, and global rankings in 2018

Nation	Level 1	Level 2	Level 3	Level 4	Level 5	Level 6	Level 7	Overall
2014	96.05	97.69	94.32	87.39	93.54	91.64	97.05	658
2016	96.52	94.34	95.41	87.09	88.63	88.27	98.54	649
2018	96.13	91.64	93.96	85.08	93.96	93.11	97.53	651
Change	+0.08	**–6.05**	–0.36	**–2.31**	+0.42	**+1.47**	+0.48	–7
Rank	2	11	5	14	10	1	4	5

Canada

In 2018 Canada ranked #9 in consciousness in the world.

Significant improvements in consciousness
The largest improvement (+3.21 points) between 2014 and 2018 was in
satisfying citizens' needs for freedom, equality and social accountability
(Level 4 consciousness).

Richard Barrett

Strengths

The main strengths of Canada are its commitment to satisfying citizens' needs for stability, well-being and happiness (Level 7 consciousness) and satisfying citizens' needs for inclusion, fairness, openness, transparency and tolerance (Level 5 consciousness). In 2014 it ranked #6 in the world at Level 7 consciousness; in 2016 and 2018 it also ranked #6. In 2014 and 2016 Canada ranked #3 in the world at Level 5 consciousness; in 2018 it ranked #9.

Things that are improving but need attention

The focus on satisfying citizens' needs for environmental quality and environmental preservation (Level 6 consciousness) needs to be sustained. There was an improvement between 2014 and 2016 and then a drop of −4.06 points between 2016 and 2018.

Things that are worsening and need attention

The most pressing need in Canada is to focus on satisfying citizens' needs for safety, protection and peace (Level 2 consciousness) and satisfying citizens' needs for inclusion, fairness, openness, tolerance and transparency (Level 5 consciousness). Since 2014 there has been a sustained decrease in consciousness in both these areas: a decrease of −3.09 points in Level 2 consciousness and a decrease of −3.12 points in Level 5 consciousness. In 2014 Canada ranked #10 in the world at Level 2 consciousness; in 2016 it ranked #11 and in 2018 it ranked #14. The key issue at Level 2 consciousness is personal safety and security. In 2014 and 2016 Canada ranked #3 in the world at Level 5 consciousness and in 2018 it ranked #9. The key issues at Level 5 consciousness are improving social cohesion and social progress.

Table 10.4: Canada: GCI scores by level of consciousness in 2014, 2016 and 2018, and global rankings in 2018

Nation	Level 1	Level 2	Level 3	Level 4	Level 5	Level 6	Level 7	Overall
2014	86.81	94.10	94.19	88.31	97.22	77.24	93.00	631
2016	87.46	91.96	93.07	87.04	94.55	80.69	96.60	631
2018	88.62	91.01	93.13	91.52	94.10	76.63	95.18	630
Change	+1.81	**−3.09**	−1.06	**+3.21**	−3.12	−0.61	+2.18	−1
Rank	13	14	6	7	9	20	6	9

170

Ireland

In 2018 Ireland ranked #8 in consciousness in the world.

Significant improvements in consciousness
The largest improvements between 2014 and 2018 were at Level 1 consciousness (+6.48 points) – satisfying citizens' needs for health care and economic performance, Level 6 consciousness (+5.81 points) – satisfying citizens' needs for environmental quality and preservation – and Level 4 consciousness (+4.47 points) – satisfying citizens' needs for freedom, equality and social accountability.

Strengths
The main strength of Ireland is its commitment to satisfying citizens' needs for inclusion, fairness, openness, tolerance and transparency (Level 5 consciousness). In 2014 Ireland ranked #7 in the world at Level 5 consciousness; in 2016 it ranked #10; and in 2018 it ranked #6.

Things that are improving but need attention
The focus on satisfying citizens' needs for education and a supportive business environment (Level 3 consciousness) needs to be sustained. There was an improvement in this area of +1.61 points between 2014 and 2016 and then a drop of –1.07 points between 2016 and 2018.

Things that are worsening and need attention
There is no level of consciousness that is significantly worsening in Ireland. There was a small decrease in Level 2 consciousness (–0.76 points) – satisfying citizens' needs for safety, protection and peace – between 2014 and 2018.

Table10.5: Ireland: GCI scores by level of consciousness in 2014, 2016 and 2018, and global rankings in 2018

Nation	Level 1	Level 2	Level 3	Level 4	Level 5	Level 6	Level 7	Overall
2014	80.83	93.55	87.39	87.50	95.59	78.37	89.49	613
2016	84.82	91.61	89.00	90.81	89.79	83.85	91.39	621
2018	86.31	92.79	87.93	91.97	96.34	84.18	91.16	631
Change	**+6.48**	–0.76	+0.54	**+4.47**	+0.75	**+5.81**	+1.67	+18
Rank	17	10	15	6	6	12	11	8

Overview

Among the four nations examined in this chapter, Ireland has been the most consistent improver. New Zealand and Canada have a good record of maintaining their level of consciousness and Switzerland has seen the largest decrease in consciousness.

Some of the largest improvements in consciousness between 2014 and 2018 in Ireland, Canada and New Zealand have been in satisfying citizens' needs for freedom, equality and social accountability (Level 4 consciousness).

Ireland also showed a large improvement in Level 1 consciousness – satisfying citizens' needs for health care and economic performance – and Level 6 consciousness – satisfying citizens' needs for environmental quality and preservation. Switzerland also showed an improvement at this level of conscious. New Zealand showed an improvement in consciousness at Level 7 – satisfying citizens' needs for stability, well-being and happiness.

Some of the largest decreases in consciousness in Canada and Switzerland have been in satisfying citizens' needs for safety, protection and peace (Level 2 consciousness). Switzerland also saw a decrease in satisfying citizens' needs for freedom, equality and social accountability (Level 4 consciousness). New Zealand saw a decrease in satisfying citizens' needs for health care and economic performance (Level 1 consciousness).

Summary

Here are the main points of this chapter.

1. Among the four nations examined in this chapter, Ireland has been the most consistent improver.
2. New Zealand and Canada have a good record of maintaining their level of consciousness.
3. Switzerland has seen the largest decrease in consciousness.
4. Some of the largest improvements in consciousness between 2014 and 2018 in Ireland, Canada and New Zealand have been

in satisfying citizens' needs for freedom, equality and social accountability (Level 4 consciousness).

5. Ireland also showed a large increase in Level 1 consciousness – satisfying citizens' needs for health care and economic performance – and Level 6 consciousness – satisfying citizens' needs for environmental quality and preservation.

6. Switzerland also showed an increase in Level 6 consciousness.

7. New Zealand showed an increase in Level 7 consciousness – satisfying citizens' needs for stability, well-being and happiness.

8. Some of the largest decreases in consciousness in Canada and Switzerland have been in satisfying citizens' needs for safety, protection and peace (Level 2 consciousness).

9. Switzerland also saw a decrease in satisfying citizens' needs for freedom, equality and social accountability (Level 4 consciousness).

10. New Zealand saw a decrease in satisfying citizens' needs for health care and economic performance (Level 1 consciousness).

11

COUNTRY COMPARISONS

The focus of this chapter is on five comparisons:

- The comparison of nations operating from the worldview of People Awareness in the Nordic nations with other nations operating from the worldview of People Awareness.
- The comparison of Norway – the most consistent improver in Nordic nations – with Sweden – the most consistent decliner in the Nordic nations.
- The comparison of New Zealand – a significant improver in consciousness in the Australasia region – with Australia – a significant decliner in consciousness in the Australasia region.
- A comparison of Canada – a maintainer of consciousness – and the US – a significant decliner in consciousness.
- A comparison of Ireland – a significant improver – and the UK – a more moderate improver.

Nordic nations and other nations

The average GCI scores for the five Nordic nations by level of consciousness compared with the average scores of other nations operating from the worldview of People Awareness in 2018 are shown in Table 11.1. The largest difference is shown in bold.

Table 11.1: Comparison of GCI scores in Nordic nations and other nations operating from the worldview of People Awareness in 2018

Nation	Level 1	Level 2	Level 3	Level 4	Level 5	Level 6	Level 7	Overall
Nordics	92.10	91.38	91.23	93.20	95.45	86.92	96.58	647
Others	90.98	92.24	92.46	90.54	95.88	85.16	94.74	642
Difference	–1.12	0.86	1.23	**–2.66**	0.43	–1.76	–1.84	–5

Overall, there is very little difference between the Nordic nations and the other nations operating from the worldview of People Awareness; the biggest difference is at Level 4 consciousness – satisfying citizens' needs for freedom, equality and social accountability. Of the four indicators making up Level 4 consciousness, the biggest difference, by a significant margin, is in the level of gender equality.

Norway and Sweden

The most conscious of the Nordic nations, and in the world, in 2018, was Norway with a GCI score of 659. Sweden was the least conscious of the Nordic nations with a GCI score of 638. In 2014 Norway and Sweden had roughly the same GCI score – Norway was 3 points higher than Sweden. In 2018 there was a 21-point difference (see Table 11.2).

Table 11.2: Comparison of GCI scores in Norway and Sweden between 2014 and 2018

Nation	2014	2016	2018	Change
Norway	646	650	659	+13
Sweden	643	642	638	–5
Difference	–3	–8	–21	–18

Table 11.3 compares the GCI scores and rankings for Norway and Sweden in 2018 for each level of consciousness. The biggest differences are shown in bold. The main differences are at Level 5 consciousness – satisfying citizens' needs for inclusion, fairness, openness, transparency and tolerance – a difference of 9.94 points, Level 3 consciousness – satisfying citizens needs for education and a supportive business environment – and

Richard Barrett

Level 7 consciousness – satisfying citizens' needs for stability, well-being and happiness – a difference of 4.15 points.

In 2018 Norway ranked #1 in the world at Level 5 consciousness and Sweden ranked #18. The biggest difference in the two Level 5 indicators was in the level of social cohesion where Norway ranked #3 in the world and Sweden ranked #22.

In 2018 Norway ranked #8 in the world at Level 3 consciousness and Sweden ranked #14. The biggest difference in the two Level 3 indicators was in the level of education where Norway ranked #4 and Sweden ranked #16.

In 2018 Norway ranked #2 in the world at Level 7 consciousness and Sweden ranked #8. The biggest difference in the two Level 7 indicators was in the level of happiness of the people. In 2018 Norway ranked #2 in the world and Sweden ranked #9.

Table 11.3: Comparison of GCI scores and rankings by level of consciousness for Norway and Sweden in 2018

Nation		Level 1	Level 2	Level 3	Level 4	Level 5	Level 6	Level 7	Overall
Norway	Score	93.25	91.50	92.52	97.10	99.41	86.00	99.03	659
Sweden	Score	94.89	89.76	88.25	94.56	89.47	86.50	94.88	638
Difference		+1.64	−1.74	**−4.27**	−2.54	**−9.94**	+0.50	**−4.15**	−21
Norway	Rank	6	13	8	2	1	10	2	1
Sweden	Rank	4	17	14	3	18	9	8	7
Difference		+2	−4	−6	−1	−17	−1	−6	−6

While Norway has been advancing in consciousness between 2014 and 2018, from a GCI score of 646 to 659, Sweden has been decreasing in consciousness, from a GCI score of 643 to 638.

New Zealand and Australia

In 2014 New Zealand had a GCI score of 651 and Australia had a GCI score of 636, a difference of 15 points. In 2018 New Zealand had a GCI score of 656 and Australia had a GCI score of 624, a difference of 28 points (see Table 11.4). The gap in consciousness between New Zealand and Australia is growing.

Table 11.4: Comparison of GCI scores in New Zealand and Australia between 2014 and 2018

Nation	2014	2016	2018	Change
New Zealand	651	659	656	+5
Australia	636	633	624	–12
Difference	–15	–26	–28	–17

Table 11.5 compares the GCI scores and rankings for New Zealand and Australia in 2018 by level of consciousness. The biggest differences are shown in bold. The main differences are at Level 4 consciousness – satisfying citizens' needs for freedom, equality and social accountability – a difference of 8.07 points, Level 6 consciousness – satisfying citizens' needs for the quality and preservation of the environment – a difference of 7.60 points, and Level 1 consciousness – satisfying citizens' needs for health care and economic performance – a difference of 7.09 points.

In 2018 New Zealand ranked #4 in the world at Level 4 consciousness and Australia ranked #11. The biggest difference in the four Level 4 indicators was in the level of gender equality. In 2018 New Zealand ranked #7 in the world and Australia ranked #35.

In 2018 New Zealand ranked #7 in the world at Level 6 consciousness and Australia ranked #16. The biggest difference in the two Level 6 indicators was in the level of quality of the environment. In 2018 New Zealand ranked #4 in the world and Australia ranked #18.

In 2018 New Zealand ranked #7 in the world at Level 1 consciousness and Australia ranked #18. The biggest difference in the three Level 1 indicators was in the level of economic performance. In 2018 New Zealand ranked #14 and Australia ranked #28.

Table 11.5: Comparison of GCI scores and rankings by level of consciousness for New Zealand and Australia in 2018

Nation		Level 1	Level 2	Level 3	Level 4	Level 5	Level 6	Level 7	Overall
N Zealand	Score	92.86	93.51	94.82	93.60	99.11	86.73	95.09	656
Australia	Score	85.77	88.83	92.02	85.53	98.47	79.13	94.74	624
Difference		**–7.09**	–4.68	–2.80	**–8.07**	–0.64	**–7.60**	–0.35	32
N Zealand	Rank	7	8	4	4	2	7	7	656

Australia	Rank	18	20	9	11	4	16	9	624
	Difference	–11	–12	–5	–7	–2	–9	–2	–32

While New Zealand has been advancing in overall consciousness between 2014 and 2018, from a GCI score of 651 to 656, Australia has been decreasing in consciousness, from a GCI score of 636 to 624. The gap between the two nations more than doubled between 2014 and 2018, from 15 points to 32 points.

Canada and the US

In 2014 Canada had a GCI score of 631 and the US had a GCI score of 576. In 2016 the level of consciousness in the US increased by 6 points to 582, whereas Canada remained unchanged. In 2018 the level of consciousness in the US decreased by 11 points to 571 and in Canada by one point to 630. The overall difference between the level of consciousness in Canada and the US increased to 10 points between 2016 and 2018 (see Table 11.6).

Table 11.6: Comparison of GCI evolution in Canada and the US between 2014 and 2018

Nation	2014	2016	2018	Change
Canada	631	631	630	–1
US	576	582	571	–5
Difference	–55	–49	–59	–4

Table 11.7 compares the GCI scores and rankings for Canada and the US in 2018 by level of consciousness. The biggest differences are shown in bold. The main differences are at Level 2 consciousness – satisfying citizens' needs for safety, protection and peace – a difference of 25.56 points, Level 4 consciousness – satisfying citizens' needs for freedom, equality and social accountability – a difference of 15.76 points, and Level 7 consciousness – satisfying citizens' needs for stability, well-being and happiness – a difference of 13.93 points.

In 2018 Canada ranked #14 in the world at Level 2 consciousness and the US ranked #65. The biggest difference in the two Level 2 indicators was in the level of violence. In 2018 Canada ranked #6 and the US ranked #106.

In 2018 Canada ranked #7 in the world at Level 4 consciousness and the US ranked #25. The differences in the four Level 4 indicators was about the same: Canada has more personal freedom, a higher level of democracy, more press freedom and more gender equality, although the level of gender equality in both countries is relatively low.

In 2018 Canada ranked #6 in the world at Level 7 consciousness and the US ranked #16. The biggest difference in the two indicators was in the level of strength, stability and legitimacy of the State.

Table 11.7: Comparison of GCI scores by level of consciousness for Canada and the US in 2018

Nation		Level 1	Level 2	Level 3	Level 4	Level 5	Level 6	Level 7	Overall
Canada	Score	88.62	91.01	93.13	91.52	94.10	76.62	95.12	630
US	Score	83.44	65.45	97.06	75.76	93.47	74.75	81.19	571
Difference		–5.18	**–25.56**	3.93	**–15.76**	–0.63	–1.87	**–13.93**	59
Canada	Rank	13	14	6	7	9	20	6	9
US	Rank	21	65	1	25	12	21	16	20
Difference		–8	–51	5	–18	–3	–1	–10	–11

While Canada maintained its overall level consciousness between 2014 and 2018, the US slightly decreased in consciousness, from a GCI score of 576 to 571. The gap between the two nations increased from 55 to 59 points between 2014 and 2018.

Ireland and the UK

In 2014 Ireland had a GCI score of 613 and the UK had a GCI score of 610, a difference of 3 points. By 2018 this difference had increased to 13 points. Ireland had a score of 631 and the UK had a score of 618 (see Table 11.8).

Table 11.8: Comparison of GCI evolution in Ireland and the UK between 2014 and 2018

Nation	2014	2016	2018	Change
Ireland	613	621	631	+18
UK	610	615	618	+8
Difference	–3	–6	–13	–10

Table 11.9 compares the GCI scores and rankings for Ireland and the UK in 2018 by level of consciousness. The biggest differences are shown in bold. The main differences are at Level 2 consciousness – satisfying citizens' needs for safety, protection and peace – a difference of 10.72 points, Level 7 consciousness – satisfying citizens' needs for stability, well-being and happiness – a difference of 10.06 points and Level 4 consciousness – satisfying citizens' needs for freedom, equality and social accountability – a difference of 6.87 points.

In 2018 Ireland ranked #10 in the world at Level 2 consciousness and the UK ranked #27. The biggest difference in the two Level 2 indicators was in the level of violence: in 2018 Ireland ranked #6 and the UK ranked #55.

In 2018 Ireland ranked #11 in the world at Level 7 consciousness and the UK ranked #17. The biggest difference in the two Level 7 indicators was in the level of strength, stability and legitimacy of the State: in 2018 Ireland ranked #11 and the UK ranked #24.

In 2018 Ireland ranked #6 in the world at Level 4 consciousness and the UK ranked #13. The differences in the four Level 4 indicators was about the same: Ireland has more personal freedom, a higher level of democracy, more press freedom and more gender equality.

There are two levels where the UK is significantly better than Ireland: Level 6 consciousness – satisfying citizens' needs for environmental quality and environmental preservation – with a difference of 7.93 points and Level 3 consciousness – satisfying citizens' needs for education and a supportive business environment – with a difference of 4.84 points.

Table 11.9: Comparison of GCI scores by level of consciousness for Ireland and the UK in 2018

Nation		Level 1	Level 2	Level 3	Level 4	Level 5	Level 6	Level 7	Overall
Ireland	Score	86.31	92.79	87.93	91.97	96.34	84.18	91.16	631
UK	Score	88.88	82.07	92.77	85.10	95.66	92.11	81.10	618
Difference		-2.57	**-10.72**	4.84	**-6.87**	-0.68	7.93	**-10.06**	-13
Ireland	Rank	17	10	15	6	6	12	11	8
UK	Rank	12	27	7	13	9	2	17	14
Difference		5	-17	8	-7	-3	10	-6	-6

While Ireland increased its overall level consciousness by 18 points between 2014 and 2018, from a GCI score of 613 to 631, the UK increased its overall level of consciousness by only 8 points, from a GCI score of 610 to 618: the gap between the two nations increased from 3 to 13 points.

Summary

Here are the main points of this chapter.

1. The biggest difference between the Nordic nations and the other nations operating from the worldview of People Awareness is in gender equality.
2. While Norway has been advancing in consciousness, Sweden has been decreasing in consciousness.
3. While New Zealand has been advancing in consciousness, Australia has been decreasing in consciousness.
4. While Canada maintained its overall level of consciousness, the US has slightly decreased in consciousness.
5. Ireland has been increasing its overall level consciousness at a faster rate than the UK. Thus, the gap in consciousness between the two nations has grown.

PART 3

THE EVOLUTION OF HUMAN CONSCIOUSNESS

The third part of the book looks to the future. Chapter 12 discusses global trends in the evolution of human consciousness and how nations can evolve from one worldview to the next. I describe the approach used by the Nordic nations to shift from Nation Awareness, through Wealth Awareness to the worldview of People Awareness. Chapter 13 describes the most important factor in shifting from the worldview of People Awareness to the worldview of Humanity Awareness – a shift in focus from social welfare programmes to a focus on psychological welfare programmes. Chapter 14 provides an overview of what would be happening in nations that embrace the worldview of Humanity Awareness.

12

GLOBAL TRANSFORMATION

Nations are like people

One of the principal conclusions arising from the GCI analysis of nations is *nations are like people; every nation has a unique psychological profile based on its 'personal' history.* Also, just like people, nations can advance from one stage of psychological development to the next; they can stagnate – remain at the same stage of development; or they can retreat to a lower stage of development and a lower level of consciousness.

Each stage of psychological development is associated with a unique worldview that reflects the level of identity/awareness of the people. We can measure where nations are in their psychological development, as well as whether they are advancing, stagnating or retreating by monitoring their GCI scores.

For example, Lithuania increased its GCI score by 47 points (+10%) between 2014 and 2018 and graduated from the worldview of State Awareness 1 to the worldview of Nation Awareness. Over the same period, Turkey reduced its GCI score by 24 points (–7%), shifting to a lower level of consciousness inside the worldview of State Awareness 1. Canada's GCI score hardly changed over the same period, staying at the lowest level of People Awareness.

Individual psychological development vs. collective psychological development

In a democratic regime the collective stage of psychological development of a nation reflects the average stage of psychological development of the people. In an authoritarian regime the collective stage of psychological development of a nation reflects the stage of psychological development of the leader. Table 3.4 in Chapter 3 shows the correspondence between the (personal) stages of psychological development and the collective stages of psychological development (worldviews).

The influence of the male ego

It is important to note that the worldviews of State Awareness, Nation Awareness and Wealth Awareness are dominated by the male ego, whereas the worldviews of Clan Awareness and Tribe Awareness are not. In these two worldviews men and women live in a state of mutual dependence. They work alongside each other to assure the group's survival and safety. The same is true for People Awareness and Humanity Awareness.

The situation that triggered the outburst of the male ego – wars over the possession of fertile territory brought on by climate change – led to the emergence of the differentiating stage of psychological development – a focus on the self-esteem level of consciousness.

In the worldview of State Awareness, the male ego knew no boundaries. It was completely focused on self-interest and personal gain. Exploitation, corruption, back-stabbing, injustice, rape and pillaging were considered normal in this worldview.

In the two succeeding worldviews there was a gradual and increasing restraint of the male ego. In the worldview of Nation Awareness, the chaos and disorder brought on by the excesses of the male ego in State Awareness were tempered by a shift from a focus on power and strength to a focus on authority and education. In the worldview of Wealth Awareness, the hierarchal and oppressive excesses of the male ego in Nation Awareness were tempered by a shift in focus from authority and education to a focus on status and (political) influence.

In the worldview of People Awareness, we begin to see the

re-establishment of mutual respect and interdependence of men and women that was present in Clan Awareness and Tribe Awareness. This is hardly surprising since the worldview of People Awareness was triggered by the demand that women have a voice and representation in the process of democratic governance.

I firmly believe that the inclusion of women in political decision-making led to an increase in the qualities of empathy and compassion, which in turn led to the implementation of social welfare programmes. The introduction of social welfare was highly significant from a psychological perspective. Social welfare created the conditions whereby everyone in the nation could theoretically satisfy their deficiency needs. This decreased the level of fear in the nation and increased the opportunity for people to focus on their growth needs.

What is now required as we evolve from People Awareness to Humanity Awareness is a shift in focus from social welfare to psychological welfare to support people in satisfying their growth needs.

Graduating from one worldview to the next

Unfortunately, there is no magic bullet for global transformation – no one-size-fits-all approach. Every nation, because of its unique history, requires its own tailored programme of psychological development: every nation must learn to master the needs of the collective stage of psychological development it is at in order to move to the next collective stage of psychological development. To this end, the year-on-year changes in the overall GCI score, the scores by level of consciousness and the scores of the 17 global indicators provide a detailed dashboard and monitoring system for measuring the evolution of consciousness of a nation.

Table 12.2 (Table 7.17 reproduced with the addition of the shift from People Awareness to Humanity Awareness) identifies the key conditions that must be met for a nation to shift from one worldview to the next. Depending on the psychological history of the nation, some of these conditions may be easy to satisfy and others may not.

Table 12.2: Key transition conditions between worldviews

From	To	Key transition conditions
People Awareness	Humanity Awareness	Increase in psychological welfare and increase in peoples' sense of meaning.
Wealth Awareness	People Awareness	Increase in gender equality, democracy, social welfare and level of support for business.
Nation Awareness	Wealth Awareness	Increase in social cohesion, decrease in corruption and increase in happiness.
State Awareness 1	Nation Awareness	Decrease in corruption, increase in press freedom, democracy, personal freedom and the strength, stability and legitimacy of the State.
State Awareness 2	State Awareness 1	Increase in happiness, strength, stability and legitimacy of the State, press freedom, and the quality and preservation of the environment.
State Awareness 3	State Awareness 2	Increase in education, social progress and health care.

Implications for global transformation?

Based on the research into societal transformation presented in this book, as well as my research into personal and organizational transformation presented in my previous books, I have arrived at the following conclusions.[53, 54, 55]

- Transformation happens one person at a time, one organization at a time and one nation at a time because every person, every organization and every nation has its own unique psychological history.
- There is a strong link between the dominant stage of psychological development of the people in a nation and the collective stage of psychological development (worldview) of a nation.
- A significant shift in the stage of psychological development of individuals (either an increase or a decrease) can promote a shift

---

[53] Richard Barrett, *Everything I Have Learned About Values* (London: Fulfilling Books), 2018.

[54] Richard Barrett, *The Metrics of Human Consciousness* (London: Fulfilling Books), 2015.

[55] Richard Barrett, *The Values-driven Organization: Cultural Health and Human Well-being as a Pathway to Sustainable Performance* (London: Routledge), 2017.

in the collective stage of psychological development of the nation, and thereby a shift in the dominant worldview.

- In authoritarian regimes, a shift in the worldview of a nation will only take place if there is a shift in the worldview (stage of psychological development) of the leader.
- In democratic regimes, a shift in the worldview of a nation will only take place if there is a shift in the worldview (collective stage of psychological development) of the masses.
- In both cases—democratic and authoritarian regimes—transformation programmes should focus on the growth and development of the leaders.
- A shift to a higher collective stage of psychological development – a higher-order worldview – can be facilitated over time by a focus on the education of children, teenagers and young adults – the future generations.

This leads me to suggest a three-pronged approach to transformation of consciousness at a national level.

A. **A long-term perspective**: Focus on the psychological development of future generations – children, teenagers and young adults who are at the differentiating stage of psychological development and entering the individuating stage of psychological development.

B. **A medium-term perspective**: Focus on the psychological development of young leaders in the private, public and civic sectors to support and mentor them through the individuating and self-actualizing stages of their psychological development.

C. **A short-term perspective**: Focus on the psychological development of the nation by using the GCI to develop policies that enable nations to focus on the issues that are preventing them from graduating to the next worldview.

This approach should be tailored to meet the specific needs of regions and nations. For example, the nations of the Arab region, for the most part, share a worldview that is different to the worldview of the nations of Sub-Saharan Africa. Similarly, the nations of the Sub-Saharan Africa region, for the most part, share a different worldview to the nations of the Nordic region. Each region should therefore have its own customized transformation programme, and each nation within each region should also have its own customized transformation programme.

Has anything like this been attempted before?

Perspective A

As far as Item A is concerned – a focus on the psychological development of future generations – the answer is a resounding yes! Was it successful? The answer again is a resounding yes!

The Bildung *approach*

In the mid-19th century, some of the key political and cultural figures in the Nordic nations recognized the need to emancipate the rural population. They foresaw that the industrial revolution would cause feudal structures to collapse resulting in a mass migration to the cities. They understood that the rural workers needed more reading and writing skills if they were to become responsible citizens and, more importantly, they would need to develop an expanded sense of collective identity – from their primarily local rural identity to a more expansive and inclusive national identity.

'They needed to develop a sense of responsibility towards self and society; they needed moral, emotional and cognitive development. The leaders wanted people to think, feel and act in different ways. They did not want to dictate what people should think or how they should act. They wanted a population that could 'author' their own lives and take part in the authoring of a new society.

What emerged was the understanding that people must be able to control their emotions, internalize the norms of society and take individual moral responsibility. In German, this kind of personal ego-development programme goes under the name *Bildung*.'[56]

In my opinion, *Bildung* is a system of education that takes people from

---

[56] Lene Rachel Andersen and Tomas Björkman, *The Nordic Secret: A European Story of Beauty and Freedom* (Stockholm: Fri Tanke Publishing), 2017.

the ego stages of development to the balancing of the ego's motivations with the soul's motivations; in other words, from the first three stages of psychological development (surviving, conforming and differentiating) into the fourth stage of psychological development (individuating).

This programme also supports people in moving from the first algorithm of evolutionary intelligence, as a way of making decisions, to the second algorithm of evolutionary intelligence – from decision-making that focuses on 'What's in it for me?' to decision-making that focuses on 'What's best for the common good?' The *Bildung* education programme laid the foundations for the development of a strong sense of social cohesion and equality.

Largely as a result of this programme, the Nordic nations moved from being at the bottom of the European economy in the 1860s to being at the top by the 1930s, and they have remained prosperous and progressive ever since. Finland made a similar journey using a customized form of *Bildung* programme starting around 1918. It achieved similar results to the other Nordic nations. Some of the principal ingredients of the *Bildung* education programme are as follows:

- Dedicated teachers.
- An understanding among the teachers of the concepts of psychological development.
- An understanding of the importance of their cultural heritage, so people feel a sense of belonging at the national level.
- Teaching what is immediately relevant to the participants – what empowers them politically and what improves their lives here and now.
- An understanding of autonomy and local self-organizing.
- Start with the 16 to 30 age group.

This last point – a focus on the young – was fundamentally important to the success of the *Bildung* programme. This age group is at the differentiating and individuating stages of psychological development: they are asking questions about recognition, responsibility and identity. They are searching for a larger sense of belonging, beyond their local

191

community, and they want to find the freedom they need to explore their gifts and talents.

The authors of *The Nordic Secret* believe that this approach, which has worked so successfully in Nordic nations, is replicable in other parts of the world.

'Poor countries can make themselves rich in less than two generations if the population gets *Bildung*. ... There was nothing unique about the Nordic nations in 1850 or Finland in 1918, quite the contrary: all four countries were poor, very religious and the rule was recently authoritarian. ... From the first successful folk high school in 1851 to when Denmark joined the economic elite took 50 years; Norway and Sweden made similar journeys and Finland did it in just 30 years.'[57]

One of the major success factors of the *Bildung* approach is that it taught people to become responsible and accountable for their lives. It helped them find ways to address their deficiency needs. By lifting themselves out of poverty, it enabled them to focus on their growth needs.

The Law of Jante

Another important factor in the formation of the culture of Nordic nations is the Law of Jante. This is a mindset[58] based on a code of conduct that has been part of the Danish, Swedish and Norwegian cultures for centuries. The Law of Jante can be summarized in one sentence: You are not to think you are anyone special or that you are better than us. Its focus is on regulating the excesses of the self-esteem level of consciousness. There are ten rules that make up the Law of Jante. You can find these rules in a book written by Aksel Sandemose entitled *A Fugitive Crosses His Tracks* published in 1936.[59] Sandemose was writing about the prevailing attitudes in his hometown of Nykōbing Mors in Denmark. The major impact of the Law of Jante is to reduce bragging, arrogance and conceit by placing emphasis on the harmony of the collective.

While there is little doubt that the Law of Jante had a significant impact in building cohesive national cultures, nowadays the rules are

---

[57] Ibid., p. 382.
[58] See Glossary for a definition of mindset.
[59] Aksel Sandemose, *A Fugitive Crosses His Tracks* (Denmark: Knopf), 1936.

coming under some criticism. The Law of Jante is perceived by some modern social commentators as inhibiting the process of individuation and self-actualization, thereby leading to high rates of depression and suicide. This in my opinion is a false argument.

Individuation is not about thinking you are better than others; it is about becoming the best version of yourself. During the process of individuation, we learn to shift from extrinsic motivation to intrinsic motivation. Therefore, the Law of Jante, which focuses on extrinsic motivation, cannot inhibit individuation and self-actualization, which are focused on intrinsic motivation.

Even though the *Bildung* programme did not continue after World War II, the Law of Jante is still alive and well throughout Nordic society. I have made it a habit over the past few years to ask every Scandinavian I meet, even when I am on holiday, if they have heard about the Law of Jante. So far, every single one of them has said yes.

It seems to me that the rules of the Law of Jante are similar to the rules found in tribal cultures. Whereas the rules in tribal cultures are designed to create internal cohesion at Level 2 consciousness (to afford safety and protection through belonging), the Law of Jante is primarily designed to support internal cohesion at Level 5 consciousness by doing away with elitism. The Law of Jante is a useful reminder to those aspiring to achieve status and notoriety, and to the rich and famous, that success does not come with being the best in the world, but being the best *for* the world, or at least the best for the community or country.

What about other nations operating from the worldview of People Awareness?

I think at this point I would like to introduce a reminder that we should not get seduced into thinking the only way for a nation to shift to the worldview of People Awareness is through embracing programmes based on the Nordic Secret and the Law of Jante. New Zealand, Switzerland, Ireland and Canada have all learned to operate from People Awareness without these two supports.

It is worth remembering that New Zealand and Switzerland currently operate from a higher overall level of consciousness than Iceland and

Sweden. Therefore, there must be other ways for nations to graduate to the worldview of People Awareness than the methods employed in Nordic nations. The routes that New Zealand and Switzerland, as well as Ireland and Canada, have taken to get to the worldview of People Awareness are different, but like the Nordic nations, their journeys are based on the unique history of their national psychological development. Despite the different routes they have taken, the nine nations operating from the worldview of People Awareness share some common strengths and weaknesses.

As far as strengths are concerned:

- Seven nations have their principal strength as satisfying citizens' needs for stability, well-being and happiness – Norway, New Zealand, Finland, Denmark, Switzerland, Sweden and Canada (Level 7 consciousness).
- Six nations have their principal strength as satisfying citizens' needs for inclusion, fairness, openness, tolerance and transparency – Norway, New Zealand, Denmark, Iceland, Ireland and Canada (Level 5 consciousness).

As far as weaknesses are concerned:

- Eight nations have their principal weakness as satisfying citizens' needs for environmental quality and preservation – all except Switzerland (Level 6 consciousness).

This analysis brings to light four important observations:

1. Nations can learn to operate from the worldview of People Awareness without necessarily following the Nordic model.
2. There are two essential levels of consciousness that must be mastered for a nation to operate from the worldview of People Awareness: satisfying citizens' needs for stability, well-being and happiness (Level 7 consciousness) and satisfying citizens' needs for inclusion, fairness, openness, tolerance and transparency (Level 5 consciousness).

3. It is also important to recognize that ability to master Level 7 and Level 5 consciousness requires a strong competency at satisfying citizens' needs for freedom, equality and accountability (Level 4 consciousness).

4. The biggest weakness in eight of the nine nations is satisfying citizens' needs for environmental quality and preservation (Level 6 consciousness).

Let's now identify other nations with strengths at Level 4, 5 and 7 consciousness. Table 12.3 shows the top ten nations satisfying citizens' needs for stability, well-being and happiness (Level 7 consciousness), inclusion, fairness, openness, tolerance and transparency (Level 5 consciousness) and freedom, equality and democracy (Level 4 consciousness).

Table 12.3: Top ten nations at Levels 4, 5 and 7 consciousness in 2018

Rank	Level 4	Level 5	Level 7
1	**Iceland**	**Norway**	Finland
2	**Norway**	**New Zealand**	**Norway**
3	Sweden	**Iceland**	**Denmark**
4	**New Zealand**	Australia	Switzerland
5	Finland	**Denmark**	**Iceland**
6	Ireland	Ireland	**Canada**
7	**Canada**	**Netherlands**	**New Zealand**
8	**Denmark**	U. Kingdom	Sweden
9	**Netherlands**	**Canada**	Australia
10	Luxembourg	Switzerland	**Netherlands**

There are only six nations that make the top ten in all three levels of consciousness – Norway, Denmark, Iceland, New Zealand, Canada and the Netherlands, three Nordic nations and three non-Nordic nations

While most of the Nordic nations have mastered Level 7 consciousness and Level 4 consciousness, it is also quite clear that Sweden (#18) and to a certain extent Finland (#11) have not yet mastered Level 5 consciousness.

Ireland has mastered Level 4 and Level 5 consciousness but has not yet mastered Level 7 consciousness. Switzerland and Australia have mastered Level 5 and Level 7 consciousness but have not yet mastered Level 2 consciousness.

Once again it becomes apparent that there are other ways to get to the worldview of People Awareness than following the Nordic model. New Zealand and Canada have done it; the Netherlands has mastered Levels 4, 5 and 7 consciousness; and Ireland, Switzerland and Australia have mastered two of these three levels of consciousness.

Perspective B

As far as Item B of the three-part programme of national transformation is concerned – a focus on the psychological development of young leaders – examples of these programmes can be found all over the world. A key aspect of these programmes is the tripartite approach of focusing on leading self, leading a team and leading an organization (or leading in society).[60] If you cannot lead yourself, you cannot lead a team, and if you cannot lead a team, you cannot lead an organization.

Such programmes almost always begin by focusing on supporting people in satisfying the needs of the individuating stage of psychological development – having the freedom and courage to answer the question, who am I? The next step is to focus on supporting people satisfying the needs of the self-actualizing stage of psychological development – connecting to the deepest levels of their self-expression and creativity.[61]

Perspective C

As far as Item C – focusing on the psychological development of the nation by using the GCI to develop policies that enable nations to tackle issues that are preventing them from graduating to the next worldview – is concerned, this has never been attempted before. The main reason being the GCI approach to identifying a nation's strengths and weaknesses only became available in 2019. Prior to this time there was no overall approach to working with the 17 indicators. In the future, I foresee the GCI approach to identifying and monitoring the transformation needs of a nation as a fundamental part of the implementation of the UN's Sustainable Development Goals.

---

[60] Richard Barrett, *The New Leadership Paradigm* (Bath: Fulfilling Books), 2010.
[61] Ibid.

Summary

Here are the main points of this chapter.

1. Nations are like people; every nation has a unique psychological profile based on its history.

2. Just like people, nations can advance from one stage of development to the next; they can stagnate – remain at the same stage of development; or they can retreat to a lower stage of development and a lower level of consciousness.

3. We can measure where nations are in their psychological development, as well as whether they are advancing, stagnating or retreating, by monitoring their GCI scores.

4. Each stage of collective psychological development is associated with a unique worldview that reflects the level of identity/awareness of the people.

5. In a democratic regime the collective stage of psychological development reflects the average stage of psychological development of the people.

6. In an authoritarian regime the collective stage of psychological development reflects the stage of psychological development of the leader.

7. The worldviews of State Awareness, Nation Awareness and Wealth Awareness are dominated by the male ego, whereas the worldviews of Clan Awareness and Tribe Awareness, as well as People Awareness and Humanity Awareness, are not.

8. Every nation, because of its unique history, needs to develop its own programme of psychological development.

9. The GCI scores by level of consciousness, plus the 17 global indicators, provide a detailed dashboard and monitoring system for measuring the evolution of consciousness of a nation.

10. In authoritarian regimes a shift in the worldview of a nation will only take place if there is a shift in the stage of psychological development of the leader.

11. In democratic regimes a shift in the worldview of a nation will only take place if there is a shift in the stage of psychological development of the masses.

12. Nations can learn to operate from the worldview of People Awareness without necessarily following the Nordic model.

13. Despite the different routes they have taken, the nine nations operating from the worldview of People Awareness share some common strengths and weaknesses.

13

FROM SOCIAL WELFARE TO PSYCHOLOGICAL WELFARE

The key to shifting from the worldview of Wealth Awareness to the worldview of People Awareness is the development of *social welfare programmes* that provide support for everyone, rich and poor alike.

The key to shifting from the worldview of People Awareness to the worldview of Humanity Awareness will be the development of *psychological welfare programmes* that provide support for everyone, at different ages and all stages of development.

This is the purpose of the three-pronged transformation programme outlined in Chapter 12, to support the psychological welfare of people, particularly the younger generations who will become the leaders of tomorrow.

The legacy of inequality

As Wilkinson and Pickett point out in their seminal publication, *The Spirit Level*,[62] the worldview of Wealth Awareness created inequalities in wealth and income between people in the same nation. This in turn led to a rise in diseases of the body and more specifically diseases of the mind.

Wilkinson and Picket are epidemiologists who have spent most of their working lives trying to understand why health gets worse at every

---

[62] Richard Wilkinson and Kate Pickett, *The Spirit Level: Why Equality is Better for Everyone* (London: Penguin Books), 2010.

step down the social ladder, so the poor are less healthy than those in the middle, who in turn are less healthy than those further up.[63] What they discovered was that 'reducing inequality is the best way of improving the quality of life for all'.[64]

They state: 'One of the key reasons why the effects of inequality have not been properly understood before is because of a failure to understand the relationship between individual psychology and societal inequality.'[65] There is a well-documented link between poor self-esteem and social insecurity, as well as a link between mental illness in the form of stress, anxiety and depression, and physical sickness.

Furthermore, 'people with insecure high self-esteem tend to be insensitive to [the needs] of others and to show an excessive preoccupation with themselves, with their success, and with their image and appearance in the eyes of others'.[66]

This 'insecure high self-esteem' is linked to narcissism – a strong focus on self rather than a focus on others. It doesn't take much to imagine what it would look like if such narcissistic people became the leaders of our nations. (There are numerous current examples we could choose from.) It would basically look like the worldviews of Wealth Awareness, Nation Awareness and State Awareness all rolled up together, because these are the stages of psychological development where the search for externally validated self-esteem is rampant among leaders.

We would be living in a world where male egos dominate government policymaking; where nations show off their might through military displays; where military budgets are higher than health and education budgets; where cries for peace are drowned out by the rattle of sabres; where men make decisions on the abortion rights of women; where women have to fight to get their voices heard; where the needs of children, those with physical and mental disadvantages and the environment are ignored in favour of cutting taxes for business owners; where the needs of our natural environment and ecology are overridden by the need to build new airport runways or new pipelines; where indigenous peoples are demoted

---

[63] Ibid. p. ix.
[64] Ibid. p. 29.
[65] Ibid. p. 33.
[66] Ibid. p. 37.

to second-class citizens; and where the needs of capitalists to make money dominate the decision-making of politicians more than the survival, safety and health care needs of the people they were elected to represent.

This description of what the world would look like if it were being run by ego-dominated male narcissists aligns closely with the average GCI score for the world in 2018. The current GCI score for the world is 444 and the GCI for the 19 nations that make up the G20[67] (not counting the EU) is 468. These scores place the world and the G20 firmly in the worldview of State Awareness 1.

Let me remind you of some of the characteristics of the worldview of State Awareness. Leaders of nations that operate from the worldview of State Awareness demand loyalty and require constant praise and adoration – they need their egos stroked. They take pride in displays of military strength and accomplishment. They need such demonstrations to feed their self-esteem: they need to feel powerful and they need to show off their strength. They will lie, cheat and manipulate to become top dog. Corruption is rife in the worldview of State Awareness.

Of course, this description does not portray every leader of the G20; it just represents the average. At this moment in time, the G20 comprises one nation operating from the worldview of People Awareness, three nations operating from Wealth Awareness, five nations operating from Nation Awareness, four nations operating from State Awareness 1 and six nations operating from State Awareness 2. With this diversity of worldviews, most of which are designed to meet the needs of the male ego, it is hardly surprising that the G20 finds it hard to agree on anything: despite the scientific evidence, they can't even agree on the causes of global warming.

The way to move beyond inequality has been fully demonstrated by the Nordic nations. By embracing the worldview of People Awareness – freedom through equality and accountability – they have created sustainable, vibrant economies that work for everyone. The approach they have used is often referred to as 'the Nordic model'.

In 1900 poverty was widespread throughout the Nordic nations. A few decades later things looked very different: they had strong economies with full employment.

---

[67] The G20 is an international forum of government leaders and governors of central banks from 19 countries and the European Union (EU).

Here are some of the Nordic model's characteristics: 'free higher education, robust support for families, a healthy work/life balance, an active response to climate change, and an abundance of high-paying jobs for young and old alike.' [68] All these benefits, including improved mental and physical health, have been achieved through a focus on freedom and equality for all. The Nordic nations have developed welfare programmes that ensure everyone can meet their deficiency needs. Therefore, everyone is free to explore their growth needs.

Psychological welfare

What the *Bildung* programme did for the Nordic nations was to support several generations of young people moving from the differentiating stage of development to the individuating stage of development. It helped them become viable independent human beings in a framework of existence that provided freedom and equality for all.

The psychological welfare programme I am proposing in Chapter 12 will not only support young people moving from the differentiating stage of psychological development to the individuating stage of development – finding freedom and autonomy to be who you really are outside your parental and cultural conditioning; it will also support people moving from the individuating stage of development to the self-actualizing stage of psychological development – finding meaning and purpose in life. It will help them to fully express their natural gifts and talents and explore their creativity.

Basically, the worldview of People Awareness is a springboard into the worldview of Humanity Awareness: we must be able to master the individuating stage of development before we can master the self-actualizing stage of development.

The worldview of Humanity Awareness is a major shift in human consciousness that takes us out of our narrowly defined sense of physical and national identity into an increasingly expansive and inclusive sense

---

[68] George Lakey, *Viking Economics: How the Scandinavians Got it Right—and How We Can Too* (London: Melville House Publishing), 2016.

of our spiritual identity. We develop a transnational sense of who we are, which embraces all races, religions and nationalities.

Basically, the worldview of People Awareness (the individuating stage of psychological development) invites us on a journey of reconnection to our source.[69] The only things blocking us on this journey are the fear-based beliefs we learned during our infant, childhood and teenage years. As we learn to master our survival, safety and security fears, we decrease our sense of separation and increase our sense of connection – this is the process that allows us to reconnect with our soul.[70] When we entered this world, we were fully connected to our souls. Gradually we lost that sense of connection as we learned to identify with our physical body and survive, keep safe and feel secure in a material world.

Similarly, when *Homo sapiens* arrived in this world we were fully connected to our souls and the spirit world. We began to lose that connection as we moved from Clan Awareness to Tribe Awareness – we started to identify with our ethnic roots and with the territory our tribe occupied. Our sense of separation increased further when we moved from Tribe Awareness to State Awareness and from State Awareness to Nation Awareness.

Our sense of separation reached its peak in the worldview of Wealth Awareness, where we let wealth and income separate us from our kin; where our love for material possessions became more important than our love for mother Earth; and where the cosmology of science (based on Darwinian meaninglessness) cut us off from all sense of a meaningful connection to a divine creator/provider. The worldview of People Awareness is the first step of the journey back into wholeness. The worldview of Humanity Awareness is the second step.

What we must remember is that all human beings are the same. They have the same hopes and fears and they grow and develop in the same way – by overcoming their fears (satisfying their deficiency needs) and thriving (satisfying their growth needs). They do this by learning how

---

[69] Richard Barrett, *What My Soul Told Me* (Bath: Fulfilling Books), 2012.

[70] Richard Barrett, *A New Psychology of Human Well-being: An Exploration of the Impact of Ego-Soul Dynamics on Mental and Physical Health* (London: Fulfilling Books), 2016.

to master each of the seven stages of psychological development at an individual level and a societal level.

The fears that prevent us from moving forward with our psychological development originate from the beliefs we learned during the first 24 years of our lives, while our body mind, emotional mind and rational mind were learning how to fit into the parental and cultural frameworks of our existence so we could master our deficiency needs.

When the community or nation we live in takes care of our deficiency needs through the implementation of social welfare programmes – when no person gets left behind and everyone is treated equally – every person gets the opportunity to embrace their growth needs.

When the community or nation we live in supports us in mastering our growth needs through the implementation of psychological welfare programmes, every person gets the opportunity to fully express their natural gifts, talents and creativity in service to the greater good.

Summary

Here are the main points of this chapter.

1. The key to shifting from the worldview of Wealth Awareness to the worldview of People Awareness is the development of social welfare programmes that provide support for everyone, rich and poor alike to meet their deficiency needs.
2. The key to shifting from the worldview of People Awareness to the worldview of Humanity Awareness will be the development of psychological welfare programmes that provide support for everyone, at different ages and all stages of psychological development.
3. One of the key reasons why the effects of inequality have not been properly understood is because of a failure to understand the relationship between individual psychology and societal inequality.
4. The worldview of Wealth Awareness created inequalities in income. This in turn led to a rise in diseases of the body and more specifically diseases of the mind.

5. People with insecure high self-esteem tend to be insensitive to the needs of others and to show an excessive preoccupation with themselves, with their success and with their image and appearance in the eyes of others.

6. Insecure high self-esteem is linked to narcissism – a strong focus on self rather than a focus on others.

7. The way to move beyond inequality has been fully demonstrated by the Nordic nations.

8. The *Bildung* programme supported several generations of young people moving from the differentiating stage of development to the individuating stage of development.

9. The worldview of People Awareness is a springboard into the worldview of Humanity Awareness: we must be able to master the individuating stage of development before we can master the self-actualizing stage of development.

10. The fears that prevent us from moving forward with our psychological development originate from the beliefs we learned during the first 24 years of our lives, while our body mind, emotional mind and rational mind were learning how to fit into the parental and cultural frameworks of our existence so we could master our deficiency needs.

11. When the community or nation we live in takes care of our deficiency needs through the implementation of social welfare programmes – when no person gets left behind and everyone is treated equally – every person gets the opportunity to embrace their growth needs.

14

HUMANITY AWARENESS

Identity has always been the slave to survival and the demon of oppression. We must find a higher-order identity that incudes everyone. Having learned to master the worldview of People Awareness by embracing the values of freedom, equality and accountability, the quest that now arises is the search for the next stage of development – the search for Humanity Awareness.

A brief overview of the origins of Humanity Awareness can be found in Chapter 4 – what it looks like, its cosmology and the principal behavioural characteristics. My purpose in this chapter is to take a deeper dive into the underlying philosophy of Humanity Awareness and show the impact that it will have on our lives.

In People Awareness the primary goal was to give people the freedom to explore their true selves by removing the survival, safety and security fears from their lives – supporting them in providing for their deficiency needs. By so doing, nations operating from the worldview of People Awareness created the conditions for people to move through the differentiating stage of development into the individuating stage of psychological development – to explore who they are outside of their parental and cultural conditioning.

Humanity Awareness takes us a step further into our psychological development; its primary goal is to create the conditions that allow people to self-actualize – to fully express their unique gifts and talents and thereby find meaning and purpose in their life.

Before we embark on the journey into Humanity Awareness, let us recognize that there are already a significant number of people operating from this worldview. These are self-actualized individuals, mostly, but not uniquely, concentrated in countries that are operating from People Awareness, who have mastered their deficiency needs, fully individuated and are now either seeking to uncover their natural gifts and talents or, having found them, make them available to the world. They have moved beyond a search for happiness and are now engaged in a search for well-being through full self-expression.

Philosophy

The central idea in the worldview of Humanity Awareness is to support full human self-expression. In Humanity Awareness we recognize that all human beings share the same identity – we are all souls experiencing life in three-dimensional material awareness, and the problems that humanity faces can only be solved in a holistic manner by involving all stakeholders.

Identity

In the worldview of Humanity Awareness, we recognize that we are all members of the human race. Not only are there no racial, religious or gender divisions in Humanity Awareness, there are also no territorial boundaries. Our home is the Earth. We are transnational and we are global. Political philosopher, historian and sociologist Hanzi Freinacht (pen name) agrees:

'The transnational way of thinking means … we know no borders, that [our] values are world-centric … the nation state or region are not the primary categories of society, but rather … train stations in a longer journey of the historical development of … human self-organization.'[71]

Full self-expression

Whereas the core purpose of the worldview of People Awareness was to find ways to satisfy our *deficiency* needs in a *national* framework of

---

[71] Hanzi Freinacht, *The Listening Society: A Metamodern Guide to Politics*, Book 1: Volume 1 (Metamoderna ApS) 2017.

existence, the core purpose of the worldview of Humanity Awareness is to find ways to satisfy our *growth* needs in a *global* framework of existence.

Holistic approach

In the worldview of Humanity Awareness our approach to solving problems is holistic and systemic. We get involved in system-wide changes. We are not blinkered by our beliefs, as people are in the preceding worldviews; we seek answers to the questions that are facing humanity through deep dialogue, intuitive insights and processes that invite our collective intelligence – processes that involve all concerned parties and align with our universal 'soul' values.[72] We are looking for solutions that address the needs of humanity.

Cosmology

At the core of every worldview is an underlying cosmology. In the worldview of People Awareness, the underlying cosmology was spirituality – a subjective experience of other dimensions of being and an exploration of the deepest values and meanings by which people live.

In the worldview of Humanity Awareness, the underlying cosmology is soul awareness – a subjective experience of our energetic reality and the source of our true being. You don't have to call it soul awareness, nor do you have to embrace the idea that you have or are a soul; what is essential if you want to embrace the cosmology of Humanity Awareness is that you feel a strong sense of connection to all human beings, exclusive of nationality, race, religion, age or gender.

Whereas the focus of spirituality is on the 'journey', the focus of the cosmology of Humanity Awareness is on the 'destination' – the retrieval of soul consciousness – the awareness we had when we were born, which we lost when the pain of being present in material awareness became too great for our soul to bear. To protect itself, the soul created the psychic

---

[72] Otto Scharmer and Katrin Kaefer, *Leading From the Emerging Future: From Ego-System to Eco-System* (San Francisco: Berrett-Koehler), 2010.

entity we call the ego to act as a buffer – to soak up the pain that comes from the experience of fear and separation.

The unique feature of the cosmology of Humanity Awareness is that it brings together psychology, spirituality and the cutting-edge theories of science into an overarching framework of understanding with the soul at the centre. In the cosmology of soul awareness, we let go of our attachment to the material dimension of existence and embrace the energetic dimension. We recognize that every human is a soul experiencing life in a human body and that we are all on the same evolutionary journey – we are just at different stations along the way.

Although we live our lives in physical awareness, we know we are not of this world. When we die, we do not lose consciousness; we simply divest ourselves of our bodies and our material awareness and move back into our full energetic awareness. Our physical body is the vehicle the soul uses to get around in material awareness, and until we recover our soul, the ego is the driver.

This understanding of the energetic nature of our being has major implications for health and healing. In the worldview of Humanity Awareness, we recognize that all mental and physical *dis-ease* arises from a lack of energetic alignment between the values and motivations of the ego and the values and motivations of the soul.[73]

Our ego is a field of conscious awareness that identifies with our body. Our soul began to create the ego towards the end of the first two years of our life. It created the ego for two purposes: to protect the soul from the pain of separation it experiences living in a fear-driven world, and to care for our body in the material dimension of existence.

Our ego is not who we are: it's who we think we are. It's the mask we wear to get our needs met in the parental, social and cultural framework of our existence. Our ego reflects the beliefs we learned during the first 24 years of our life while our mind was developing and our brain was growing. We must remove the ego mask – by letting go of our fears – if we want to live in soul awareness.

Because the ego believes it lives in a material world, it thinks it can die.

---

[73] Richard Barrett, *A New Psychology of Human Well-being: An Exploration of the Influence of Ego-Soul Dynamics on Mental and Physical Health* (London: Fulfilling Books), 2016.

Because it thinks it can die, it thinks it has needs, and because it thinks it has needs, it develops fears about not being able to get its needs met. We must learn to master these fears if we wish to live in soul awareness. The degree to which we overcome the fears of the ego is the degree to which we live in alignment with our soul.

Because the soul identifies with our energy field and not with our physical body, it knows it cannot die. Therefore, it has no fears. When we die, we don't lose consciousness; we simply lose awareness of the three-dimensional material world. When we leave this physical world, we return to the energetic dimension of reality from whence we came.

The level of ego–soul alignment we achieve determines our mental and physical health and our sense of well-being. The degree to which we can let go of the fear-based energies of the ego is the degree to which we are able to experience the love-based energy of our soul.

Souls incarnate into the three-dimensional material awareness to fulfil three desires: to fully express their gifts and talents; to connect with other souls to make a difference in the world; and to contribute to the well-being of humanity and the planet. The degree to which we fulfil these desires significantly affects our mental and physical well-being.[74]

Governance

In the worldview of Wealth Awareness, we made a brave attempt to embrace democracy, but the results were disastrous.

'We have conducted a 40-year experiment with neoliberalism. The evidence is in, and by any measure, it has failed. And by the most important measure – the well-being of ordinary citizens – it has failed miserably.'[75]

We lost sight of our humanity because our underlying cosmology was science. In the cosmology of science, we deny any spiritual identity; we see no connection between humans, and we find no purpose in life because

---

[74] https://www.aahv.global/living-your-soul-s-destiny.html

[75] Joseph E. Stiglitz, a Nobel laureate in economics, is University Professor at Columbia University and chief economist at the Roosevelt Institute. He is the author, most recently, of *People, Power, and Profits: Progressive Capitalism for an Age of Discontent* (W.W. Norton and Allen Lane).

we embrace the concept of Darwinian meaninglessness – a world built on random mutations.

In Wealth Awareness we were still living in the age of self-esteem consciousness where the male ego was dominant. Our governance systems reflected this situation: they were polarized, combative and based on the principle of winner takes all.[76] We aligned ourselves with political parties that reflected the needs of the dominant subgroups in our society – the rich versus the poor, and the owners of industry versus the workers.

Politics in the worldview of Wealth Awareness was all about money. The high-income people had their political party and the low-income people had their political party. Political fights were mostly about finding ways to seduce the middle-income people while also serving the needs of the rich (corporate interests) or the poor (the disadvantaged), depending on which party you belonged to.

Governance in the worldview of People Awareness solved this problem by focusing on the basic needs of everyone – not the rich, not the poor, but everyone. All political parties shifted their focus to the centre.

However, as Hanzi Freinacht points out: 'There is no [political] "centre" in any strict, analytical sense [but] ... an uncompromising acceptance of the market economy and an equally uncompromising acceptance of the welfare state.'[77]

As a result of the acceptance of this core ideology, it has become increasingly difficult to distinguish between political parties (the 'Left' from the 'Right') in nations that operate from the worldview of People Awareness. The worldview of People Awareness shifted national governments from two-party adversarial politics to multi-party cooperative coalitions.

In the worldview of People Awareness there was a universal agreement on the basic principles of governance: freedom, equality and personal accountability, along with full employment, care for the disadvantaged and the rehabilitation of the natural environment.

Money is no longer the central issue in the worldview of People

---

[76] Watch the debates in the Houses of Parliament in the UK if you want to see how ego-driven, partisan politics works.

[77] Hanzi Freinacht, *The Listening Society: A Metamodern Guide to Politics*, Book 1: Volume 1 (Metamoderna ApS), 2017.

Awareness; the welfare and the well-being of citizens are uppermost in every politician's mind. The government takes care of everyone's basic needs by providing free education and free health care and ensuring everyone has the skills to find a job. There is also a focus on the needs of families – long parental leave for both men and women, free kindergarten care for children and access to bank loans for housing.

This raises the question, what are the values that support the worldview of People Awareness? In my book *Everything I Have Learned About Values*,[78] published in 2017, I presented the results of a global values survey of half a million people. The results are startling in their clarity. Out of the top five values, four are situated at the level of relationship consciousness – family, caring, respect and friendship. These are the values that are central to the worldview of People Awareness.

Out of the next five values, four are located at Level 5 consciousness, the level of internal cohesion – trust, commitment, enthusiasm and creativity. These are the values that are central to the worldview of Humanity Awareness. The tenth value is located at Level 4 consciousness – continuous learning.

These results clearly indicate the primacy of relationship values (Level 2 consciousness). Once these values are established, people want to explore their internal cohesion values (Level 5 consciousness). Among these values we see an emphasis on social cohesion – trust – and an emphasis on self-expression – creativity.

Internal cohesion has two meanings in Humanity Awareness, an external meaning – social cohesion – and an internal meaning – ego–soul alignment. The tenth value in my global values survey – continuous learning – bears witness to the desire for people to focus on their growth and development.

The key issue in Humanity Awareness is to create a governance system that deliberately develops and carefully cultivates 'a deeper kind of welfare system that includes the psychological, social and emotional aspects of human beings, so that the average person, over the length of his or her

---

[78] Richard Barrett, *Everything I Have Learned About Values* (London: Fulfilling Books), 2017, p. 3.

lifespan, becomes much more secure, authentic and happy'.[79] The key question for me is, what would such a governance system look like?

We can derive an answer to this question by exploring the evolutionary journey of our collective psychological development to see where it leads. In the worldview of State Awareness, governance focused on meeting the (self-esteem) needs of the leader – security through power and strength. *Do as I say and don't argue with me if you value your life.*

In the worldview of Nation Awareness, governance focused on meeting the (self-esteem) needs of the political and religious establishment – security through authority and education. *There is only one right way, so if you don't agree get out of the way.*

In the worldview of Wealth Awareness, governance focused on meeting the self-esteem needs of the rich and wealthy. Wealth Awareness led to combative, polarized two-party politics. Interactions between parties were dominated by confrontation and debate. *We are engaged in a competition where winner takes all.*

In the worldview of People Awareness, governance focused on meeting the individuation needs of the people – freedom through equality and accountability. People awareness led to multi-party coalitions and consensus. Interactions between parties were dominated by dialogue and discussion. *Everyone must be a winner.*

Hanzi Freinacht comments:

'No longer is there any real choice between the different parties, between the Left and the Right … The different parties and their ideologies are all shifting positions, trying to find themselves, trying to find visions and goals to latch on to, copying them from one another. In the process, they come closer and closer to each other.'[80]

The closer political parties get the less relevant they become. The next step will be to do away with party politics altogether. The worldview of Humanity Awareness will lead us into direct representation by the people around the core idea of finding meaning through self-expression and well-being for everyone.

Professional politicians – mostly (but not all) self-serving elites – will

---

[79] Hanzi Freinacht, *The Listening Society: A Metamodern Guide to Politics*, Book 1: Volume 1 (Metamoderna Aps), 2017.
[80] Ibid.

disappear altogether. They will be replaced by delegates representing different stages of psychological development (age groups) and different geographic areas.

Whereas the last four stages of psychological development will be represented by people in their thirties (the individuating stage), forties (the self-actualizing stage), fifties (the integrating stage) and sixties (the serving stage), the infants, children and teenagers will be represented by agencies that support their growth through the first three stages of psychological development.

Why elect people from different stages of psychological development? Because people at each stage of psychological development have different needs, and because they have different needs, they prioritize different values. The governance system in Humanity Awareness will find ways to reflect the different needs and values of all age groups.

Hanzi Freinacht further comments:

'Once the average person is much more secure, authentic and happy, he or she also tends (on average) to develop into a braver, more mature, more idealistic and reasonable person who cooperates more easily with others and makes better priorities, both individually and politically. Such people can then recreate society in a myriad of ways, solving many of the complex, wicked problems that we are facing today.'[81]

To this end the focus of governance in the worldview of Humanity Awareness will be on the implementation of psychological welfare programmes particularly for children, teenagers and young adults – the future generations. The job of us 'oldies' is to open the door to a new future by equipping young people for the job of creating that future.

With this focus on the needs associated with the different stages of psychological development we will need new metrics. Among the key new metrics will be indicators that focus on the level of well-being of the people;[82] the physical and mental health of different genders and age groups; the level of empathy and compassion in the community and the larger society; the level of kindness of people; and the incidence of suicide and homicide in each age group.

---

[81] Ibid.

[82] The tasks and needs that contribute to well-being at each stage of psychological development are shown in Table 3.2.

Laura Burgis, President of Human Values Center, believes we urgently need to make compassion a universal goal. She says: 'Compassion is essential to human relationships and to a fulfilled humanity. It is the path to enlightenment, and indispensable to the creation of a just economy and a peaceful global community.' Furthermore, there are now over 430 urban areas worldwide that have passed resolutions to officially become a 'compassionate city'. These cities span 54 countries and represent 660 million people worldwide.[83]

Other sectors

Having provided a description of the philosophy, the cosmology and the governance system in Humanity Awareness, let's now explore how the concept of 'finding meaning through self-expression and creativity' shows up in other sectors. I want to begin with what I regard as the four most important components of any worldview, namely gender relations, parenting, education and health.

Gender relations

Gender relations is an extremely complex topic. It includes romance, desire, physical and emotional intimacy, and so on. However, what I am speaking about here is none of these. What I want to focus on is the relationship between adult men and adult women in public life – at work, in social gatherings and all other forms of transactional encounters.

It is sad, but true, that men have been dominating and deprecating women in public life for more than three millennia. This is still the case in nations that embrace the worldviews of State Awareness, Nation Awareness and Wealth Awareness.

Women are treated like servants, slaves and sexual objects in the worldview of State Awareness. In the worldview of Nation Awareness, they are 'tolerated' but not encouraged to contribute. They are only revered if they are a successful warrior (Joan of Arc), a successful monarch (Queen Elizabeth I) or can beat men at their own games. In the worldview of

---

[83] From an email exchange. For more information: www.charterforcompassion.org

Wealth Awareness, women are only considered useful if they contribute to the economy, but their work is not valued as highly as men's.

In People Awareness, women got an equal voice, equal opportunities and equal status to men in public life – equality is still a work in progress in business life. So, what's next? What will happen to gender relations in the worldview of Humanity Awareness?

In the worldview of Humanity Awareness, women and men are no longer collaborators, they are partners. They each acknowledge the others' respective strengths and use them in appropriate circumstances. They are open and honest with each other, particularly about their feelings. They learn how to engage in challenging conversations that require emotional fearlessness; something neither men nor women are good at for different reasons.

Both men and women work on their weaknesses. In this regard the two sexes have much to teach each other, particularly in the domain of evolutionary intelligence. Men tend to be good at dealing with threats through power and strength – overcoming attack or opposition and regaining stability through force; not necessarily physical force, but through manipulation, debate and a determination to win at all costs. Let's call this the way of Yang.

Women tend to deal with threats through bonding and cooperation – overcoming threats and regaining stability through dialogue and discussion by finding win–win scenarios. Let's call this the way of Yin. It is important to recognize that both the Yin and Yang approaches can be valid depending on the situation. In the worldview of Humanity Awareness, both men and women learn to balance their Yin and Yang energies; sometimes more Yin, sometimes more Yang, but always appropriate for the circumstance.

Thus, the key to gender relations in the worldview of Humanity Awareness is not external equality (that is, what we learned in People Awareness), but internal equality – each gender becoming whole through the integration of female energies of Yin in the male, and the integration of male energies of Yang in the female.

Parenting

Let me begin with a quote from Kahil Gibran, a favourite philosopher of mine, which aligns with the essence of the cosmology of the worldview of Humanity Awareness:

'Your children are not your children. They are the sons and daughters of Life's longing for itself. They come through you but not from you. And though they are with you, yet they belong not to you.'[84]

There is no doubt in my mind that you are wonderfully privileged if you have a child. The soul of your child has chosen you as its steward to help it to learn how to master being in a material awareness and fully express its purpose. Your stewardship begins the moment your child is conceived; it continues until your child is ready to take responsibility for its life as an independent adult. When this time arrives, you must let go.

'You must give them your love but not your thoughts, for they will have their own thoughts. ... You may strive to be like them but seek not to make them like you.'[85]

You may have much to teach your child, but never forget for a moment that your child may have much to teach you. Just like you, your child is a soul. You are equal in this regard. You share the same origins and at the deepest level of being you share the same universal values, but you do not share the same gifts and talents. In this regard, every soul is unique. Every soul has its own form of self-expression. Your job is to nurture and support your child's self-expression, just as it was your parents' job to nurture and support yours.

That is your primary role as a parent – to give your child's soul the opportunity to express its unique character: not to fashion it; not to mould it or make it into a replica of you, but to give it the space to grow and flourish in a fear-free environment so your child may become all it can become. You must also teach your child how to connect with other children and contribute to the well-being of their peer group.

Always treat your child as an equal. You may bring your experience and learning to the relationship but allow your child to make its own informed choices: allow it to learn the repercussions and responsibilities

---

[84] Kahil Gibran, *The Prophet* (London: Pan Books) 1991, p. 22.
[85] Ibid., p. 22 and 25.

involved in decision-making. If you can do this, you will be setting your child up to make responsible choices later in life. Your job is to assure your offspring's survival, safety and security during its infant, childhood and teenage years, so that it grows up without a self-critical voice and without subconscious fears.

Once your child has left home, your job as a parent is not finished. You must become their trusted advisor – someone your child can turn to when they get embroiled in the vicissitudes of life. The soul of your child has its own destiny: you must allow and support it in its unfolding. In this regard it is important that you are aware of the seven stages of psychological development – the journey the soul goes through in its attempt to find fulfilment in our three-dimensional material plane of awareness.[86]

Although the search for well-being is a lifelong task, it begins as soon as you are conceived. Therefore, the initial onus for our well-being falls on our primary caregivers. The Flourish Project[87] recognizes this fact and provides models and tools to help caregivers to both attend to the vital importance of their own well-being and to ensure that the earliest years of children's lives establish the conditions for later flourishing.

Education

It is important to recognize that school systems are organized to teach children what they need to know to support the dominant worldview. Thus, in the worldview of State Awareness there is a strong focus on physical fitness, sports, strategy and combat skills. In the worldview of Nation Awareness there is a strong focus on reading, writing and religious knowledge. In the worldview of Wealth Awareness there is a strong focus on mathematics, science, economics and business skills. In the worldview of People Awareness there is a strong focus on gender relations and emotional skills.

In the worldview of Humanity Awareness our education systems will focus on the development of the whole child. We will have child-centred education programmes that support children in staying close to their souls. Such programmes will seek to identify and support the development of our

---

[86] See my forthcoming book, *Parenting the Soul of Your Child*.

[87] www.flourishproject.net

children's natural gifts and talents; to connect with others in unconditional loving relationships; and to contribute to the well-being of the community.

In addition, there will be a strong support for the emotional and mental health of our children by teaching them how to make values-based decisions, practise mindfulness and engage in daily meditation and support for them as they transition through the conforming, differentiating and individuating stages of psychological development.

In Humanity Awareness, education systems will extend beyond the normal school years. We will be engaged in lifelong learning programmes that support people in mastering each of the adult stages of psychological development – individuating, self-actualizing, integrating and serving.

Health

In the worldview of State Awareness, herbs and plants were used for healing. In the worldview of Nation Awareness, sacrifice and prayers were used for healing. In the worldview of Wealth Awareness, surgery and drugs were used for healing. In the worldview of People Awareness, in addition to surgery and drugs, we begin to see the introduction of alternative healing modalities involving the mind–body connection.

In the worldview of Humanity Awareness, we will see a significant increase in psychotherapeutic and energy approaches to healing as well as a focus on health maintenance and disease prevention. This will come about through a deeper understanding of the impact of ego–soul dynamics on the human energy field;[88] the importance of cultural and environmental factors on physical and mental well-being; and the need to shift to organic methods of food production. We will also see a merging of Eastern and Western approaches to medicine.

In the worldview of Humanity Awareness, surgery and drugs will become the healing modalities of the last resort. Health practitioners will be trained in the care of the soul. There will be a shift in the understanding of who we really are. We will recognize that we are primarily energetic beings living in material bodies. We will come to realize that health

---

[88] Richard Barrett, *A New Psychology of Human Well-being: An Exploration of the Influence of Ego-Soul Dynamics on Mental and Physical Health* (London: Fulfilling Books), 2016.

disorders, mental and physical, reflect the energetic misalignment between the energy behind our ego's motivations and the energy behind our soul's motivations.

Having explored the impact of the worldview of Humanity Awareness on gender relations, parenting, education and health, let us now turn our attention to the business sector and leadership.

Business sector

The focus of business in Humanity Awareness will be on creating a meaningful economy – one that allows people to thrive in psychologically healthy cultures[89] with work that supports human evolution and the ecology of the planet. To this end, all businesses will sign up to the UN's Sustainable Development Goals.[90]

The authors of *The Rise of the Meaningful Economy*,[91] Mark Drewell and Björn Larsson, stress that it is no longer just a small number of the privileged elite who can look for meaning and express that in their economic decision-making; millions more people, particularly the younger generation and people in nations operating from the worldview of People Awareness, are looking for meaningful work. They are also being more conscious in how they spend their money. Drewell and Larsson state that meaning is a new economic force – a new currency.

In *Reinventing Organisations*,[92] Frederic Laloux also talks about the importance of evolutionary purpose. He states: 'Teal organizations [those operating from the worldview of Humanity Awareness] are seen as having a life and sense of direction of their own. Instead of trying to predict and control the future, members of the organization are invited to listen and understand what the organization is drawn to become, where it naturally wants to go.'

In Humanity Awareness, business will be organized around three core

[89] Richard Barrett, *The Values-driven Organisation: Cultural Health and Human Well-being as a Pathway to Sustainable Performance* (London: Routledge), 2017.
[90] https://sustainabledevelopment.un.org
[91] Mark Drewell and Björn Larson, *The Rise of the Meaningful Economy: A Megatrend Where Meaning is the New Currency* (Stockholm: Amazon), 2017.
[92] Frederic Laloux, *Reinventing Organisations* (London: Nelson Parker), 2014.

principles – social purpose, personal and professional development, and social and environmental accountability.

Social purpose

Every industry and business sector will have a governing body that regulates the operations of companies according to an agreed list of universal human values and an overarching social purpose that supports the well-being of humanity and the planet.

The purpose of the governing body will be to provide a framework of values and rules, from within which competition in every industry and business sector can be organized in a similar way to the Olympic Games – agreement at a global level on the framework within which competition takes place.

Personal and professional development

Every organization (for profit and not-for-profit) in addition to having a social purpose will have a deliberately developmental framework of education[93] and training for personal development (soft skills) and professional development (hard skills) for all employees.

Employee development and leadership programmes will be designed to support workers in mastering the adult stages of psychological development – individuating (releasing subconscious fears and limiting beliefs); self-actualizing (developing the individual's gifts and talents); integrating (connecting with others in unconditional loving relationships); and serving (contributing to the well-being of humanity and the planet).

Laloux refers to this as 'wholeness'. He states: 'Teal organizations have developed a consistent set of practices that invite us to drop the [ego] mask, reclaim our inner wholeness, and bring all of who we are to work.'[94]

Social and environmental responsibility

Every organization will be responsible and accountable for its social and environmental impact – external costs that are now borne by society will be internalized. Businesses will recognize they are wholly owned subsidiaries

---

[93] Robert Kegan and Lisa Laskow Lahey, *An Everyone Culture: Becoming a Deliberately Developmental Organisation* (Harvard Business School Publishing: Boston), 2016.
[94] Frederic Laloux, *Reinventing Organisations* (Nelson Parker: London), 2014.

of society, and society is a wholly owned subsidiary of the environment. If we lose our environment, our society will collapse, and our businesses will suffer.

Businesses will also recognize that they are agents for peace – bringing stability through wealth creation and contributing to the support of national welfare programmes. To this end, organizations will seek out full spectrum leaders – leaders who aspire to be the best *for* the world rather than the best *in* the world. Selfish business behaviours that compromise the future of our global society will not be tolerated in Humanity Awareness.

Leadership

Our research at the Barrett Values Centre˚ over the past 20 years has shown that the most successful leaders operate from full spectrum consciousness.[95] They always stay calm because they can handle any situation that arises. They propose solutions that care for the needs of all stakeholders and they have signed up to support the UN's Sustainable Development Goals.

Full spectrum leaders have the courage to face their fears, challenge the status quo, persevere when things get tough, risk everything for the cause they believe in, and do all these things without any regard for personal gain. They want to create a better future for everyone. Their goal is 'to make everyone fully powerful'[96] so the organization can become self-organizing. 'The traditional roles of the CEO fall away – there are, for example, no targets, no budgets to approve, no executive team to chair, no promotions to decide on. ... A critical role therefore of the founder/CEO is to "hold the space" for Teal structures and practices.'[97]

To become a full spectrum leader, you must first learn to lead yourself: if you can't lead yourself, you can't lead a team. You must then learn how to lead a team: if you can't lead a team, you can't lead an organization. You must then learn how to lead an organization. Full spectrum leaders have a personal touch. They stay in contact with their colleagues. They manage by values; they measure their culture; and they focus on their

---

[95] https://www.valuescentre.com/tools-assessments/#leadertools
[96] Frederic Laloux, *Reinventing Organisations* (Nelson Parker: London), 2014.
[97] Ibid.

own psychological development as well as the psychological development of their people.[98]

At the core of the transition of business in Humanity Awareness will be a shift in focus from short-term financial results to long-term societal goals. Increasingly, businesses will be organized around cooperative principles.

This quote from Daniel Goleman sums up the type of leadership we will find in Humanity Awareness.

'Great leaders do not settle for systems as they are, but see what they could become, and so work to transform them for the better, to benefit the widest circle. Then there are those rare souls who shift beyond mere competence to wisdom, and so operate on behalf of society itself rather than a specific political group or business. They are free to think far, far ahead. Their aperture encompasses the welfare of humanity at large, not a single group; they see people as We, not as Us and Them. And they leave a legacy for future generations – these are the leaders we remember a century or more later.'[99]

I now want to focus on two sectors that play an important role in supporting social cohesion – justice and the arts – and the sector that is the fundamental key to our future survival – the environment.

Justice

The fundamental purpose of justice has always been *to protect the internal stability of a society* by punishing and preventing actions that could destabilize the dominant worldview.

In the worldview of State Awareness, justice is focused on protecting the power of the elites. Severe punishments act as a fear-based deterrent for stabilizing the power of the ruling aristocracy. Torture as a means of getting to the truth is considered acceptable. Instantaneous punishment by death and physical maiming are common practice in the worldview of State Awareness.

In the worldview of Nation Awareness, justice is focused on supporting moral righteousness. Courts are made up of religious or high-ranking State

---

[98] Richard Barrett, *The New Leadership Paradigm* (Bath: Fulfilling Books), 2010.
[99] Daniel Goleman, *Focus: The Inner Driver of Excellence* (New York: HarperCollins), 2013.

officials. This leaves the courts open to manipulation by the elites. In this worldview, the elites tend to get less severe punishments than the common people. The ultimate punishment in this worldview is the death penalty.

In the worldview of Wealth Awareness, justice is focused on moral and economic fairness. Justice is administered by independent courts and suitably qualified citizens who decide on the outcome of a trial. Punishment for serious crimes can include heavy fines and long periods of incarceration. There is no capital punishment in nations that operate from the worldview of Wealth Awareness.

In the worldview of People Awareness, justice is also focused on moral and economic fairness; even though punishments involve fines and/or incarceration, a strong emphasis is placed on rehabilitation so that wrongdoers can reintegrate into society and recidivism is reduced. There is no capital punishment in the worldview of People Awareness.

In the worldview of Humanity Awareness, there is a recognition that people commit crimes because of the psychological conditioning they experienced during their childhood and teenage years. The focus of the justice system is restoring people to wholeness. All those who commit crimes in the worldview of Humanity Awareness undergo a psychological evaluation and are helped and supported in their psychological rehabilitation. Every prisoner is assigned a mentor/coach – someone they can turn to for support as they attempt to individuate and self-actualize.

A key component of the justice system in Humanity Awareness will be inter-generational fairness – a shift from a focus on societal short-term gains to long-term benefits that support both people and the environment. For this to happen, we must encourage long-term social and environmental investing; and, most importantly, we must give the young a voice in key decision-making. Theirs is the future; they must have a say on the world we are creating (see the section on Governance).

Arts sector

The arts have always held a special place in society because their purpose is to make public the inner workings of our souls.

Most of us do not let our light out, because we are afraid that our offering will not be good enough; that it will be judged unworthy. So, we look at and listen to the works of the courageous souls who are attempting to make their perfect offering, secretly hoping that through their inspiration we can find the courage to access our own light within. We fail only because we lack the courage to embrace our unique gifts and talents, or we prioritize success over well-being, or status over self-expression.

The arts can be used to mirror our inadequacies and inspire us to become more fully who we are; to access our gifts and talents and make them public. Most importantly, the arts can be used to tell inspiring stories about how Humanity Awareness is creating a better world for everyone.

The arts holds the key to the flourishing of Humanity Awareness, because Humanity Awareness corresponds to the fifth stage of psychological development – self-actualization, the stage where we learn to access our soul's self-expression. The arts provides an avenue for us to express our unique gifts and talents in service to the growth and well-being of humanity. In the worldview of Humanity Awareness, children are encouraged to creatively express their natural skills and talents.

Finally, perhaps the most important sector we need to focus on for the future of humanity is the physical environment. It is so important that it will, very soon, evolve into its own worldview – the worldview of Earth Awareness.

The environment

In Wealth Awareness we depleted the Earth's resources in search of profits. In People Awareness we began to correct our ways: although our main concern was correcting inequality, we started to recognize the adverse impacts we were having on our environment and began to focus on environmental sustainability. This led to the creation of the Green Parties.

The first Green Parties were created in the 1970s. There are now Green Parties in more than 90 countries. The Global Greens Charter lists six guiding principles: ecological wisdom, social justice, participatory democracy, nonviolence, sustainability and respect for diversity. In the worldview of People Awareness, we began to focus on recycling and reducing carbon emissions.

In Humanity Awareness we will go much further. We will design our businesses and our homes to harness natural energy, minimize energy consumption and generate zero waste. We will replace all plastics with biodegradable alternatives; we will eliminate the use of pesticides; we will go beyond sustainability to focus on ecological resilience; we will attempt to repair the damage we did to our environment in the worldview of Wealth Awareness; and we will begin to recognize that the Earth has much to teach us, such as the importance of nurturing diversity and the interdependence of all living systems. In Humanity Awareness we will learn to steward the Earth and conserve its natural resources. We will make sure all our plans take account of the needs of future generations.

We will all spend more time in nature, particularly with our children; we will rely on nature to nurture our souls; and we will not let economic gain get in the way of preserving and enhancing our natural environment. The quality of the air we breathe, the water we drink and the food we eat will be our top priority. There will be no food products that are not organic. In addition to focusing on our own health, we will start to focus on the health of all living creatures and the planet itself.

Call to action

In November 2017 I invited a group of 12 people from around the world to a four-day meeting near Oxford to discuss this question: What would a community or nation look like if it was operating from the worldview of Humanity Awareness? Based on the success of the first meeting, in November 2018 I organized a second meeting, this time with 28 participants. The results of these meetings are reflected in the preceding text.

It is my intention over the next few years to continue to explore and deepen these conversations by creating a Humanity Awareness Initiative and forming action groups to implement the worldview of Humanity Awareness in countries all over the world. As I write (summer of 2019) there are two groups beginning to form, one in Sweden and one in Brazil. If you would like to start such an action group, please contact me at info@barrettacademy.com.

Summary

Here are the main points of this chapter.

1. The central idea in the worldview of Humanity Awareness is to support human self-expression.

2. The approach to solving problems in Humanity Awareness is holistic and systemic.

3. The underlying cosmology is soul awareness – a subjective experience of our energetic reality and the source of our true being.

4. All human beings share the same identity – we are all souls experiencing life in three-dimensional material awareness.

5. Whereas governance in the worldview of People Awareness focused on social welfare programmes, governance in the worldview of Humanity Awareness focuses on psychological welfare programmes.

6. The soul of your child has chosen you as its steward to help it to learn how to master being in a material awareness and fully express its purpose. Your stewardship begins the moment your child is conceived.

7. Education systems will focus on the development of the whole child. We will develop child-centred education programmes that teach children to creatively express their natural skills and talents.

8. We will see a significant increase in psychotherapeutic approaches to healing. This will come about through a deeper understanding of the impact of ego–soul dynamics on the human energy field.

9. Business will be organized around three core principles – social purpose, personal and professional development, and social and environmental accountability.

10. Leaders will manage by values; they will measure their culture; and they will focus on their own psychological development as well as the psychological development of their people.

11. All those who commit crimes in the worldview of Humanity Awareness will undergo a psychological evaluation and be helped and supported in their psychological rehabilitation.

12. The arts provide an avenue for us to express our unique gifts and talents in service to the well-being of humanity.
13. We will design our businesses and our homes to harness natural forms of energy, minimize energy consumption and generate zero waste.

GLOSSARY

Algorithm

An algorithm is an established process or set of rules to be followed for problem-solving. The concept of algorithm has existed for centuries. Nowadays, it is mainly used in data processing.

Beliefs

Beliefs are assumptions we hold to be true. They may or may not be true; that is why they are called assumptions. Our principal beliefs are formed in the specific physical, social and cultural frameworks of existence that we are brought up in during the first 24 years of our lives, when our minds and brains are growing and developing – when we are learning how to get our deficiency needs met.

Cosmology

A cosmology is a system of beliefs that defines who we are; our place in the universe; the origin and structure of our material world; our relationship to other dimensions of existence; and, most importantly, how to conduct and align ourselves with whomever or whatever we consider to be the divine creator/provider so that we can get our needs met in this life and the next.

Cultural entropy

Cultural entropy in an organizational setting is the amount of energy that employees consume in doing unnecessary or unproductive work – the amount of conflict, friction, stress and frustration that employees encounter in their day-to-day activities that prevent them from meeting the needs of the organization. Cultural entropy in a national setting is the amount of frustration and stress that citizens encounter in attempting to get their needs met. The higher the level of cultural entropy, the lower the level of well-being.[100]

Culture

The culture of a group of people is a set of shared characteristics encompassing language, religion, cuisine, social habits, music and arts, which identifies them as separate from other groups of people. The beliefs of the culture define how people relate to other members of the group and how people should conduct themselves to get their needs met. People who share the same culture have a common ethnic and social heritage and normally live in a specific territory that they regard as their cultural home.

DNA

Viewed through the lens of 3-D material awareness, deoxyribonucleic acid (DNA) is a molecule that carries the genetic instructions used in the development, functioning and reproduction of living organisms. Viewed through the lens of 4-D energetic awareness, DNA is an energetic field of information and instructions that belong in part to the energy field of the species and in part to the energy field of the soul templates of the parents that make a child. In 3-D material awareness, specific parts of a DNA molecule are called genes. In 4-D energetic awareness, genes are specific aspects of the energy field of a DNA molecule.

---

[100] Richard Barrett, *The Values-driven Organization: Cultural health and employee well-being as a pathway to sustainable performance* (Second edition) (London: Routledge), 2017, pp. 16–18.

Ego

Our ego is a field of conscious awareness that identifies with our physical body. Because the ego believes it inhabits a body and lives in a material world, it lives in three-dimensional reality and thinks it can die. Because it thinks it can die, it thinks it has needs; and because it thinks it has needs, it develops fears about not being able to get its needs met. The principal needs of the ego are survival, safety and security. The ego mind is the creation of the soul mind. The soul creates the ego to protect itself from the pain (energetic instability) it experiences from being present in three-dimensional material awareness.

Full spectrum

Full spectrum consciousness is the ability to operate successfully from all seven levels of consciousness and handle any situation that arises without fear. A full spectrum nation is one that satisfies peoples' deficiency needs, transformation needs and growth needs.

Mindset

Whereas a worldview is an overarching belief system – how we believe we need to act to get our most important needs met in the group we belong to – a mindset is a belief system that usually reflects our personal history and/or the history of our group – the common attitudes found in our group culture.

In England, one of the dominant collective mindsets is 'the stiff upper lip'. In this mindset, people display fortitude and stoicism in the face of adversity, or exercise self-restraint in the expression of their emotions. In Serbia there are two dominant collective mindsets – a belief that things are not possible, and a strong sense of us (family) against them (the rest of the world). In Denmark, Norway and Sweden there is a collective mindset known as the Law of Jante. This refers to a mentality that denigrates individual achievement and places emphasis on the collective.

Individual mindsets are based on personal beliefs. Some common mindsets we find in people all over the world are: I don't have enough; I am not loved enough; and I am not enough. These three mindsets correspond to the limiting beliefs that we formulate during the first 24 years of our lives when we are learning how to survive, keep safe and feel secure in the parental and cultural framework of our existence.

Soul

Our soul is an individuated aspect of the universal energy field. We don't have a soul. We are the soul. For the first three months of life in utero – from the moment of conception to the formation of the reptilian mind/brain – the soul mind is the dominant (conscious) interface with the embryo's external world – the mother's womb. The species mind, which is the subconscious of the soul mind, guides the development of the embryo into a foetus and creates a functioning body mind (reptilian mind/brain) by around the first trimester of gestation.

When the body mind becomes operational, it becomes the new conscious interface with the external world, and the soul mind becomes the subconscious of the body mind.

The problem the foetus or the newly born baby has is that it still believes it is living in an energetic field of connectedness and love – the world of the soul – because it has not yet learned about separation. The baby gradually learns through the experience of uncomfortable sensations that it is no longer living in that world, and it begins to fear separation. For the soul, the feeling of separation equates to a lack of love.

At this point, usually around 18 months to two years, the 'pain' associated with the feeling of separation becomes too much for the soul to bear. It filters out this pain by creating the psychic entity we call the ego. The ego's role is to buffer the soul from the world of separation and enable us to become a viable independent entity in the material framework of our existence.

Values

Values are a shorthand way of defining whatever it is we think we need in our lives – what is important to us. Whatever we need is what we value.

Values are the energetic drivers of our aspirations and intentions. They are the source of all human motivations and decision-making.

Well-being

Well-being is the feeling we get when we can satisfy the needs of the stage of psychological development we are at and also satisfy the needs of the stages of psychological development we have passed through.

Worldview

A worldview is more than a culture. People all over the world can share the same worldview but have different cultures. For example, even though the worldview of Tribe Awareness can be found in ethnically homogenous groups all over the world, each group (tribe) has its own culture, which shows up in different characteristics such as language, dress code, rituals, traditions, etc.

Similarly, even though several nations have adopted the worldview of Wealth Awareness, each of the nations that ascribe to this worldview have their own cultures – the UK, France, Austria and Belgium are all culturally different and have their own traditions and customs.

Thus, the term culture refers to the common ethnic and social heritage of people living in or associated with a specific territory that they call home. The term worldview, on the other hand, refers to an overarching philosophy for living – a way of being, seeing and interpreting the world.